Praise for *The Redeemed Reader*

The Redeemed Reader is exactly the kind of thoughtful, grace-filled resource Christian families need today. Much like the website I've trusted for years, the authors don't shy away from hard questions or complex books. Instead, they offer wise, grounded guidance for navigating literature with conviction and curiosity. This book doesn't ask parents to compromise their values—it equips them to engage deeply with the stories shaping our culture while honoring their conscience. Reading *The Redeemed Reader* felt like sitting down with my most bookish, insightful friends—only these friends come prepared with years of literary wisdom and spiritual discernment. The pages brim with rich conversation about stories, ideas, and how we help our kids (and ourselves!) read well in a complex world. If reviews came with sound effects, you'd hear me whistling, laughing, crying, questioning, and smiling my way through this gem. It's a revelatory and celebratory read. This book is a rare treasure: it encourages Christian families to wrestle honestly with contemporary books rather than retreat from them. The authors neither dismiss nuance nor demand compromise—they model how to explore a wide range of literature with both discernment and delight. *The Redeemed Reader* reminds us that reading is not just safe or unsafe—it's an opportunity to grow, to ask questions, and to form readers who are both wise and compassionate.

AMBER O'NEAL JOHNSTON
Author of *Soul School* and *A Place to Belong*

The Redeemed Reader is an excellent resource from a trustworthy band of wise women. I am grateful for their faithfulness and generosity, their clarity and kindness. Thoughtful parents looking for help in navigating the world of children's literature will find here good words from faithful friends.

S. D. SMITH
Author of The Green Ember Series

As a long-time follower and supporter of Redeemed Reader, I am thrilled to see and read this book. It seems both right and fitting that this team of writers would expand their work to a book-length product. Now that they have done so, I am certain it will benefit both readers and future readers.

TIM CHALLIES
Pastor, speaker, and author of *Epic: An Around-the-World Journey Through Christian History*

This valuable resource for parents, teachers, and librarians presents a framework for viewing stories and literature in the context of biblical truth. It illustrates how this approach guides the selection of reading materials across genres. The book addresses "messy topics" with courage and sensitivity, aiding in appropriate book selection for a child's age and emotional maturity. Crafted in a graceful and thought-provoking style, *The Redeemed Reader* is a welcome contribution to discussions on selecting and introducing books for your child.

MARK HUNT
Coauthor with Gladys Hunt of *Honey for a Child's Heart, Updated and Expanded*

JANIE CHEANEY, BETSY FARQUHAR,
HAYLEY MORELL & MEGAN SABEN

THE
REDEEMED

READER

Cultivating a Child's Discernment and
Imagination Through Truth and Story

MOODY PUBLISHERS
CHICAGO

© 2025 by
Janie Cheaney, Betsy Farquhar, Haley Morell, Megan Saben

All rights reserved. No part of this book may be reproduced in any form without permission in writing from the publisher, except in the case of brief quotations embodied in critical articles or reviews.

Scripture quotations are from the ESV® Bible (The Holy Bible, English Standard Version®), © 2001 by Crossway, a publishing ministry of Good News Publishers. ESV Text Edition: 2025. The ESV text may not be quoted in any publication made available to the public by a Creative Commons license. The ESV may not be translated in whole or in part into any other language. Used by permission. All rights reserved.

Scripture marked as nkjv taken from the New King James Version®. Copyright © 1982 by Thomas Nelson. Used by permission. All rights reserved.

All emphasis in Scripture has been added.

Edited by Amanda Cleary Eastep
Interior design: Puckett Smartt
Cover design: Faceout Studio, Molly von Borstel
Cover graphic of tree copyright © 2025 by CSA-Images/Getty Images (158392235). All rights reserved.
Cover graphic of ornamental frame copyright © 2025 by CSA-Archive/Getty Images (1003178450). All rights reserved.

Library of Congress Cataloging-in-Publication Data

Names: Cheaney, J. B. author | Farquhar, Betsy author | Saben, Megan author
    | Morell, Hayley author
Title: The redeemed reader : cultivating a child's discernment and
    imagination through truth and story / Janie Cheaney, Betsy Farquhar,
    Megan Saben, and Hayley Morell.
Description: Chicago : Moody Publishers, [2025] | Includes bibliographical
    references. | Summary: "The Redeemed Reader offers insight into how to
    build discernment in children and provides practical tips, examples, and
    booklists for their literary journey. Passionate about shepherding
    imaginations and young hearts, the authors read ahead so that you can
    confidently choose books for your children"-- Provided by publisher.
Identifiers: LCCN 2025012012 (print) | LCCN 2025012013 (ebook) | ISBN
    9780802436139 paperback | ISBN 9780802468727 ebook
Subjects: LCSH: Parenting--Religious aspects--Christianity | Child
    rearing--Religious aspects--Christianity | BISAC: FAMILY & RELATIONSHIPS
    / Education | RELIGION / Christian Living / Parenting
Classification: LCC BV4529 .C438 2025 (print) | LCC BV4529 (ebook) | DDC
    248.8/45--dc23/eng/20250701
LC record available at https://lccn.loc.gov/2025012012
LC ebook record available at https://lccn.loc.gov/2025012013

Originally delivered by fleets of horse-drawn wagons, the affordable paperbacks from D. L. Moody's publishing house resourced the church and served everyday people. Now, after more than 125 years of publishing and ministry, Moody Publishers' mission remains the same—even if our delivery systems have changed a bit. For more information on other books (and resources) created from a biblical perspective, go to www.moodypublishers.com or write to:

Moody Publishers
820 N. LaSalle Boulevard
Chicago, IL 60610

1 3 5 7 9 10 8 6 4 2

Printed in the United States of America

For Emily, who started this ball rolling. ~ J.B.C.

For Ethan, my Renaissance man. ~ B.F.

For Joel, forever and always. ~ H.M.

For Michael, my beloved hero. ~ M.S.

CONTENTS

The Chapter Before the First — 9

PART ONE: TRUTH AND STORY

Section 1: Shepherding the Imagination

1. Foundations: Discovering Truth and Story — 17
2. Developing Discernment and Delight: What to Read When — 31
3. Something for Everyone: Reading Levels and Genres — 41
4. Discussion Starters: Worldview and Discernment in Literature — 55

PART TWO: RAISING READERS

Section 2: Reading the Classics

5. A Fresh Look at Old Books: The Risks and Rewards of Reading the Classics — 65
6. To Be, or Not to Be: Literary Retellings — 79
7. Graphic Novels: Are They Literature? — 89
8. "Savages" and "Slaves": Historical Racism in Children's Books — 97

Section 3: Contemporary Issues

9. "Messy" Books: What Do We Do with Them? — 107
10. Dominion vs. Demolition: Environmentalism in Children's Literature — 123
11. Of Every Tribe and Nation: The Beauty and Challenge of Diversity — 135
12. Who Am I? Identity and Representation — 147
13. Turn on the Light: "Dark" YA Fiction — 161

Section 4: Ages, Stages, and Genres

14. The Pictures Matter! Enjoying Picture Books — 171
15. The Emerging Reader:
    Nurturing a Love of Stories and Reading — 183
16. Just for Laughs: Kid Humor — 191
17. Delight and Wisdom: The Joy of Poetry — 199
18. Weird New Worlds: Sci-Fi and Dystopia — 207
19. The Horns of Elfland: On Reading Fantasy — 219
20. Beyond Ever After: A Vision for Christian Romance — 227

Section 5: Practical Application

21. Bibles and Beyond: Choosing Christian Resources — 239
22. Who Is My Neighbor? Loving Authors — 257
23. Finding Book People: Loving Your Library — 265
24. When the Headlines Strike:
    Loving Your Neighbor and Your World — 271
25. Piles and Stacks: Personal Library Management — 279

The Chapter After the Last — 293
Starred Reviews: The Best of the Best — 297
Acknowledgments — 317

THE CHAPTER BEFORE THE FIRST

In which we meet our heroines, readers are introduced to Redeemed Reader, and you learn how to read this book.

> Once upon a time, a very long time ago now, about last Friday, Winne-the-Pooh lived in a forest all by himself under the name of Sanders.[1]
>
> —A. A. Milne, *Winne-the-Pooh*

Once upon a time, not long ago, in 2011, a former book editor and a children's author began a conversation. The editor, Emily Whitten, had a literary blog, but she wanted something more. The author, Janie Cheaney, was facing a dry spell after publishing four novels for children. Both women wanted to do something with their literary gifts, something that connected their love of books and their Christian faith. What did it mean to be a redeemed reader of children's books? To explore this question, they created a website.

In search of a logo, Emily found a dove carrying an olive branch. The image reflected the hopefulness of their mission, a reminder of God's redeeming work. The website grew, with a stream of book reviews and reflections on reading and culture. While Emily brought a knowledge of the children's

---

1. A. A. Milne and Ernest Howard Shepard, *The Complete Tales of Winnie-The-Pooh* (Penguin Young Readers Group, 1994), 2.

book industry, Janie's insight reflected her experience as an early homeschool pioneer, creator of the Wordsmith writing curriculum, and her decades as a columnist at *World* magazine.

Soon, a young homeschool graduate on the hunt for Christian book reviews stumbled upon the website. A regular commenter, Hayley eventually joined the team, first as an intern, then as executive assistant and staff writer. Known as the "babysitter with the book bag," Hayley brought experience from studying at Boyce College and the World Journalism Institute. As Redeemed Reader was forming, two college friends were blogging about children's literature while their young children were napping. Megan Saben and Betsy Farquhar became good friends during their undergraduate years at Covenant College, and both went on to get master's degrees in children's literature and library science. In the fall of 2012, after first engaging in the comment section and then guest posting, Megan and Betsy joined the Redeemed Reader team.

Time passed, books were reviewed, and opportunities came and went. In 2016, Emily felt called in a different direction and stepped away from Redeemed Reader, passing the "managerial reins" to Betsy.[2] Though the early years were a time of growth and transition, the core mission of Redeemed Reader remained steadfast.

A Hopeful Philosophy & Purpose

Redeemed Reader, from the beginning, had an ambitious goal: It wasn't going to be just another book blog. Instead, it was a place for Christians to engage with culture through children's books. The website's first tagline was "Christ, Culture, and Kids' Books."[3]

Today, the team at Redeemed Reader brings a philosophy of children's

---

2. Redeemed Reader, *The Redeemed Reader's Companion: Provocative Posts, Lively Lists, and Top Titles* (Redeemed Reader, 2018), 6.
3. Redeemed Reader, "Christian Children's Book Reviews | Redeemed Reader," archived April 10, 2013 at the Wayback Machine, https://web.archive.org/web/20130410055301/http://www.redeemedreader.com/.

literature they've honed for more than a decade. We are a place for Christian parents and educators to engage with children's books because we know you want to choose the best books for your children and teens and help shepherd their imaginations as they mature.[4] With thousands of book reviews and a deep archive of reflections and resources, our website is full of information. But at our core, we are book lovers, not screen lovers, and we know the value of a book in hand when you're at the library, looking for recommendations. We wanted to create a book to serve readers and help share our philosophy, experience, and yes, many, many books!

On our website, there are some books we unreservedly recommend: Our starred reviews represent the best of the best. But all the books we review fit within our mandate:

> *At Redeemed Reader, we want to shape redeemed readers who engage both mind and heart in dialogue with the culture around them. Humans are story-loving and story-telling; that's the way God made us. He Himself is a storyteller (and we may infer, a story-lover); why else would He create a universe as a stage and a tumultuous cast of varied and prolific, plot-making and plot-reacting characters called humanity? But every story has a shape and a theme, and as we grow we need to learn to recognize what a story is trying to tell us.[5]*

Redeemed Reader is the story of a group of women who are faithful Christians, faithful members of their local churches, and faithful readers of children's books. From the beginning, we each brought something unique to the table. Hayley brought a youthful willingness to read Young Adult (YA) fantasy. Janie outstripped the rest of the team in her middle grade fiction reading. Betsy brought a love of middle grade nonfiction. Megan loved picture books.

---

4. "Our Beliefs," Redeemed Reader, accessed November 10, 2024, https://redeemedreader.com/our-beliefs/.

5. *The Redeemed Reader's Companion: Provocative Posts, Lively Lists, and Top Titles*, Redeemed Reader, 8.

Over the years, as Redeemed Reader has grown, so have our friendships as a team. We've rejoiced and grieved together. We've shared daily life: We've moved multiple times; Megan published two picture books; Betsy sent her first child off to college; Janie updated her homeschool writing curriculum and published two more children's novels; and Hayley met a book lover and got married. All along, Redeemed Reader has been there.

Together our team forms a cohesive whole with a unified front, yet with a broad range of literary taste. When we get together, we laugh about the books we have read and not read. We laugh over the fact that three of us love the Lord of the Rings and the other simply cannot get into it. We are individuals with particular loves and gifts.

That is what we share with our readers, as we read ahead for them.

The Christian Critic

Kate Lucky, the culture editor at *Christianity Today*, discusses the unique task of a Christian critic. Because of individual consciences, Christians do not always have a cut-and-dried reason for recommending what they love. As Lucky writes:

> *This makes the task of the Christian critic at once more difficult and more interesting. Our job is not to justify our taste in culture but to explain what we see from a vantage point oriented to Christ. Not, This art is actually kinda Christian, but rather, Here's what I realized as a Christian encountering this art.*[6]

At Redeemed Reader, we read widely. We review a lot of books in the mainstream industry because that is where most books are published. We believe:

---

6. Kate Lucky, "Taste and See If the Show Is Good," *Christianity Today*, September 13, 2024, https://www.christianitytoday.com/2024/09/taste-and-see-if-the-show-is-good-emmys-breaking-bad-baby-reindeer/.

> "As Christians, we are called not to retreat from the world, but to be salt and light in the world, and raise up our children to be the same. This means interacting with our culture, praising the good and admonishing the bad. It means finding hope within ourselves and within others and explaining that hope with gentleness and respect (1 Peter 3:15). It means walking with Jesus along the library shelves, into the schools, over the Internet. His common grace shines in every true work, even if it's by an unbelieving author or artist—In His light we see light (Psalm. 36:9)."[7]

In addition, we believe that good literature illuminates truth we already know and awakens us to truth we might pursue. Good literature warns us away from falsehood and provides unforgettable examples of how now to live. We've all heard that reading broadens our horizons, and so it does. But first we have to learn to recognize what horizons we're encountering. In other words, we have become readers.[8] But how does one become a reader? Where should we start? What should we read, and what shouldn't we be reading? We believe in finding God's Truth and Story in children's literature. In the following chapters, we invite you to join us on this adventure.

How to Read This Book

In writing this book, we each drafted different chapters and then worked together to edit the chapters as a whole. And, of course, we assembled lots of booklists for you.

While we know you might want to (or already have!) flip ahead to read a certain chapter, we have structured this book intentionally.

Part 1: Truth and Story establishes a framework upon which the following chapters rest.

---

7. "Our Philosophy and Practice," Redeemed Reader, https://redeemedreader.com/our-philosophy-and-practice/.
8. Text previously published in Redeemed Reader, *The Redeemed Reader's Companion*, 8.

Part 2: Raising Readers builds upon the foundation of Part 1 in a series of short, topical chapters. These can be read independently though they do build upon each other, and we believe reading them in order will be beneficial. You might notice we have chapters on some specific genres, like fantasy and science fiction, while not covering others, like realistic fiction, historical fiction, or mysteries. We focused on genres for which we receive the most questions, such as fantasy and dystopia. While realistic fiction is a popular genre, we don't single it out; instead, we cover realistic fiction in our chapters on contemporary issues such as sexuality, racism, messy books, and diversity.

Each of our chapters concludes with a micro booklist for further reading. These books are intended to build on the chapter and are not always stand-alone recommendations. Rather, they provide a way to dig deeper with an additional resource for adults along with select children's and teens' books that reflect the chapter. Each has been reviewed on Redeemed Reader if you want more information.

Now that we've told you about the book, and a bit about ourselves, let's dive in!

Janie, Betsy, Hayley, and Megan

Abbreviations of publishing categories used throughout this book:

PB   Picture Books, ages 3–8
ER   Easy Readers, ages 4–8
CB   Chapter Books, ages 7–10
MG   Middle Grade, ages 8–12
YA   Young Adult, ages 13–17

PART ONE

TRUTH AND STORY

SECTION 1
Shepherding the Imagination

CHAPTER 1

FOUNDATIONS: DISCOVERING TRUTH AND STORY

> "It isn't Narnia, you know," sobbed Lucy. "It's you.
> We shan't meet you there. And how can we live, never meeting you?"
> "But you shall meet me, dear one," said Aslan.[1]
>
> —C. S. Lewis, *The Voyage of the Dawn Treader*

Although Megan was indisputably the most voracious reader in her family, somehow she managed to graduate from high school having read only *The Lion, the Witch and the Wardrobe* out of the entire Chronicles of Narnia. Maybe it was the '70s style cover art with the weird line of people who seemed to be falling upward on the cover of *The Magician's Nephew* that turned her off to the rest. Yes, children do judge books by their covers.

It wasn't that she didn't enjoy reading fantasy. Her librarian grandmother had sent *The Magic Bicycle* by John Bibee and *The Tower of Geburah* and *The Iron Scepter* by John White, and she loved reading the delightful stories with redemptive themes that were reminiscent of the single Narnia book she had read.

While Megan's younger sister, a slower reader, admired Puddleglum in *The Silver Chair*, Megan rushed through volumes of inspirational historical fiction and swooned over the *Anne of Green Gables* TV miniseries instead of

---

1. C. S. Lewis, *The Voyage of the Dawn Treader* (Harper Collins, 1980), 247.

reading the books. It wasn't until her senior year at Covenant College, when she and Betsy were taking a children's literature class taught by Ethan Pettit, that she finally got around to finishing The Chronicles of Narnia.

Mr. Pettit, the assistant librarian, was known for serving tea to students who visited his office. Having been influenced by Francis Schaeffer and Madeleine L'Engle, he explained the difference between capital "T" Truth versus lowercase "t" truth and capital "S" Story versus lowercase "s" story to the class. Combining Truth with Story is very different than Truth and "story" or "truth" and Story, and "truth" with "story" lacks substance.

One of the assignments was to keep a reading journal of children's books. So, Megan worked her way through picture books and middle grade novels, including the familiar story of *The Lion, the Witch, and the Wardrobe*, followed by *Prince Caspian*, then *The Voyage of the Dawn Treader*.

Sitting on the floor of her room, leaning against the bottom bunk, she read the last chapter in which Edmund and Lucy arrive on shore and find a Lamb waiting for them on the beach. The Lamb invites them to join him for breakfast, then transforms into their beloved friend, Aslan. But their joy turns to sorrow when Aslan reveals that this is their last visit to Narnia.

"It isn't Narnia, you know," sobbed Lucy. "It's you.
We shan't meet you there. And how can we live, never meeting you?"

"But you shall meet me, dear one," said Aslan.

"Are—are you there too, Sir?" said Edmund.

"I am," said Aslan. "But there I have another name. You must learn to know me by that name. This was the very reason why you were brought to Narnia, that by knowing me here for a little, you may know me better there."[2]

As Megan tells it now, "I stopped. I read the words again. I read them a third time, tears flowing down my cheeks. Tears still come to my eyes when I

---

2. Ibid.

remember that day because my life has never been the same. I had professed faith in Christ for years, but for the first time, I was beginning to realize the power of children's literature to speak Truth to me through a Story, and I could hear Christ, through Aslan, calling me 'Dear one.'"

The more we read, the more we discover that the voice of His Truth not only speaks through books that are written, published by, and marketed to Christians, but also in other many kinds of literature because the Holy Spirit breathes through common grace. Truly, every good gift and every perfect gift is from above (James 1:17).

The Unformula

What is Truth? What is Story? Definitions are elusive because there is no formula. There are essentials and common elements, but each author brings a unique voice and experience to his or her writing.

We're using capital "T" Truth here to refer to the ultimate Truth found in God's Word, and capital "S" Story to mean the grand biblical narrative of creation, fall, redemption, and restoration. Fragments of Truth and echoes of the great Story can be found even in secular works, owing to God's common grace. As we explore these ideas, we recognize that each of us is accountable to his or her own conscience (Rom. 14:12), and our personal experiences will shape how we read and understand Truth and Story.

TRUTH

There are two ways of looking at Truth in literature. When we speak of God's Truth, what the Bible calls wisdom, manifested through creation and redemptive history as God has ordained it, we capitalize the "T" for emphasis. Anywhere we read of goodness, hope, light, loving one's neighbor, good triumphing over evil, forgiveness and redemption, healthy family relationships, friendships, and beauty and order in creation, we see Truth, and our hearts rejoice. Because we were made in God's image, we cannot help but love what God loves.

We find examples of Truth in picture books like *Last Stop on Market Street* by Matt de la Peña, in which a boy's grandmother opens his eyes to love his neighbor and practice kindness. In *Heckedy Peg* by Audrey Wood, a mother's love for her children makes her bold and wise. *Bartholomew and the Oobleck* by Dr. Seuss is a wonderful story of pride and humility, and *Yellow and Pink* by William Steig shows the absurdity of evolution.

> *Books that hold the most Truth not only show that we need a savior, but that there is a Savior, and therefore we have hope.*

Books that hold the most Truth not only show that we need a savior, but that there is a Savior, and therefore we have hope. They point to our deep desire for peace with God and with one another.

Stories that reflect the fallen nature of our world reveal Truth wherever a redemptive ending unfolds. A broken family finds forgiveness in *The Star That Always Stays* by Anna Rose Johnson, and a lazy, alcoholic father is converted at the end of *Strawberry Girl* by Lois Lenski. A boy without parents is taken in by a father figure who cares for him in *The Season of Styx Malone* by Kekla Magoon, and a proud rabbit is humbled and becomes a Christ figure in *The Miraculous Journey of Edward Tulane* by Kate DiCamillo. In the Rabbit and Robot books by Cece Bell, friendship undergoes tension and reconciliation.

Truth in nonfiction may be found in books that explain how to solve a math problem or that joyfully describe nature, leading us to delight in God's creation. Recent trends in picture book biographies and nonfiction have turned bland facts into engaging literature such as *The Day-Glo Brothers* by Chris Barton, *The Boys in the Boat* by Daniel James Brown, *Fallout* by Steve Sheinkin, or *The Girl Who Drew Butterflies* by Joyce Sidman.

truth

Many crowd-pleasing, trite-but-harmless books such as branded spin-offs, books by celebrities, or watered-down fairy tales, only contain "truth," not real Truth. Although these may be heavily promoted by marketing departments, they don't leave a lasting impression on the audience. They often feature pop-culture characters and offer positive affirmation and "character training" rather than bestowing delight.

Such "truth" may also be found in popular stories that are clean of sex, foul language, and violence such as a fun mystery series. These may be fun for young readers and are generally harmless, even if they don't nourish the soul. There is nothing objectionable about the I Spy or Where's Waldo books, and *Mr. Fox's Game of "No!"* by David LaRochelle or *The Monster at the End of this Book* by Jon Stone are interactive crowd-pleasers.

Other books that claim to present "truths" clearly oppose God's Truth. Half-truths and falsehood masquerade as "truth" in books that claim there is no real goodness in the world and there are no trustworthy allies among adults. Books that promote gender fluidity or same-sex relationships are contrary to God's design for men and women that is revealed in Scripture.

WINSOME VESSELS

Do you have a collection of mugs? How do you decide which one to use for your favorite morning beverage? Do your children have particular favorites?

In the same way that there is no formula for the Truth/Story framework, no formula can guarantee the design of a perfect vessel. You could drink tea out of a ceramic cup with a promotional logo instead of a thoughtfully fashioned pottery mug and it would still be comforting. Part of our subjective preference is the objective quality of workmanship, and part of it is personal taste.

Does it matter if you drink homemade chai or locally roasted coffee in a Styrofoam cup? Although the difference in taste might not be discernible to everyone, much of the pleasure is lost by drinking from a generic, disposable cup.

What if you chose one of your favorite mugs and prepared a cup of store-brand hot chocolate mix using water instead of milk? Could the smooth curve and fond memories of a well-crafted vessel redeem the flavor of a watery, artificially flavored, overly sweet beverage? Absolutely not.

Likewise, Story is the winsome vessel of Truth.

STORY

Scripture sets the standard for the best Story elements that draw us in. God begins His narrative thread with creation in which He opens history, showing delight in a beautiful setting and in enjoying fellowship with the people He made.

Plot twist: Eve was deceived and desired the fruit she wasn't supposed to have because the serpent desired to destroy God's plan.

Inciting event: God expected this and had already arranged a deeper, richer Story.

Rising action: The Old Testament, in all its interwoven genres.

Climax: Jesus' crucifixion, burial, and particularly His resurrection.

Falling action: The book of Acts, continuing through the last two millennia to the present.

Conclusion: The people of God are living in the denouement, waiting for the marriage supper of the Lamb.

PLOT DIAGRAM OF SCRIPTURE

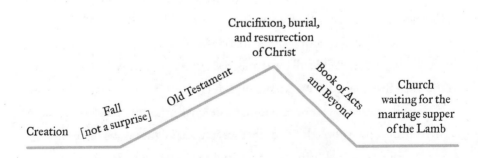

Story, at its core, reflects the experience of the human condition, while Truth within the Story points to God's ultimate reality. In the midst of this grand narrative that centers on the glory of Jesus Christ, the Bible provides many Stories within the whole Story including character sagas (Abraham, David, Paul), cautionary tales (Lot's wife, Achan), romance (Boaz and Ruth), and vivid historical events (the ten plagues, Daniel in the lions' den, Esther rescuing her people), as well as poetry, wise sayings, parables, and even trickster tales (Jacob, Delilah, or Hushai in 2 Sam. 16). Sometimes it is hard to see how God is working, but because we know that God is sovereign, we anticipate a redemptive ending. For example, although God is not specifically mentioned in the book of Esther, His providence is clear in the midst of exile, and we see reflections of God's justice in the execution of Haman and the exaltation of Mordecai and Esther.

In literature we find many examples that echo the Story of the Bible. *The Lion, the Witch and the Wardrobe* clearly mirrors the Story of Jesus who redeems sinners living under the curse through a mediator's atoning death and resurrection. Fairy tales emphasize motifs that we also find in Proverbs, such as the consequences of wise and foolish behavior. Picture book biographies, thoughtful narrative nonfiction, and intricate descriptions in nature lore (whether or not it's identified as "creation") invite our young readers into the Story that God is weaving through people and places. Engaging memoirs abound for young people. Some of our favorites include *Brown Girl Dreaming* by Jaqueline Woodson, *El Deafo* by Cece Bell, and *Everything Sad Is Untrue* by Daniel Nayeri.

Sometimes it is hard to separate Stories from Truth because the Story narrative can be exceptionally well-told. Even when the conclusion is flawed, we can still delight in the craftsmanship. Neal Shusterman's young adult Arc of the Scythe trilogy has strong Story elements because it grapples with the nature of humanity, but it contains "truth" that does not reflect God's Truth.

story

Not every book has to be a Story to be worthy of reading. Some readers might delight in a "story" that others don't appreciate, and some "stories" offer little more than simple pleasure or interesting subject matter. These are appropriate as appetizers or dessert in your family's literary menu. A little is fine, but not really satisfying.

Sometimes a "story" suffers from too much good intention. Inspirational picture books and novels may try too hard to communicate Truth while the author's care in storytelling falls short of richness, beauty, and depth.

Some excellent literature is cheated of greatness when it is simplified, with mediocre results. This is common in retellings of Bible stories, fairy tales, and in franchised "new adventures of" popular characters such as Thomas the Tank Engine, Clifford, Curious George, Little Bear, etc. Modern easy-reader variations such as the newer *Little House on the Prairie* stories sacrifice rich language for controlled vocabulary, which is no delight to read.

Certain "stories" are not without value when they are used to encourage young readers to gain confidence and discover a desire to read more. Do Garfield comics contain Truth and Story? No, but humor in a few panels can motivate a young reader to persevere in decoding words. Continuing to surround him with a variety of books that are rich and delightful is part of the process of learning to appreciate better Stories as he matures.

The axis in the following graph demonstrates how books may be arranged in different quadrants based on certain criteria, while allowing for personal taste.

Foundations: Discovering Truth and Story

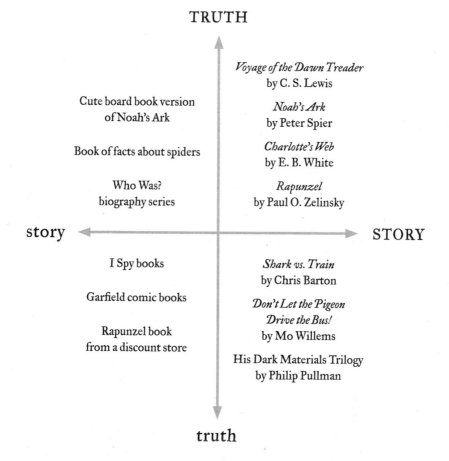

In the upper right corner, we find easily recognizable examples of Truth revealed through Story in *Voyage of the Dawn Treader* and a gorgeous wordless picture book version of *Noah's Ark*. *Charlotte's Web* is a beloved classic that weaves themes of friendship and loyalty with the deeper Truth of sacrificial love. *Rapunzel*, retold and illustrated by Paul Zelinsky, enriches a well-known fairy tale full of symbolism with lavish illustrations and tender emotion.

Moving down, we find "truth" and Story in *Shark vs. Train*, a picture book about two boys pitting the strengths and weaknesses of their favorite toys against each other. *Don't Let the Pigeon Drive the Bus!* is a fun read-aloud and a crowd pleaser without significant Truth. *His Dark Materials* is an engaging trilogy in which the author's antagonism toward the church is evident. Can we enjoy reading these books? Certainly, while applying varying degrees of discernment (or assuming that they're just plain fun[3]).

The lower left corner includes books that are "truth" and "story." These may be favorites for a season, and there's nothing seriously offensive, but they soon lose their charm with minimal nostalgic residue.

The last quadrant in the upper left contains books that are Truth and "story." These may include cute board books of Noah's ark that poorly represent the biblical account but still introduce children to a man who obeyed God and, with his family, was delivered from judgment.[4] Factual books that are popular or highly visual also fall in this category.

God, the Author of Truth and Story

Pontius Pilate looked wearily into the eyes of Jesus and asked, "What is truth?" (John 18:38a). He did not expect an answer. Before him stood the very incarnation of love, goodness, justice, mercy, compassion, and the Savior of the world—the perfect embodiment of Truth and any virtues we glimpse in the best children's stories. But Pilate was blind.

We still live in a world that is blind to the Truth, that denies the reality of God's design and authority over His creation. But if our ears hear the One who declared, "I am the way, and the truth, and the life. No one comes to the Father except through me" (John 14:6), our eyes can be opened to see the goodness of God everywhere, including in literature for children.

Why do we respond so viscerally to stories? The classic plot arc of the Bible, as we've already seen, is hard-wired in human consciousness: setting, conflict, development, climax, resolution. Story puts flesh on these bare bones of Truth. Stories that include descriptions of beauty in nature reflect the seeds

---

3. See chapter 16, "Just for Laughs: Kid Humor."
4. The Ark Encounter in Kentucky has an impressive display of problematic picture book retellings of Noah's ark. As always, use discretion.

of creation. Where nature is ravaged or weeds crop up, that is a result of the fall; planting a garden is a redemptive act of faith. Where we read of a happy family, beginning with marriage that is between one man and one woman, that is a gift that was God's idea. Where there is divorce or death of a parent, the pain, separation, and longing are evidence of the fall. There may or may not be restoration in the conclusion, but we look for signs of grace in other caring adults who come alongside the hurting child, bringing healing and hope in the midst of difficult circumstances.

Is our duty to be didactic, expecting to stop and make spiritual application while we're reading? Not necessarily. Children who have been made in the image of God will naturally be drawn to manifestations of His character in Truth, and experiencing delight in many Stories will have the cumulative effect of helping lift the veil of delighting in Him. Part of our role as parents and educators means being prepared when the occasion does arise to point out both positive and negative aspects of characters; not as moral guides (don't betray your siblings for candy like Edmund did!) but recognizing that although we are imperfect, our hope of redemption is in Jesus Christ.[5]

Jesus is the Word made flesh who dwelt among us. As the creator of the perfect Story arc, He knew how effectively stories communicate. He knew, as good preachers do, that His audience's understanding was limited, and that parables would help those who had ears to hear. He knew that Truth soaks into the soil of the soul through Story, especially when it is grounded in reality.

Sometimes Truth and Story do not gloriously soar off the page together. We do not always find them shining from happy pages of books that are teaching character values, nor in secret, subtle themes veiled in clean literature that is "safe" for anyone to read. Christians can read a wide variety of literature, both sacred and secular, but we need discernment when doing so.

As much as we would like to enjoy children's books that are described as "inspirational," they are often saccharine, lacking realistic emotion and

---

5. See chapter 21.

the well-crafted narrative of a Story. Since everything is put under Christ's dominion, we can learn to read to the glory of God, always looking for Truth and Story wherever it may be found. Pleasure is a gift that comes from God, and it is the first indication of the presence of Truth and/or Story. If there is no delight, we ask ourselves why.

On Reading and Story

A love of Stories begins with *hearing* them, not independently reading them. It takes a lot of reading aloud from literature that provides rich language and delightful stories before a child is ready to learn to read. Delight is a great motivator.

When we look at the whole wide world God has made, when we cultivate our children's imaginations, we are offering them a reason to want more Stories. We can tell them Stories, show them Stories, read them Stories, and nurture a love for Story long before children have the developmental skills necessary to read the words on their own. Long before a child can read, he or she should develop a taste for the Stories that will make the effort worthwhile.

Stories connect us to God. He reveals Himself through His Word and the unfolding of history, and through seeing how He works in our own and in our children's lives.

Stories connect us to others, to family members who relate past experiences, to shared culture and inside jokes. To friends who are eager for us to read the same book, who make memories with us, or whose lives are nothing like our own. Stories connect us to strangers, to their experiences in the past or in another country or culture.

Oral storytelling has been around for millennia, and reading aloud with a child is a priceless experience, not merely because of the book, but especially for the development of loving relationships with a caregiver. In *The Enchanted Hour*, Meghan Cox Gurdon writes, "The act of reading together secures people to one another, creating order and connection, as if we were quilt squares tacked together with threads made of stories."[6] Bonding over a shared, well-narrated audiobook can provide a modern alternative to sitting around a fire (although s'mores are a marvelous reason to build relationships if you don't have a traveling bard handy). Hearing good stories can make any child's soul hunger for more. Taste and see.

READING AS WORSHIP

Discerning appreciation of literature, from picture books to lengthy classics, comes from learning to recognize these elements and how they resonate. There may be Truth told in "story," or a Story may only contain "truth." Reading is an act of redemption by those who seek to wonder and to worship God by offering up all our activities with our families in every area of life.

God made a magnanimous offer to Solomon when he was made king, and Solomon asked for one thing: wisdom. God is still the source of all wisdom, and He gives each of us the opportunity to glorify Him in our reading. This means choosing some books, but not others, discussing questions that arise along the way, and being gracious while holding different opinions and humble enough to see how we can shine gospel light into our understanding of Truth and Story in all kinds of literature.

Ultimately, finding Truth and Story is an act of worship, beginning with asking for wisdom (James 1:5). Let us seek to find what is true and good in the books that we read.

---

6. Meghan Cox Gurdon, *The Enchanted Hour* (Harper, 2019), 47.

BOOKLIST FOR CHAPTER 1

Further Reading

    Echoes of Eden, Jerram Barrs

For Children/Teens

    Bartholomew and the Oobleck by Dr. Seuss (Picture Book)
    The Golden Plate, Bernadette Watts (PB)
    Last Stop on Market Street, Matt de la Peña (PB)
    The Girl and the Bicycle, Mark Pett (PB)
    The Watcher, Nikki Grimes (PB)
    Ben Washington series, Jasmine Mullen (Chapter Book)
    Mikis and the Donkey, Bibi Dumon Tak (CB)
    All-of-a-Kind Family, Sydney Taylor (Middle Grade)
    The Charlatan's Boy, Jonathan Rogers (MG)
    Miraculous Journey of Edward Tulane, Kate DiCamillo (MG)
    Words by Heart, Ouida Sebestyen (MG)
    The Mythmakers, John Hendrix (Young Adult/Graphic Novel)
    Once a Queen, Sarah Arthur (YA)

CHAPTER 2

DEVELOPING DISCERNMENT AND DELIGHT: WHAT TO READ WHEN

> He held up a book then. "I'm reading it to you for relax."
> "Has it got any sports in it?"
> "Fencing. Fighting. Torture. Poison. True Love. Hate. Revenge. Giants. Hunters. Bad men. Good men. Beautifulest Ladies. Snakes. Spiders.... Pain. Death. Brave men. Cowardly men. Strongest men. Chases. Escapes. Lies. Truths. Passion. Miracles."
> "Sounds okay," I said.[1]
> — William Goldman, *The Princess Bride*

I magine sitting down to your family's Thanksgiving meal. Your three-year-old pushes his mashed potatoes around, waits for you to cut up his turkey, and complains about the green bean casserole. Meanwhile, your seven-year-old begs to eat dessert first because she remembers loving Grandma's pumpkin pie, please Mom? You, however, remember that same seven-year-old turning up her nose when you first offered her the same pie years ago.

---

1. William Goldman, *The Princess Bride: An Illustrated Edition of S. Morgenstern's Classic Tale of True Love and High Adventure* (Harper, 2013), 10–11.

Raising readers is like training our children not only to eat (ability), but enjoy (taste), the Thanksgiving meal. We willingly work to train ability and taste because we know the result is worth it: a group of family and friends gathered around a bountiful table for feasting and fellowship. "Ability and taste" translate to "discernment and delight." Our goal is raising readers who delight in story and can discern truth, not ones who are "well-read" by arbitrary, non-biblical standards.

Children are drawn to sweet, easy stories, like dessert, before they develop an appreciation for more savory dishes, like roasted Brussels sprouts. Children are not abnormal simply because they do not fully appreciate the Thanksgiving feast for a few years. The literary feast is no different.

We are tempted to parade our children's reading habits as badges of good parenting or good educational training. Conversely, we are tempted to panic if our children are not reading on "their level." What if your daughter hasn't read *The Hobbit* yet? Is she "behind"? What is her reading level anyway? Does it matter?

What Is a "Reading Level"?

Reading levels are bunk.

There. We said it. Academic reading levels are artificial metrics designed to help parents and educators know a book's general difficulty level or a child's approximate reading ability.[2] Great effort is made to match a child at a particular age or grade to precisely the right academic reading level with less effort given to holistically determining a child's developmental readiness (as opposed to the broader publisher "reading levels" that span a larger age range). But these graded reading levels only measure comprehension and decoding (sounding out/recognizing words) skills. As children's author Katherine Paterson laments, "The basic task of education is the care and feeding of the imagination. . . .

---

2. Academic reading levels are not the same thing as publisher reading levels, but they overlap. We'll cover publisher reading levels more in chapter 3.

Education has chosen to emphasize decoding and computation rather than the cultivation of the imagination."[3]

One popular reading program is Accelerated Reader (AR). Schools around the country, both public and private, use this system to help students read "on their level." Prizes and points are awarded after children read books on their assessed reading level and take a short comprehension quiz. Classrooms compete with other classrooms, making reading more a competitive sport than a source of pleasure or enlightenment.

In theory, AR levels mirror grade levels. For example, books marked a 5 should equal a fifth grade level; the number after the decimal indicates how many months into the corresponding school year.[4] For example, 5.6 indicates the sixth month of fifth grade. But these reading levels do not address content, nor a reader's conscience, developmental stage, or maturity.

For example, *The Hundred Dresses*, *The Magician's Nephew*, *Ramona and Her Father*, *Roll of Thunder, Hear My Cry*, *The Hunger Games*, and *To Kill a Mockingbird* are each assigned a 5.+ reading level in the AR system. Granted, *The Hunger Games* and *To Kill a Mockingbird* are listed as "upper grades interest level" (grades 9–12) and the rest are "middle grades interest level" (grades 4–8). A simple list like this reveals how inadequate numerically driven reading levels are when choosing books for children and teens. Language Arts curricula tend to be more thoughtful, placing *The Hundred Dresses* somewhere around third or fourth grade, and *Roll of Thunder, Hear My Cry* around sixth or seventh. Those books align with those ages. Why? Because their content suits the general maturity of students in those grades, regardless of technical reading levels.

Quantifying reading levels is but one tool for evaluating a book's suitability for a particular child. Content maturity levels, complexity of theme, and your

---

3. Katherine Paterson, *A Sense of Wonder: On Reading and Writing Books for Children* (Plume, 1995), 198.
4. Anyone can look up a book in the AR system online. (Lexile levels are used similarly.) "Renaissance Accelerated Reader Bookfinder," Renaissance Learning, 2023, https://www.arbookfind.com/.

child's unique training and experience are impossible to quantify. As adults, we want to shepherd our children's imaginations, not merely equip them to recognize words on a page.

C. S. Lewis makes a similar point regarding publishers' age recommendations:

> *This neat sorting-out of books into age-groups, so dear to publishers, has only a very sketchy relation with the habits of any real readers. Those of us who are blamed when old for reading childish books were blamed when children for reading books too old for us. No reader worth his salt trots along in obedience to a time-table.*[5]

Why start this chapter in the weeds of AR book levels? The AR program illustrates our cultural framework for raising readers without considering the whole child. If your child is not ready for the Thanksgiving feast, they will neither feast nor give thanks. We don't consider calories as the sole determination of overall deliciousness and desirability. Might we consider how to take delight in the feast itself?

Waiting for maturity means just that: *waiting*. We want to say with Gerald of Elephant and Piggie fame, "GROAN! I am *done* waiting."[6] As parents and educators, we want our children to read all the great books, all our personal favorites. In our eagerness to share this feast with our children, too often we rush the process. We toss books at children because they are exceptional students! But your eight-year-old might not be ready for *A Wrinkle in Time*, even if he reads at a fifth grade level. *And that is okay.*

In practice, this means paying attention to our individual children and students. Life experience, academic ability, developmental readiness (particularly in abstract thinking), conscience sensitivity—all play into a child's maturity level and their ability to enjoy and benefit from a given book. Readers are individual souls; varying maturity levels are normal.

---

5. C. S. Lewis, "On Three Ways of Writing for Children," in *Of Other Worlds: Essays and Stories*, ed. Walter Hooper (Harcourt Brace and Co., 1994), 28.
6. Mo Willems, *Waiting Is Not Easy!* (Hyperion, 2014), 30–32.

Cultivating Ability and Taste

Rather than focusing on academic reading levels and which books your child can decode easily and fluently, ponder which books foster delight in your home or classroom. Scholar Junius Johnson explains that first understanding what engages a child helps us to wisely "provide channels for their wonder and imagination."[7]

> *Each book opens another channel, and we want to open as many as we can, for the Spirit of God is abundant enough to flow through infinitely many. These things hold open the spaces in our soul where the Spirit inspires and encourages us. They make us magnanimous, and on this spiritual immensity we can build the character that will help our children grow into the fullness of virtue. Good stories keep the soul awake, forewarning it of danger and populating it with heroes and heroines whose examples of courage and character give us strength to see ourselves standing against similar foes and refusing to yield to evil. Story has always been and remains our greatest tool in crafting wise and great people.*[8]

Delight and discernment are our primary goals as we shepherd the young imaginations in our care and help them grow into "wise and great people" who are "magnanimous," possessing the "fullness of virtue." Reading levels are servants in this goal, not shepherds. Remember, the Holy Spirit is at work, and He defies quantification! Pray about how best to foster delight and discernment in each of your young readers, research the books available, and keep the bigger picture in mind.

Dr. Jill P. May, children's literature scholar and professor, urges educators to pay attention to their elementary-aged students instead of merely following

---

7. Junius Johnson, "Afterword: Imagination, Mystery, Wonder," in *Wild Things and Castles in the Sky: A Guide to Choosing the Best Books for Children*, eds. Leslie Bustard et al. (Square Halo Books, 2021), 283.
8. Ibid.

grade-level lists of "important" books. Her advice is just as valid for parents. What do young readers notice in the books they read? How can we invite them into conversation? The more we ask our children what they think, the more they will begin to pay attention as they read. May writes that "children will grow up to be adults who will pick books that best fit their own needs—or they will grow up to be nonreaders. That choice will largely depend on how they perceive literature and its meaning."[9]

> *Delight and discernment are our primary goals as we shepherd the young imaginations in our care.*

C. S. Lewis agrees: "The child as reader is neither to be patronised nor idolised: we talk to him as man to man."[10]

The process of noticing features of a book (pictures or text), critiquing it together, laughing or crying together, wondering whether an ending "works" or a character seems true to life—such involvement invites our young readers to be discerning readers, whether they are reading picture books at age ten or huge novels at age six. This is how we foster delight.

Ruth Sawyer, author of the Newbery Award–winning *Roller Skates*, writes in her memoir:

> *When we bring that which appeals to the imaginative, creative mind and spirit of the child, it appeals to the subconscious as well as to the conscious— to the emotions. These children want to feel, to gather in the beauty, the sense of something hidden, to be revealed later. First delight—then wisdom.*[11]

Sometimes we will strike out, and sometimes we will hit a home run. Our children will not always enjoy the same titles we do, but by reading widely and

---

9. Jill P. May, *Children's Literature and Critical Theory* (Oxford University Press, 1995), 189.
10. Lewis, *Of Other Worlds*, 34.
11. Ruth Sawyer, *The Way of the Storyteller: A Great Storyteller Shares Her Rich Experience and Joy in Her Art and Tells Eleven of Her Best-Loved Stories* (Penguin Publishing Group, 1976), 189.

often, we will cultivate readers who are not only eager to read, but thoughtful about their reading.

This process of shepherding young imaginations is a dangerous journey, filled with temptations to Vanity Fair and battles with Apollyon. Our training of young readers must include consideration for both their delight and their growing discernment as we evaluate which books they are ready for holistically.

Books serve a distinct role in instructing one's conscience.[12] Author Leslie Bustard writes: "Stories train our imaginations and help us grow in empathy and sympathy, but stories can also help us understand how we fit into the kingdom of God, as well as prepare us for a life of being molded by the word of God."[13]

A Holistic View

Are you fretting that your son is reading less than he used to? Are you concerned that your daughter is reading the wrong sorts of books?

Words are important! Jesus is called the Word of God, the Word made flesh. God spoke creation into being using words. The Lord has revealed Himself to us through His creation and His Word. Reading is only a tool; it should never be an idol. Our ultimate priority is to know the Lord and nurture our children to do so likewise, not to read all the right books.

It is easy to elevate the act of "reading good books." When we fret over our children's reading levels, fear that we did not assign the correct book, or lament that a particular out-of-print copy is unavailable, it is time for a heart check. Are we worrying unduly? Have we gotten our priorities out of whack?

Parents and teachers rightly want to ensure that the children and students in their care are receiving a sound education, are exposed to cultural excellence, and are developing steadily toward proficiency and maturity. However,

---

12. The idea of "instructing one's conscience" comes from *Ourselves* by Charlotte Mason.
13. Leslie Bustard, "Introduction," in *Wild Things and Castles in the Sky: A Guide to Choosing the Best Books for Children*, eds. Leslie Bustard et al. (Square Halo Books, 2021), 9.

unhealthy concern creeps in when we add spiritual overtones to these fears, worrying that the "right" book is essential for our child's spiritual development—that reading a particular title at a particular age is a sign of being a good Christian.

Part of our reading recommendations as parents and educators must factor in the whole life: If your formerly eager reader seems to be losing enthusiasm, what else is going on in that child's life? Is this simply a busy season with soccer practice, a new baby sibling, extra homework, or a part-time job? Reading comes and goes for children and teens. Many good things can crowd out time to read, and it will rightly take second place in certain seasons.

If your child has put reading aside, or if your family had a good read-aloud habit in place but cannot find the time right now, it is okay. Step back and evaluate the whys: Laziness is one thing; a full schedule is a different issue.

Practical Tips

You are willing to wait until your child is ready to read *The Hiding Place* or *The Faithful Spy*, but what do you read in the meantime?

As young children begin with soft food and finger foods, we begin with easier texts that are approachable to children, and we read aloud the harder texts until our children can read them on their own. A feast is composed of multiple flavors, textures, and courses. Take time to enjoy funny books, serious books, spiritual resources, beautiful pictures, stories of derring-do and adventure and excitement. Just as we do not prepare our children for Thanksgiving by only eating turkey every day of the year, we don't need to read every children's version of Homer's *Odyssey* with them.

Author N. D. Wilson explains that because human beings are "narrative creatures,"[14] stories nourish us like food:

---

14. N. D. Wilson, *Death by Living: Life Is Meant to Be Spent* (Thomas Nelson, 2013), 11.

For years, all we do is feed. We don't control what our parents feed us for dinner, we don't control what they read to us (or don't read to us). . . . We are loaded full with every kind of tale. . . . When we begin to make our own choices, when we become an active character in our own narratives, all of that soul food is behind us. . . . Souls will be fed and shaped from the inside out.[15]

And so, we cultivate the love of a good story because it helps children love *the* Story. We read Scripture together, reminding ourselves that this Story is True in every sense. Reading well does enable us to read God's Word more astutely. The Bible is a tremendous work of literature, in addition to the inspired rule for our faith and practice. But reading is only one piece of who we are.[16] Stories themselves are more important than mere words on a page. And shepherding children's imaginations is more important than whether a child is a "reader."

As children grow, they will naturally move from *The Story of Ferdinand* the bull, to *St. George and the Dragon* (preferably the version by Margaret Hodges), to *The Hobbit* and to *Beowulf*. Dragons are real and terrible, but we do not begin with lengthy poetry and lopping off the arms of monsters. We begin with Ferdinand, sitting "just quietly and smell[ing] the flowers."[17]

---

15. Ibid.
16. We firmly believe "reading well" is a tool for enabling us to read God's Word better. But we also want to acknowledge that not everyone is a "reader." In other words, not everyone will read thoughtfully and/or voraciously by choice. That's okay!
17. Munro Leaf, *The Story of Ferdinand* (Puffin, 1936), n.p.

BOOKLIST FOR CHAPTER 2

Further Reading

Honey for a Child's Heart, Gladys Hunt

For Children/Teens

These books have wide age appeal and work well for read-alouds or independent readers.

John Ronald's Dragons: The Story of J. R. R. Tolkien, Caroline McAlister, Eliza Wheeler (Picture Book)
Skunk and Badger, Amy Timberlake (Chapter Book)
Too Small Tola series, Atinuke (CB)
Astrid the Unstoppable, Maria Parr (Middle Grade)
Echo, Pam Muñoz Ryan (MG)
The Hobbit, J. R. R. Tolkien (MG)
The Many Assassinations of Samir, the Seller of Dreams, Daniel Nayeri (MG)
The Miraculous Journey of Edward Tulane, Kate DiCamillo (MG)
Where the Mountain Meets the Moon, Grace Lin (MG)

CHAPTER 3

SOMETHING FOR EVERYONE: READING LEVELS AND GENRES

> So please, oh please, we beg, we pray,
> Go throw your TV set away,
> And in its place you can install
> A lovely bookshelf on the wall.[1]
>
> —Roald Dahl, *Charlie and the Chocolate Factory*

A literary genre designates the type of literature that appeals to a given reader.

"I'm really into fantasy," one reader may say, while another counters,

"I get lost in fantasy—all that grandiose language and made-up names. I like realism."

"Well, I love language, and what great authors can do with it. Doesn't matter if it's fantasy or realism, just sweep me away with great characters and dialogue."

"Who cares about language?? Sweep me away with a swoony guy and the girl who can't stand him but falls for him in the end. I'm talking about amour!"

---

1. Roald Dahl, *Charlie and the Chocolate Factory* (Puffin, 1998), 141.

"Well, if I'm going to read a book at all, it had better make me laugh."

Even reluctant readers have an idea of what kind of stories they like, but before parents head to the library or grandmas head to the big chain bookstore, they need to know where their readers are in age and developmental readiness. Publishers sort their children's inventory into six very general groups, according to the age of the reader:

- **Board Books** (ages 0–3), marketed for babies and toddlers.
- **Picture Books** (ages 3–8), usually (but not always!) designed for reading aloud.
- **Easy Readers** (ages 4–8), intended to help preschoolers through second graders gain ability and confidence in independent reading. "Leveled" readers, which adhere to strict vocabulary guidelines, fall into this category.
- **Chapter Books** (ages 7–10), for children with a more sustained interest level than the picture book set.
- **Middle Grade** (MG; ages 8–12), the broadest category and the bulk of children's publishing, for independent readers.
- **Young Adult** (YA; ages 12–17), with the largest age appeal. YA is targeted to readers ranging from age 12 all the way up to adult.

Note that *publisher* reading levels are much broader than the academic reading levels discussed in chapter 2. In our book reviews at Redeemed Reader, we use publisher designations when indicating the reading level, but also include a "Recommended for" designation reflecting our best judgment about appropriate ages for the subject matter.

Picture books can be simple enough for a two-year-old to understand (think *Goodnight Moon*), or dense enough to challenge a fifth grader, like the many science- or history-related picture books we review.

Easy Readers straddle a wide line between picture and chapter books. They range from very simple with just a few words per page (like Mo Willems' Elephant and Piggie series) to more complex stories with multiple episodes

Something for Everyone: Reading Levels and Genres

—the Frog and Toad books are a classic example, or more recently, Tedd Arnold's Fly Guy series. Leveled Readers are usually published in series and clearly marked with the grade level, like the "I Can Read" books.

Chapter books are sometimes hard to distinguish from Easy Readers, with similar large type, wide margins, and illustrations on almost every page. The main difference is that chapter books tell a single story rather than a series of episodes, reflecting the greater attention span of older readers. The Lulu series by Hilary McKay is an outstanding example.

Middle Grade is usually what comes to mind when we think "children's literature" (and "Newbery Award"). It's targeted toward "the bicycle years," when kids begin to feel a sense of independence. The publishing industry has prepared them with tricycles (leveled readers) and training wheels (chapter books); now they are able to take off on their own, developing their own literary tastes and abilities. A lot of growing up takes place in the years between third and seventh grade, and it can be hard to determine where a child is on the reading-level scale. In general, we think of lower MG as ages eight to ten (think *Charlotte's Web* or, more recently, the Green Ember series by S. D. Smith) and upper MG as ages ten to twelve (*A Wrinkle in Time*, *Things Seen from Above*). Many of the MG books we review would be interesting to older readers as well, all the way up to age fifteen.

Hi-Lo is a sub-group between MG and YA. The tag stands for "high interest, low reading level," meaning subjects of interest to older kids with underdeveloped reading skills. Nonfiction used to dominate this level, but the field has expanded to include fiction in all genres, such as the popular I Survived series. Literary quality has improved also.

YA has at times been the hottest and trendiest category—also the most controversial. No topic is considered out of bounds for YA. The only requirement is that the main characters be in their teens, usually between sixteen and eighteen. Romance used to be the YA staple; now fantasy vies with general realistic fiction for domination in the field.

But What Do They *Like*?

"Genre" applies to any reading level and refers to the type of literature a reader prefers, such as westerns, historical fiction, romance. Some genres are rigidly defined, while others are broad and fluid. This is as true for children's literature as it is for the adult market.

Nonfiction

Nonfiction is obviously defined as "anything that isn't fiction." It used to be the bread and butter of the publishing industry, meeting the demand for practical information like cookbooks and self-help. But in an age of YouTube and food bloggers, who needs books? It's a different story in children's publishing, especially since the Common Core initiative of the 2010s expanded the demand for nonfiction in the classroom, and in addition to quantity, we're seeing more quality.

School librarians divide nonfiction into five major categories:

Traditional Nonfiction

This is the kind we all grew up with and is still standard today. Examples are the Landmark history series of the baby-boomer generation, the many National Geographic series of today, and countless stand-alone titles like *Courage Has No Color* and *We've Got a Job*. Traditional nonfiction often strives for drama, but the purpose is expository: communicating information in an interesting way.

Browsable Nonfiction

DK (Dorling Kindersley) created this category in the 1990s beginning with their Eyewitness series books. They are useful as reference: to introduce a subject, fill in knowledge gaps, or create interest in a particular topic. The author is secondary; sometimes not even named. Page layouts feature illustrations, photographs, short blocks of text (including side bars), and visual aids like charts, graphs, and timelines.

They're not meant to be read straight through but are perfect for random browsing. They are also great for kids who feel overwhelmed by pages of solid text, especially those who gravitate to hands-on projects and video games. National Geographic Kids and other series books follow the DK pattern.

Narrative Nonfiction

In the 1950s and 60s, the Childhood of Famous Americans history series were written like novels, with scenes and dialogue spun from the barest facts. By the mid-1990s, more authors were using the elements of fiction to tell exciting stories about pivotal historical events or scientific discoveries. In adult publishing, narrative nonfiction is such a popular genre that "young reader" editions of titles like *Hidden Figures* and *Unbroken* have done well in juvenile sales. Steve Sheinkin writes narrative nonfiction directly for young teens, such as *Fallout* and *Impossible Escape*.

Expository Literature

What distinguishes this category is the author: a writer first (as opposed to a scientist or historian who writes), with a passionate interest in the subject. Sometimes the author is directly involved, like Sy Montgomery in her Scientists in the Field series. The prose style may be distinctive, as in *The Adventurous Life of Myles Standish* by Cheryl Harness. Jason Chin combines his interests with outstanding artwork in *Gravity* and *Grand Canyon*. The author may even use poetry to combine history and personal experience, as Nikki Grimes does in *One Last Word*.

Active Nonfiction

These are books to get kids involved. The category isn't new, but it's expanding beyond science experiments and cookbooks. The "For Kids" books published by Chicago Review (like *Michelangelo for Kids* and *The White House for Kids*) combine history or biography with twenty-one activities that correlate in some way with subject matter.

The Scholastic True or False series takes a subject and walks readers through it, challenging them to answer true/false questions along the way. National Geographic Field Guides encourage kids to get out and discover for themselves.

To these five, we might add one more:

Graphic Nonfiction

"Graphic," in this case, refers to the format, not the content. Information presented comic-book style goes as far back as the educational comics handed out by General Electric or the US Treasury department. The best graphic nonfiction combines artistry and design with sound information and often beautiful writing as well. Nathan Hale's Hazardous Tales are a good example (see *Treaties, Trenches, Mud, and Blood*). Nick Bertozzi (*Shackleton: Antarctic Odyssey*), Don Brown (*Drowned City*), and Matt Phelan (*Bluffton*) are reliably excellent. History and biography are natural subjects for graphic nonfiction, but Kingstone Comics' *The Book of God* adds theology and Bible literacy.

Some readers prefer nonfiction; for others it may be an acquired taste. We recommend the Dewey Decimal Dare. Periodically, challenge your kids (and yourself!) to browse one Dewey Decimal section of your local library and find at least one interesting title to read and recount. Broad sections are designated by hundreds: 000 is "General Knowledge" (including Weird but True facts—always a kid favorite); 100s is Philosophy and Psychology (including self-help); 200s is Religion, 300s is Social Science, etc.

In the children's section, the 100s and 200s are sparse, and worthy of caution. Self-help from a secular perspective may not be all that helpful, and while it's useful to learn about other religions, be wary of exaggerations and misrepresentations.

In the fiction field, anything that can be thought of can also be written about, and the lines separating genres are permeable and easily combined.

Realistic Fiction

Realistic fiction can be light-hearted, adventurous, silly, cozy, or serious as a heart attack. Some may even include heart attacks, or cancer, or accidents that steal the life of a beloved friend or family member (see *Bridge to Terabithia*).

Realistic fiction is often the genre of choice for addressing current issues, like sexual assault (*Speak*), parental neglect and abuse (*Fighting Words*), transgenderism (*Too Bright to See*), feminism and lesbianism (*When You Trap a Tiger*)—as such, it frequently dominates annual "Best of" lists and ALA award categories.

Adventure

This is a subgenre of realistic fiction, including travel stories, survival stories, and war stories. Classic adventure tales are a staple of youth literature, at least since *Treasure Island*. Modern-day examples include *Peak*, *Hatchet*, *The Explorer*, and *Northwind*.

Mystery and Suspense

Classic mystery novels present a puzzle to be solved—anything from a missing link to a murder—and a series of clues to be followed up until the puzzle is solved. The basic formula works even in chapter books, like *Aven Green, Sleuthing Machine*, and Easy Reader comics like the Detective Sweet Pea series. Subgenres include cozy mysteries (e.g., *Aggie Morton, Mystery Queen*), puzzle novels (*The Westing Game*, *Encyclopedia Brown*), and suspense/thriller (*The Mysterious Benedict Society*, *One of Us Is Lying*).

Historical Fiction

Historical Fiction used to score big wins with Newbery committees: *Carry on, Mr. Bowditch*; *Rifles for Watie*; *Johnny Tremain*; *The Witch of Blackbird Pond*; etc. Today it's not as popular—or so the publishing line goes, even though *Freewater*, a novel about a clandestine colony of runaway slaves, captured the Newbery Award in 2023.

Straightforward historical fiction titles are not as prevalent as they used to be. It's more common to add time travel or other fantasy elements (*Egg & Spoon*) and even goofy humor (*Abraham Lincoln, Pro Wrestler*). Genre-blending can help draw history-resistant readers into the infinite variety and nuance of the world of the past, though be wary of historical fiction that puts twenty-first-century attitudes in the minds of historical characters. Feminism has a way of sneaking into otherwise realistic narratives, sometimes to ridiculous lengths, as in *The True Confessions of Charlotte Doyle* (the twelve-year-old heroine who, while sailing to America in the 1820s, sparks a mutiny and eventually takes control of the ship!).

Fantasy

Fantasy has its roots in legends (e.g., King Arthur), myths (*The Iliad*), and folk/fairy tales. Now it's one of the bestselling genres in children's publishing, and definitely the broadest. Not so long ago, "fantasy" meant medieval settings, wizards, and quests, but traditional varieties have sprouted contemporary ones and lots of blending into other genres.

Fairy tales provide the fantasy breeding ground. Grimms' fairy tales still sell in their original form, but updated versions appear every season. Examples are the Lunar Chronicles (Cinderella), *Briar and Rose and Jack* (Jack and the Beanstalk), *Thornwood* (Sleeping Beauty), and many more. Some retellings push contemporary themes like feminism, but don't miss original contemporary fairy tales like *The Princess Bride* and *Howl's Moving Castle*.

High (Epic) and Low (Realistic) High fantasy employs the aforementioned medieval settings, wizards, and quests. *The Hobbit* and The Lord of the Rings set the standard, followed decades later by The Dark Is Rising Sequence and Lloyd Alexander's Chronicles of Prydain. "Low," unlike "high," imports fantasy elements into realistic settings, such as plastic figures coming to life in *The Indian in the Cupboard*, *Miss Hickory*, and the Doll People series by Ann Martin.

Animal Tales are fantasy stories about animals that talk (or at least communicate with each other) and may affect human clothing and manners. *Watership Down*, *Mrs. Frisby and the Rats of NIMH*, and *The Tale of Peter Rabbit* are classic examples. *The Eyes and the Impossible* and The Mistmantle Chronicles are more recent and highly recommended.

Magical Realism features supernatural intervention in ordinary lives. "Magic" moves the action in *Savvy*, *Flora & Ulysses*, and *When You Trap a Tiger*, though there's no hint in any of these where the magic comes from.

Paranormal Romance This sub-genre is confined to YA fiction. The success of the Twilight series made this the fastest-growing fantasy genre in the early 2000s, with werewolves, zombies, fallen angels, and even mermen joining vampires as love interests. "Romantasy" is the latest evolution.

Urban Fantasy is set in a modern-day (not always urban) setting, and the stories tend to be dark and gritty and often include romance as a subplot. Characters are usually witches, vampires, werewolves, etc., locked in mortal combat with rival factions or families. The Mortal Instruments series is one example.

Steampunk fantasy worlds function via mechanical inventions projected backward into a quasi-Victorian setting. The Larklight, Airborne, and Leviathan trilogies are outstanding examples.

Space Fantasy The difference between space fantasy and science fiction can be hard to distinguish since this fantasy category features spaceships, alien species, and interplanetary travel. The telling element is some form of supernatural magical power that can't be explained, such as the "Force." The Force puts Star Wars in the space fantasy category, while Star Trek is closer to science fiction. *A Wrinkle in Time* is even harder to categorize, but the invention of Mrs Who, Mrs Whatsit, and Mrs Which as mediums nudge it into fantasy territory.

Christian Fantasy is prolific enough to deserve its own subgenre and includes examples from almost all of the subcategories above. Most are series books, such as The Ashtown Burials, Jack Zulu, The Wilderking Trilogy, and The Dream Keeper Saga. The best Christian fantasy includes parallels to biblical truth or echoes of the great redemption narrative.

Science Fiction

The question to ask when distinguishing certain types of fantasy from science fiction is, could this conceivably happen in the known universe? Might it be possible to travel at light speed, encounter alien races, even jump time? Or might certain trends today lead to a dystopian future right here on earth? Science fiction, perhaps more than any other category, grapples with big questions such as what it means to be human and the limits of science.

Space sci-fi takes place on other planets or galaxies and can be grittily realistic, like *The Martian*, or wildly speculative, like *We're Not from Here*.

Futuristic sci-fi takes place on earth and is often tech-related. Jules Verne practically invented the genre with *Journey to the Center of the Earth* and similar titles. *Ender's Game* is a prime example, as is *Origin* by Jessica Khoury and Kenneth Oppel's Overthrow series. Alternative history can fall into this category, such as Terry Pratchett's *The Nation*.

Dystopian stories take place on earth after a modern apocalypse has upended the social order. *The Giver* and The Unwanteds series are middle grade examples. YA dystopias are grimmer and grittier, like *The Hunger Games* and *Divergent*.

Romance

Romance fiction is huge in the adult market, as evidenced by display racks of fuzzy pink borders, swirling titles, and dashing heroes. Some YA romance today is of the light-hearted, meet-cute variety, although "romantasy," blending romance and fantasy, is capturing more of the market. Books marketed as "sex-positive" present sexual experimentation as natural, largely harmless, and just part of growing up, as in Jason Reynolds' *Twenty-Four Seconds from Now*.

Novels described as "queer" are found in all YA genres, but often with a romantic angle. "Sapphic" romance (lesbian relationship) novels outnumber gay love stories, although the Heartstopper graphic novels featuring Nick and Charlie are so popular they've spun off coloring books, calendars, and a Netflix series.

Some teen novels—not necessarily classified as "romance"—thoughtfully explore love vs. infatuation or the mystery of attraction itself: *Hattie Big Sky, Buffalo Flats*, and *Enemies in the Orchard* (all historical fiction) are good examples. *Love and Other Great Expectations* is a fun teen read that's not overly starry-eyed about romance.

Romance, or faint stirrings of it, can also appear in middle grade fiction. Sadly, though, the romantic feelings depicted in some general market MG fiction today are often directed toward the same sex.

Horror

Horror can be considered "dark fantasy," particularly if ghosts, vampires, or undead villains provide the chills. But sometimes it's a psychotic killer on the loose—or nothing but the characters' overactive imaginations.

The Goosebumps series is for middle grade readers who love the scares; teen horror is more serious and also scarier. Much of it aims solely at shock value with cliffhanger pauses, terrifying clues, and a big payoff of blood and/or further mayhem. But horror can be a thoughtful medium for older readers to explore the human capacity for evil. One example is *The Apprenticeship of Victor Frankenstein* (two volumes), which details how a promising young man from a good German family becomes a student of the dark arts.

Humor

Some children's literature serves no higher purpose than to make kids laugh. Classics like the McBroom and Amelia Bedelia series have delighted young readers for at least two generations. Newer titles like *The Diary of a Wimpy Kid*, *The Terrible Two*, and *The Best of Iggy* may have some thoughtful takeaways but mainly serve up laughs.

Most parents are delighted when their reluctant reader gloms on to a category or author they can't get enough of. But both reluctant and eager readers should be encouraged to broaden their reading tastes.

Reading aloud to multiple family members or classrooms can introduce children to a variety of genres. What if the boys want to hear *The Diary of a Wimpy Kid*? Well, it's funny. And you and your listeners can debate the pros and cons of Greg Heffley's behavior as you go along. If your horror fans want to read Goosebumps #476 next, humor them as far as you can—because then you can choose *Anne of Green Gables*. For the next round, tell your Wimpy-Kid enthusiast he'll enjoy *Holes* and suggest *Lockwood & Company* for the scares—similar laughs and creepy thrills, but more literary value.

Literary genres are as rich and varied as life itself—try to encourage a variety of reading matter while the children are still young, and it will serve them well throughout life.

BOOKLIST FOR CHAPTER 3

To illustrate one genre over multiple publisher reading levels, this list is all mysteries!

Further Reading
   Gaudy Night, Dorothy Sayers

For Children/Teens
   Spot, the Cat, Henry Cole (Picture Book)
   King and Kayla series, Dori Hillestad Butler (Easy Reader)
   Aven Green, Sleuthing Machine, Dusti Bowling (Chapter Book)
   Homer on the Case, Henry Cole (lower Middle Grade)
   The Father Brown Reader: Stories from Chesterton,
      Nancy Carpentier Brown (MG)
   Magnolia Wu Unfolds It All, Chanel Miller (MG)
   The Mysterious Benedict Society, Trenton Lee Stewart (MG)
   The Westing Game, Ellen Raskin (MG)
   The Bletchley Riddle, Ruta Sepetys and Steve Sheinkin (MG)
   The Code of Silence, Tim Shoemaker (MG/Young Adult)
   *The Mona Lisa Vanishes: A Legendary Painter, A Shocking Heist,
      and the Birth of a Global Celebrity*, Nicholas Day (MG/YA)
   A Pocket Full of Murder, R. J. Anderson (MG/YA)

CHAPTER 4

DISCUSSION STARTERS: WORLDVIEW AND DISCERNMENT IN LITERATURE

> Well, it was worth finding the courage . . . to give people hope.
> To show them that the world is not all ugliness,
> but holds beauty and goodness.[1]
> —Pam Muñoz Ryan, *Mañanaland*

In the old days, we like to think that American culture was largely Christian. That didn't mean everyone, or even a majority of Americans, were sincere believers, but that the wider world our children grew up in subscribed to the same general moral code. In the early 1960s, politicians who divorced might be passed over for higher office, cheating on a test was always wrong, and going to church was a good thing. But those community standards were already shifting.

---

1. Pam Muñoz Ryan, *Mañanaland* (Scholastic, 2020), 96.

What Keeps Us Up at Night

The Christian worldview of original sin and divine redemption is foreign to most Americans. As much as we try to share and model the gospel for our sons and daughters, many of them go astray once they've moved out. We've seen too many young people raised in Bible-believing homes reject their parents' faith, wrestle with doubts about their own faith, or seek worldly pursuits. If Christian parenting won't absolutely guarantee Christian offspring, what will?

Two points to make here: First, the general culture was never Christian and never will be. Christianity is always countercultural, even in straitlaced societies where almost everybody goes to church. There's nothing more contrary to the human spirit than dethroning self to follow Christ, even to the point of suffering injustice patiently and handing over your spare cloak. There's always some angle of Christianity the culture opposes, and every generation of Christians needs to be aware of that sticking point in order to counteract its temptations.

Second, it's easy to underestimate the power of sin. Christian parents and grandparents may remember the times they stumbled and failed, and we long to spare our children those pitfalls. But every generation will encounter its own pitfalls. Many, by God's grace, will avoid permanent damage, but there will also be those who can't seem to reconcile what they've been taught with what they perceive to be true. Or what they really, truly want to do. Rebelliousness is inherent in all of us, just more obvious in some.

Young people need to know both what's outside in the world and what's inside their own hearts. The Bible is our first resort, always, for "teaching, for reproof, for correction, and for training in righteousness" (2 Tim. 3:16–17). But literature that truthfully reflects life as it's lived in the world can be a useful secondary resource—even if we're a little uncomfortable with the content. Novels, biographies, and memoirs that don't necessarily fall in line with Christian teaching can still be worth reading and talking about if they realistically reflect the world—especially the power and effects of sin. That's why we call them "discussion starters."

GETTING OUTSIDE OUR OWN HEADS

To students—and adults—who don't naturally read for pleasure, literature can seem like a useless frill. Why waste time reading *Great Expectations*, or *Crime and Punishment*, or even *The Hunger Games* when we could be studying something practical? We've shown how Truth and Story relate. But even literature that conflicts with biblical truth at some points can be worthwhile if it is honest about the human condition. We can disagree with the characters' conclusions and evaluate their personal choices. We can debate whether they understand the reality they're living in. We can try to discern what the author believes about free will and personal responsibility and human nature. Good literature allows readers to get inside another person's mind and understand the world from another point of view. For example:

> Where does the protagonist of *The Fault in Our Stars*, a teenage girl with terminal cancer, find hope?
>
> How can white readers sympathize with the black teen who narrates *The Hate U Give*, and how will her experience always seem foreign to them?
>
> How would it feel, as an *American Born Chinese*, to establish a connection with your cultural heritage? What spiritual insights can you see in Gene Luen Yang's depiction of the Monkey King?
>
> How desperate would we have to be, like the protagonist of *Beast Rider*, to hop a freight train known as La Bestia and risk its many perils?
>
> What sort of dystopia might lie ahead if things go very wrong? Would it be more like *The Hunger Games*, *Divergent*, *The Giver*, or *The Knife of Never Letting Go?* Or if none of these seem likely, what do they say about what our society fears now?
>
> What do the Shakespearean heroines of *Enter the Body* conclude about love and male/female relationships? Is there anything we can learn from them?

Loving the Creature

The Bible is clear that God loves His creation: "God saw that it was good" at every step of putting the universe together. Does He love all the people in it? Though "angry with the wicked every day" (Ps. 7:11 NKJV), His love extends to them too. "The LORD is good to all, and his mercy is over all he has made" (Ps. 145:9).

God's Son displayed the same lovingkindness while on earth: "When he [Jesus] saw the crowds, he had compassion on them, because they were harassed and helpless, like sheep without a shepherd" (Matt. 9:36).

"Harassed and helpless" could describe many a YA and middle grade protagonist. A gifted author, whether Christian or skeptic, can not only get inside her characters' minds but also make those characters real, as though they had lives beyond the page. By entering the story, readers gain sympathy for a well-written fictional character, even as they learn to recognize the flaws in their reasoning and choices. Sympathy becomes compassion when readers are confronted with the real-life "characters" they see at Walmart, at sports events, in the airport, and on social media.

This is not to say that every book that expresses unbiblical worldviews is worthy of our attention. Readers should be on the lookout for warning signs, such as:

Agenda-driven fiction

"Agendas" aren't bad in themselves. After all, Christians have an agenda to glorify God and proclaim Christ. But a Christian novel that pictures conversion as the solution to all of life's problems would be agenda-driven, i.e., attempting to drive the reader toward a desired conclusion.

Both readers and authors can misunderstand the purpose of fiction. It is not to provide correct answers to life's problems, but to raise appropriate questions. Nonfiction can teach and direct; the best fiction can illuminate and suggest, allowing readers to come to their own conclusions.

That said, children's authors often have some reassuring message to share with young readers who don't have the benefit of adult experience; this is natural and right. But some authors use characters as mouthpieces and bend the plot toward an obvious takeaway. For example, *George* (later titled *Melissa*) and *Too Bright to See*, both highly lauded middle grade novels, depict transgenderism as healthy and life-affirming with no profound medical or emotional consequences.

Serious matters treated frivolously

Humor is a saving grace and can leaven an otherwise gloomy tone. But a comic novel about a road trip from Missouri to New Mexico to get a legal abortion? That's a capsule definition of *Unpregnant* (2019). Judy Blume's *Forever* (1975) isn't exactly a comic novel, but it makes light of teen sex as something kids just naturally do, with little or no emotional consequence as long as they use "protection."

Sensationalism

Some novels reach for headlines by going to extremes. For example, several years ago, a YA novel called *Rainbow Party* caught the attention of outraged rightwing talk-show hosts everywhere. Here's the nutshell description: "A cautionary tale about a group of teens faced with the prospect of attending a party involving oral sex."[2] Perhaps it's a well-written, thoughtful examination of casual sex and its consequences. Or perhaps it's a sensationalist tale that goes over the top in order to sell more books. Impossible to say without reading the book for oneself, but life is short and there are better choices to consume our reading time.

---

2. "Rainbow Party: About the Book," Simon & Schuster, https://www.simonandschuster.com/books/Rainbow-Party/Paul-Ruditis/9781416902355.

Gloom and doom

Some YA novels are so dark they might bring the cheeriest reader to the brink of despair. This doesn't mean that all "downer" novels are completely without merit or should be avoided. *Lord of the Flies* (to take one classic example) raises interesting questions about human nature. But immersing readers in downer literature for the sake of "realism" is neither healthy nor real. We'll discuss this further in chapter 13.

> *How do we spot books that may be based on—and even promote—unbiblical ideas and values?*

How do we spot books that may be based on—and even promote—unbiblical ideas and values? Often checking an online synopsis and scanning reader reviews will be enough. Proactively, get to know authors who can be trusted to treat serious subjects in a thoughtful way that raises thoughtful questions. Contemporary authors (many of whom are Christians) who do this well are M. T. Anderson, Neal Schusterman, Nikki Grimes, Francisco X. Stork, Gene Luen Yang, Gary Schmidt, and Mitali Perkins.

So Let's Talk About It

How to discuss a "discussion starter"? First, wait until children are old enough to start thinking for themselves, often around the ages of eleven to thirteen. Some children mature earlier than others. Some readers will be drawn to "problem" novels about protagonists facing serious life issues like a death in the family, a mentally ill parent or sibling, drug addiction, or even abuse. Others avoid those subjects like boiled Brussels sprouts and steer toward humorous fiction, nonfiction, or practical how-tos. Obviously, young people shouldn't drown in negativity. But they might benefit from an occasional read-along with a parent, peers, or siblings, accompanied by fruitful discussion.

Second, don't overdo it—leave some of the discovery up to young readers.

Learning to discern for themselves is the goal, and since you don't have time to pre-read everything, an inappropriate book may slip by your radar. No need to panic; a well-supported and reasoned worldview won't be overturned by one book, and if communication lines are open, your teens may come to you first with their own concerns and questions.

That said, some books are worth reading together—not only the affirming ones but also the challenging ones (see chapter 9 on Messy Books). You might read ahead and make a few notes before passing the book along to your teen. Or keep pace with each other by reading one chapter at a time. Once read, here are some questions to consider:

- Who are the "good" guys?

- How does the author present less sympathetic characters through speech or action?

- What does the protagonist believe? What seems most important to him or her?

- What, if anything, do the main characters believe or say about God?

- What have they learned, or how have they changed by the end?

- What characters would you like to be friends with? Why?

- What characters do you find yourself arguing with?

- What choices do they make that you would disagree with?

These questions are suggestions—don't try to ask all of them! They're a means of getting to an author's point of view and major themes. Once those are understood, they can be critiqued from a Christian framework.

BOOKLIST FOR CHAPTER 4

Further Reading

The Pop Culture Parent: Helping Kids Engage Their World for Christ, Ted Turner, E. Stephen Burnett, and Jared Moore.

For Children/Teens

(Some of the YA titles have significant language issues; please check our Redeemed Reader review to determine the appropriateness for an individual child.)

Beast Rider, Tony Johnson (MG; immigration)
Sunny Side Up, Jennifer Holm (MG graphic novel; sibling drug use)
Starfish, Lisa Fipps (MG graphic novel; obesity and body positivity)
Posted, John David Anderson (MG; bullying; social media)
All American Boys, Jason Reynolds and Brendan Kiely (YA; racial tensions)
Challenger Deep, Neal Shusterman (YA; mental illness)
Dancing at the Pity Party, Tyler Feder (YA graphic novel; death of a parent)
Gay Girl, Good God, Jackie Hill Perry (YA; same-sex attraction)
The Hate U Give, Angie Thomas (YA; racism)
The Hunger Games, Suzanne Collins (YA; nihilism)
On the Hook, Francisco X. Stork (YA; crime and revenge)
Ordinary Hazards, Nikki Grimes (YA; neglect; sexual abuse)

PART TWO

RAISING READERS

SECTION 2
Reading the Classics

CHAPTER 5

A FRESH LOOK AT OLD BOOKS: THE RISKS AND REWARDS OF READING THE CLASSICS

> Of making many books there is no end.
> —Ecclesiastes 12:12b

There is only one required book. Look at all the recommended booklists online, including those on Redeemed Reader. Or titles suggested by your child's curriculum, mentioned by well-meaning church friends, or balanced precariously on your own teetering "TBR" (to-be-read) pile. All of them are optional.

How can we at Redeemed Reader, avowed "book people," make such a statement? In short, we book people are people of *the* Book. God's Word is the only inspired, infallible text, and, as such, is the only required reading. The Bible, in God's marvelous providence, is for all times, places, and people groups. When you find yourself fretting over a particular title you have not read yet (or read to your child), ask yourself if you are elevating books too highly. Books and stories impact readers, but they do not save readers.

Jesus saves. Jesus can and does save without a single work of fiction, a single

> *It's tempting to lean on older titles because they seem "safe." But we must read discerningly and evaluate each book in light of its content and its reader.*

poem, a single "classic." Books certainly aid us in our growth and maturity as Christians, but they are only books. We are under grace, not law. We are free to choose books based on our circumstances, our readers, our understanding of God's word and its standards.

Shepherding young readers is challenging. Choosing books is challenging. It's tempting to lean on older titles because they seem "safe." But we must read discerningly and evaluate each book in light of its content and its reader. Booklists from respected sources help reduce decision fatigue, but booklists are suggestions, not requirements. And when they contain primarily books published long ago, look carefully. No one book is automatically more wholesome, Christian, or "right" than another because of publication date. Old books offer many rewards, but, as with contemporary books, they also require reader discernment.

Rewards: Delight and Virtue

Books that stand the test of time are well-written, address the human condition, and are memorable. "Well-written" depends, of course, on the literary conventions of the day; for instance, modern authors are more likely to write novels in verse (collections of short poems that, together, tell a story) than epic poems like Homer.

We regularly overlook dated literary conventions when we read memorable stories about memorable people because we connect with the human condition. The human condition includes our depravity, our hopelessness without Christ, our need for redemption, the hope of redemption, and a taste of future glory. Many books we now regard as classics expertly illustrate aspects of this.

The Bible is, of course, the preeminent story, the first "fairy tale" of a prince rescuing his future bride (and it happens to be true!). The best earthly stories reflect the Bible's first story, as we discussed in chapter 1. Christian college professor Donald Williams reminds us:

> *Christians alone understand why human beings, whether "literary" types or not, are impelled to make, tell, and hear stories. . . . That is why we not only learn from literature but enjoy it: it delights as it teaches. And it conveys its kind of truth through the creation of concrete images which incarnate or embody ideas which would otherwise remain abstract and nebulous.*[1]

Sadly, many schools are bowing to pressure and removing these great stories.[2] As activists in our broader culture seek to remove classics from the curriculum, we at Redeemed Reader would urge readers to keep reading old books. So do countless respected authors. Karen Swallow Prior, Vigen Guroian, and Mitali Perkins each remind us that the classics inspire us to pursue virtue.[3] Author Pahtyana Moore offers a helpful definition of virtue as "the avenue by which we reflect the character of God in our everyday lives and impact all who cross our path. A life of virtue is our strongest and surest witness of His presence in every society from the beginning of time."[4] Thus, we read Homer's

---

1. Donald T. Williams, "Christian Poetics, Past and Present," in *The Christian Imagination*, ed. Leland Ryken (Waterbrook Press, 2002), 11.
2. For example, a California School District considered removing books like *To Kill a Mockingbird*, *Roll of Thunder, Hear My Cry*, *Adventures of Huckleberry Finn*, and others. "California School District Considers Ban on Classic Books," National Coalition Against Censorship, December 4, 2020, https://ncac.org/news/california-book-challenge-2020. For similar efforts in Florida regarding *Paradise Lost* and *A Midsummer Night's Dream*, see Olivia Jones, "Florida Schools Removed Classics Works of Literature by John Milton Including *Paradise Lost* and Restricted Some Shakespeare including A Midsummer Night's Dream Under State's New Law, Teacher Claims," Daily Mail, July 6, 2023, https://www.dailymail.co.uk/news/article-12270015/Florida-schools-remove-classic-works-literature-states-new-law-teacher-claims.html.
3. See *On Reading Well* by Karen Swallow Prior, *Tending the Heart of Virtue* by Vigen Guroian, and *Steeped in Stories* by Mitali Perkins.
4. Pahtyana Moore, "The Heartbeat of Humanity: Virtue," in *Wild Things and Castles in the Sky*, eds. Leslie Bustard et al. (Square Halo Books, 2021), 171.

Iliad and recognize our own sin in Achilles' petulance. Homer's *Odyssey* shows us the beauty of marital love and faithfulness in Penelope's long-suffering, or the desperate need we have for divine intervention as we, like Odysseus, are beset by suffering. *Beowulf* illustrates the ultimate defeat of the dragon, hinting at the final book of Scripture and the defeat of another dragon.

Children's classics hold a special place in our hearts; many are excellent fare for children who are advanced readers or for parents who want a great bedtime read-aloud. Children today are bombarded by images, short snippets of text or audio commentary, and often see schoolwork in bite-size chunks on a screen. Higher education professionals at prestigious universities bemoan the lack of attention in today's students.[5] One of the great gifts older titles offer is the foundational skill of learning to pay attention.

Children who read classic literature do more than boost their attention skills, however. Before they realize it, they have messed about in boats with Mole and Rat, gone on adventures with Bilbo, fallen down the rabbit hole with Alice, or set up camp on an island without their parents. Hundreds of pages later, when the tale ends, children have shored up their moral courage alongside their power of attention.

Do not throw out the classics. But do consider that older titles, like newer titles, demand discernment.

Risks: Philosophy and Perspective

Anytime we read any book other than the Bible, we may encounter unbiblical ideas. No other book is inerrant, inspired by God. But we tend to read older books, especially from the Western canon, a bit less critically than newer ones—our guard is down. Every era reflects different prevailing cultural philosophies and trends; earlier eras are not automatically more biblical. Sin

---

5. Rose Horowitch, "The Elite College Students Who Can't Read Books," *Atlantic*, November 2024, https://www.theatlantic.com/magazine/archive/2024/11/the-elite-college-students-who-cant-read-books/679945.

masquerades in many guises, including cultural attitudes toward ethnicities, the treatment of the poor and needy, assumptions about what makes life worth living, and how we gain spiritual enlightenment.

Sin in literature is not limited to sex, drugs, and rock-and-roll. Some historical titles are guilty of racism. Others promote pagan philosophy, but we give them a "pass" simply because the educated elite have read these same titles for thousands of years. Perhaps our biggest risk when we read old books is simply that we do not read discerningly. Out of fear, we look to these older, "trusted" titles because they seem safe and have been vetted. We think, *These books are recommended by all these respected sources. They're not like the books at my library that promote transgenderism and evolution.* That may be true; however, even beloved Victorian children's classics are products of their time and place.

Thus, we encourage you to consider the following four risks.

Risk #1: Unbiblical Ideas and Philosophy

Romantic and naturalist philosophical ideas embodied the spirit of the Victorian age. Drawing on the work of John Locke ("The child is born as a blank slate"), Jean-Jacques Rousseau encouraged the Romantic ideal that children develop fine on their own if their environment alone is ideal, without overt instruction from adults. *The Secret Garden* clearly demonstrates this.[6] The protagonist Mary Lennox flourishes in a lovely environment with little to no meddling from grown-ups. While her original environment included less than exemplary parental figures, the answer is not to remove authority or circumvent it. Children (like grown-ups) have sinful hearts, and left to their own devices, do not automatically grow in wisdom and stature and favor with God and man (Luke 2:52). Romantic philosophy is more subtle than overt depictions of something like transgenderism, but its very subtlety can be just as harmful.

---

6. Recognizing philosophical issues does not mean we do not like these books! It means we must be wise in our handling of them. *The Secret Garden* happens to be Betsy's favorite book from childhood.

At the height of the Industrial Revolution, amidst child labor issues, urban housing issues, and poor infrastructure and sanitation, children's novels like *The Wind in the Willows* that delighted in unspoiled nature were a welcome breath of fresh air. The natural world is not bad; God created this beautiful world for us in which to live. But newer books set in modern cities are not less spiritual simply because they are not set in nature.

The exiled Israelites during Jeremiah's day were instructed to "seek the welfare of the city" where God had sent them into exile, to "pray to the LORD on its behalf, for in its welfare you will find your welfare" (Jer. 29:7). Revelation reminds us that we are looking forward to a heavenly *city* (Rev. 21:2). Balance those lovely nature stories with delightful urban stories, like the Book Scavenger series by Jennifer Chambliss Bertman (which includes online tech) or *Hope in the Valley* by Mitali Perkins (which includes urban housing issues).

Risk #2: Limited Ethnic and Cultural Representation

Authors naturally write stories based upon personal experience. We cannot expect British nationals in Victorian England to include people groups unknown to them. We *can* expect those patriotic Brits and proper Victorians to write enthusiastically of anyone British and disparagingly of all other "uncivilized" peoples—even the French! Their treatment of the "other," regardless of who the other was, was often deplorable and sinful.

In God's marvelous, creative providence, His church is composed of people from all eras and cultures, of all ages, colors, shapes, and sizes. Each person is made in the image of God, but each is uniquely gifted and creative. When we promote books by and about one cultural group from one time to the near exclusion of others, we limit our view of God's image bearers. What about Christians in our churches who look different from the majority, whether they are from another country or just up the road?

When Betsy taught senior English at a Christian school, her class studied *Their Eyes Were Watching God* by Zora Neale Hurston. Midway through the book, one of her black students approached her after class, exclaiming how much she liked the book. She said it was the first time in her twelve years at that school that she'd been assigned a book about someone who looked like her. The student body was about 30 percent black, but even if the school was 100 percent white, God's church is not. What a disservice we do to our young people if our assigned reading, especially from Christian schools and in Christian homes, does not help readers see the magnificent diversity in God's people.

We can (and should) lament the many factors influencing the lack of non-white representation in older books, but we need not toss all older titles that do not portray biblical attitudes. Instead, discuss potential issues as the need arises.[7] As author Eréndira Ramírez-Ortega writes:

If we only introduce children to books from within our own tradition, we deny our children encounters with the richness and variety of what exists beyond their atmosphere.[8]

Newer titles often have more biblical representation of different ethnic and cultural groups. Hilary McKay's charming chapter book series about a girl named Lulu features a young black family as compared with the all-white family in the Ramona books. The Vanderbeekers series stars a multiracial family who lives in a brownstone in New York City, much like the favorite classic *All-of-a-Kind Family* features a Jewish family.

Risk #3: Misplaced Nostalgia

Spending all our time with Laura Ingalls and Caddie Woodlawn can make us long for "simpler times." We think: Life was easier, less complicated. Neighbors talked to each other. Modern life is too noisy and hectic.

Some of that may be true, but it is also true that modern life has many

---

7. See Chapter 8 on historical racism in books for more.
8. Eréndira Ramírez-Ortega, "Latino Literature," in *Wild Things and Castles in the Sky*, eds. Leslie Bustard, et al., 193.

conveniences few of us would give up. Ma Ingalls did not have an electric washing machine or a grocery store with such exotic foods as pesto or pineapples. In God's providence, we and our children are living in *this particular time and place*.

Misplaced nostalgia also creeps in when we assume older titles always portray stable families. It is right and good to lament the increasing divorce rates and the breakup of families. But we must also recognize that "absentee fathers"[9] in books are not new. Older children's classics also include many titles with missing fathers. *The Railway Children* are missing their father while he is unjustly imprisoned. *Strawberry Girl* by Lois Lenski includes an alcoholic father. Children are more likely in twenty-first century America to experience divorce (in their own families or a classmate's) than they are to have a father off at war, but both experiences are valid subjects for stories, and children today benefit from reading about both. Indeed, many new books do feature protagonists who are missing a father. For instance, the protagonist of *The Labors of Hercules Beal* by Gary D. Schmidt grapples with grief over the loss of both parents. The main character in *The Star That Always Stays* by Anna Rose Johnson must confront the social backlash from her mother's recent divorce and remarriage. Instead of bemoaning absentee fathers, look deeper: *Why* is the father absent? And is the book celebrating his absence or lamenting it? That is of more concern than simply a parent's absence.

Risk #4: Assuming Old Conventions Are Better than New

Old books might be wonderful literary specimens, but they are products of their time, both in the writing style and the way the book was manufactured. For example, Jane Austen wrote witty novels about the social conventions of her Georgian society upbringing. Contemporary authors seeking to comment on current social mores will not create characters who speak as elegantly because the average human today does not speak like Lizzie Bennet. Author

---

9. This issue is not limited to absentee fathers alone, but at Redeemed Reader, we hear more complaints about absentee fathers than mothers.

Becky Dean, in *Love & Other Great Expectations*, speaks cleverly into current high school students' lives about love, relationships, and life; fittingly, her characters sound like contemporary people.

The prose in older novels is often longer and more complex than today's spare prose. More words don't necessarily make for better prose but might reflect the absence of revising technology (who wants to rewrite all of *Moby Dick* by hand?) or the way an author was compensated (Dickens was paid by the word!). Our digital age has encouraged fewer words, but poetry, the height of literary expression, has used minimal words to communicate deep truth and riveting story for centuries.

Similarly, printing technology has added a whole new dimension to today's picture books, enhancing the text with bright colors. The technology to print books with multiple colors and hues developed over the past century. Robert McCloskey made marvelous picture books in the early twentieth century; Jerry Pinkney in the early twenty-first century. Where McCloskey created a world with limited colors, highlighting details between Sal and the bear through his careful drawings, Pinkney painted exuberant watercolor illustrations to accompany well-known folk tales and fables.

In addition to book production conventions, older texts feel disconnected from current experience because they do not show current technology. More people live in big cities now than 150 years ago. We have explored space, invented robots, and use mini, handheld computers every day. The recent book, *A Rover's Story*, explores the idea of an artificially intelligent Mars rover who grows sentient. This well-told story raises interesting questions about the future of space exploration and the issues around the latest technology. It also subtly raises questions about the nature of disability. Hand this title to your reluctant reader who is passionate about the newest Mars rover. Consider discussing it in addition to a nineteenth century adventure novel.

God made people in His image; a significant part of that image-bearing is the ability to create. Our children live in a world that uses digital tools to create in ways we can still only imagine. As visual media changes, where will they look for inspiration? John Hendrix creates intriguing graphic novels; a favorite of ours is *The Mythmakers* about C. S. Lewis and J. R. R. Tolkien. It looks nothing like biographies for young people that were published pre-1950. Or pre-2000 for that matter! Reading current Christian authors like Amanda Cleary Eastep, Mitali Perkins, S. D. Smith, or Daniel Nayeri helps give children a vision for pursuing a creative calling today as an outworking of their Christian faith.

Special Considerations for School Booklists

School booklists—particularly from Christian schools—that focus on books published before 1975, unwittingly reinforce some of these risks if they do not balance old with new. Classics have lasted partly because they are timeless in their treatment of the human condition, even if they are outdated in their views of racism, roles of women, or similar subjects. But there is nothing inherently wrong or inferior with new books, either.

Adding newer titles to elementary and middle school booklists is easy, particularly if parents or teachers are reading aloud to their students. High school booklists feel more permanent and immovable. The implicit assumption is that students will progress through certain familiar books by the time they graduate high school, emerging well-read and well-educated. Standard American literature courses historically included *The Scarlet Letter* by Nathaniel Hawthorne and *The Red Badge of Courage* by Stephen Crane, alongside twentieth-century titles like *Native Son* by Richard Wright or *I Know Why the Caged Bird Sings* by Maya Angelou. British literature courses might include *The Heart of Darkness* by Joseph Conrad, *Hamlet* or another Shakespearean tragedy, *Lord of the Flies* by William Golding, and *Great Expectations* by Charles Dickens. Today, we see additions like *The Kite Runner* by Khaled Hosseini as well.

These books contain heavy subject matter: adultery and other sexual sin, violence, death, financial ruin, suicidal thoughts, evil perpetrated by one part of society onto another.

Does this mean we should never read "dark" classics with students? Of course not. Sometimes, the "darkest" books pave the way for the brightest discussions. Adults know evil exists; teenagers do too. Adults have the opportunity and responsibility to present biblical hope to teenagers when they read books like these with them. If a teen is studying a Shakespearean tragedy, remind them that the "point of no return" for Shakespeare's characters and their tragic flaws does not exist for God's children: We are never too far gone to be out of reach of His grace. The climax in a Shakespeare play that leads to inevitable falling action is not applicable for Christians: Jesus' death on the cross was our story's climax, and His coming again is the triumphant conclusion.

Similarly, for a book like *Lord of the Flies*, a grim book if ever there was one, we can discuss our desperate need for redemption alongside a discussion of the nature of sin and the fall. Without Christ, we are the boys on the island. We need that saving grace from outside ourselves just as much as those boys needed that boat at the end of the novel.

Shedding gospel light on serious and disturbing classics is part of the answer to the school booklist dilemma. Supplementing the booklist with lighter books is also part of the solution.

Do not throw out the old books; *do* balance your reading diet.

BALANCING OLD AND NEW

When choosing any book to read to or with our children and students, first consider their hearts. We have precious souls to shepherd. When in doubt, stop and ponder, even if the book in question is a classic.

Consider Philippians 4:8: "Finally, brothers, whatever is true, whatever is honorable, whatever is just, whatever is pure, whatever is lovely, whatever is commendable, if there is any excellence, if there is anything worthy of praise, think about these things."

Singer/songwriter Matthew Clark reminds us:

> *Those images that populate our imaginations have a lot to do with what we acquire a taste for as well, whether it's goodness or badness. As Fred Rogers indicates, it's very important to collect good images to pin on our corkboard, because they form a taste for the things of God and they bring good choices within reach for us. . . . The more good stories, characters, music, and beautiful experiences we internalize, the greater our resource for godly feeling and action becomes (Phil.4:8).*[10]

Gentle, cardigan-clad Mr. Rogers, sitting in his living room and inviting us to be his neighbor, might be a fading image. But whether you picture a corkboard of images or a feast with different foods, ensure the overall reading diet you offer your children and students is balanced. Reading about the human condition involves reading about sin and darkness, but the way in which an author handles that sin is important.

Sin is occasionally recounted more graphically in newer books than older ones, but sin is sin. When we encounter sin in a work of literature, whether old/classic or new/contemporary, we look to Scripture for a benchmark. Does the work of literature portray sin as sin? Does the sinner repent? Is justice served? Is the matter handled with the discretion we see in Scripture? Is hope offered? Is redemption possible? We can put no sweeter image on our corkboard than Christ redeeming wretched sinners.

Ecclesiastes reminds us that there is nothing new under the sun. If Genesis were made into a true-to-the-book movie, the Redeemed Reader team would not allow our children to watch it; we might abstain as well. Tongue-in-cheek, perhaps, but it is true: Sin in all its ugliness has been with us a long time. It existed on the nineteenth-century prairie, it exists in twenty-first-century Atlanta. Reading books that grapple with today's issues can help equip children to wrestle with the ways sin manifests itself today. Consider adding a book like *The Season of Styx Malone* by Kekla Magoon to your lineup after

---

10. Matthew Clark, "The Fragrance of the Blessed Realm: Goodness," in *Wild Things and Castles in the Sky*, eds. Leslie Bustard, et al., 221.

Caddie Woodlawn for an utterly different read that is no less affirming to the ideas of family unity and loving one's neighbor.

Likewise, virtue remains the same at its core, but its manifestations look different in different times and places. Stories from long ago show children acting kindly and dealing with bullies (such as *The Hundred Dresses*), but new stories also show children acting kindly and bravely facing bullies (*The Watcher* by Nikki Grimes). Older readers might enjoy *Save Me a Seat*, about two boys who come to realize they have more in common than they originally thought; or *Somebody on This Bus Is Going to Be Famous* by J. B. Cheaney, in which an entire group of middle schoolers gains a renewed appreciation for one another.

In addition to considering a book's content, also consider the reader. Is the reader ready for this classic? If the title in question is a children's classic, the answer might be a resounding "Yes!" It might be a "Let's wait a bit and see." If the book in question is standard fare for a high school literature class, consider *why* the book is listed on high school syllabi before handing it to a sixth grader who reads "above grade level." The content may be more suitable for high school audiences even if the words can be decoded easily by a middle school student.

Because there is no required book, we are free to swap in more hopeful titles for any of the standard options. If a given title is not the right fit for our circumstances, we look for a better one. Consider requesting some hopeful titles, either old or new, the next time you are offered the chance to give feedback on a school booklist. Suggest swapping a Shakespearean comedy such as *Much Ado About Nothing* for one of the many tragedies. Students will receive a well-rounded education even if it means they miss *Romeo and Juliet* or *Hamlet* in high school. Suggest *A Tale of Two Cities* for *Great Expectations*; tragedy still occurs, but the ending is rich with redemptive overtones. Graphic novel retellings are not true substitutes, but they offer solid alternatives for stories you wish to simply introduce but not dwell on. Graphic novels may also free up time for a lighter, more hopeful work in addition to more serious titles.

It is easy to gloss over worldview issues in familiar classics that everyone has read. But all books portray a worldview and each much be evaluated in light of its content and its reader. Let us always remember that books don't save; only Jesus saves.

BOOKLIST FOR CHAPTER 5

Further Reading

Wild Things and Castles in the Sky, edited by Leslie Bustard, Théa Rosenburg, and Carey Bustard

For Children/Teens

Rabbit and Robot, Cece Bell (Easy Reader; pair with the Henry and Mudge books)

Lulu and the Duck in the Park, Hilary McKay (Chapter Book; pair with *Beezus and Ramona*)

The Tales of Deckawoo Drive, Kate DiCamillo (CB; pair with *The Boxcar Children*)

A Rover's Story, Jasmine Warga (Middle Grade science fiction; pair with *Around the World in 80 Days*)

The Boy Who Became Buffalo Bill, Andrea Warren (MG nonfiction; pair with *Little House on the Prairie*)

The Faithful Spy, John Hendrix (MG NF graphic novel about Bonhoeffer; pair with *The Hiding Place*)

Where the Mountain Meets the Moon, Grace Lin (MG fantasy; pair with *The Wizard of Oz*)

The Carver and the Queen, Emma Fox (YA fantasy; pair with *The Silver Chair*)

Everything Sad Is Untrue, Daniel Nayeri (YA memoir; swap in for titles like Angelou's *I Know Why the Caged Bird Sings* or Hosseini's *The Kite Runner*)

CHAPTER 6

TO BE, OR NOT TO BE: LITERARY RETELLINGS

> I dreamed that I saw a man, with his face turned away
> from his own house—a book in his hand, and a great burden
> on his back. I looked and saw him open the book and read therein;
> and as he read, he wept and trembled; and not being able to
> contain himself, he broke out with a lamentable cry, saying:
> *What shall I do to be saved?*[1]
>
> —Oliver Hunkin, *Dangerous Journey: The Story of Pilgrim's Progress*

Historic Biltmore Estate in Asheville, North Carolina, is the largest privately owned mansion in the United States. Guests pass slowly through the house, admiring its grandeur from behind red velvet lines. One visit is not adequate to absorb the marvelous library, elaborate decor, and precious works of art.

Imagine that the trustees of the estate hired a marketing expert with new and original ideas to advise them on how to attract a future generation of visitors. Were they offering enough? What would inspire young children and interest them in a place like Biltmore if they have grown up on screens and fun digital cartoons?

The expert has an exciting plan, an innovative strategy.

Introducing ... the Biltmore bounce house, situated proudly on the front

---

1. Oliver Hunkin, *Dangerous Journey: The Story of Pilgrim's Progress* (Eerdmans, 1985), 8.

lawn! The bounce house would be the shape of Biltmore but brightly colored and fun!

Does this sound preposterous? What would be a better way to bring a masterpiece to life for children?

Three Seventeenth-Century Books That Changed Your World

Three "literary Biltmores" were published within seventy years of each other. The seventeenth century was a pivotal era for the prosperity of the English language and literary culture, and we owe it a debt of gratitude for the King James Bible, Shakespeare's First Folio, and *The Pilgrim's Progress*.

Scripture holds its place alone. But what is particularly interesting about all three is that they were published for the common people and continue to be accessible to all.

Children can learn to appreciate Truth and Story in the language of the King James Version, several of Shakespeare's plays, and *The Pilgrim's Progress*, and thankfully many excellent retellings and illustrated versions are available to help them along the way. But because there is a ready market for all three, publishers offer a wide range of editions to choose from. Which ones are worth adding to your home library? What should you look for in a retelling of Bible stories, Shakespeare, or *The Pilgrim's Progress*, either in picture book or short story format?

When you are ready to introduce younger children to stories from these works, finding a literary retelling that respects both the original work and the developing imagination of the audience makes all the difference.

Bible Story Retellings

Bible story retellings must be excellent and beautiful by the standards of whatever art style you choose, whether you prefer realistic, detailed pictures or more stylized and symbolic illustrations. The vocabulary and craftsmanship of the story should be literary, showing and not merely telling, written with an ear for the sound of words and winsome appeal to the imagination.

On the website we've reviewed a wide range of Bible story books and picture book editions for all ages. Many are stronger on text than illustrations, so we do our best to focus on those that most accurately reflect Scripture. Remember that most of the Bible was set in the Middle East, so try to include books with authentic-looking characters of color in your collection.

An interesting range of illustration styles is available in Bible story books. *The Read-Aloud Bible Stories* by Ella Lindvall, illustrated by H. Kent Puckett, don't show Jesus' face and are accessible to young children without cheapening the narrative. Catalina Echeverri's illustrations (*The Garden, the Curtain, and the Cross*) are fresh, vibrant, and culturally appropriate. Stylized earth-toned art like the Howdeshells' in *The Story of Us* by Mitali Perkins or the jewel-toned palette by Don Clark in Kevin DeYoung's *The Biggest Story Bible Storybook* have unique appeals that work for some children.

Options like *Christmas Is Here* by Lauren Castillo portray Luke 2 with a modern pageant. *Miracle Man* and *Go and Do Likewise* by John Hendrix visually awaken the drama of familiar events and teaching in the life of Jesus. Even rocks make a great art medium, as Patti Rokus shows in *A Savior Is Born: Rocks Tell the Story of Christmas* and *He Is Risen: Rocks Tell the Story of Easter*.

When the text is handled with reverence and the narrator and artist are not condescending toward their audience, the results can be extraordinary.

SHAKESPEARE RETELLINGS

God in His wisdom has endowed certain authors with such common grace and insight into human nature that their work has made a deep impression on culture. Shakespeare is one of those gifted men whose tragedies and comedies have appeared not only on stage, but also in child-friendly retellings, including picture books and graphic novels.

Shakespeare wrote his plays for the populace, not the cultured elite, and they were popular from the end of the sixteenth century through the beginning of the seventeenth. Seven years after his death, his friends compiled manuscripts from most of his plays and published them in the First Folio in 1623. Why would we introduce Shakespeare's work to children now? Three reasons: his insight into human nature, his use of beautiful language, and his enduring cultural references.

Human behavior in a fallen world apart from Christ is accurately represented in Shakespeare's works. He had remarkable insight into what motivates his characters: love, lust, revenge, greed, power . . . these are the same issues that Jane Austen and Agatha Christie wrote about and that we continue to see in our current culture. His stories are relevant. How many teenagers do we know who, like Romeo and Juliet, fall in love with someone despite their parents' advice? They don't listen, and lo, something tragic happens. This is an old story; there is nothing new under the sun. But from a Christian standpoint, we recognize that our tragic flaws are not destiny. Because Jesus Christ is our hope, Christians are never past the point of no return.

Shakespeare's language is beautiful and rich. His plays are the source of more familiar phrases than any other author in the English language; only the King James Bible surpasses him. But aren't the plays hard to understand? For those well-grounded in singing traditional hymns, the vocabulary, structure, and meter are easier to grasp. Familiarity with the Bible and hymns help us understand Shakespeare, and being knowledgeable of his stories provides a deeper understanding of who we are and life in this world.

References to Shakespeare's *Hamlet* alone abound in popular culture. If children have no knowledge of this tragedy about the young prince of Denmark, they will not understand or appreciate allusions to it in *The Lion King, A Christmas Carol*, and even in a Sesame Street segment with renowned Shakespearean actor Patrick Stewart.[2]

---

2. Patrick Stewart, "Sesame Street: Patrick Stewart Soliloquy on B," YouTube, September 10, 2008, https://www.youtube.com/watch?v=hA7lv1SDzno.

The Stratford Zoo graphic novel versions of *Macbeth* and *Romeo and Juliet* set two of his most famous tragedies in nighttime performances at a zoo, with animals playing the roles and adding humorous commentary. Marcia Williams created a comic-book style collection that contains more of the plays as well. Both are fun introductions for younger children.

Bruce Coville's Shakespeare picture book retellings are excellent because he honors both the story and the audience. For longer narrative versions, Charles and Mary Lamb, Tina Packer, and Leon Garfield are literary storytellers who provide more detail and direct quotations.

THE PILGRIM'S PROGRESS RETELLINGS

The Pilgrim's Progress by John Bunyan is one of the most recognizable, most translated, most sold works in the English language. In fact, *The Pilgrim's Progress* has never been out of print since it was first published in 1678.

Bunyan was a bold Baptist preacher in a time when the state-approved church was not Baptist (it was what today we call Anglican). When he didn't stop preaching the Word of God, Bunyan was arrested. Being in prison didn't hinder him; he merely continued via the written word.

First published as *The Pilgrim's Progress from This World, to That Which Is to Come*, *The Pilgrim's Progress* is an allegory, a story in which nearly every fictional character, scene, and situation is a stand-in for real truth, real people, and real places. As Christian travels on his journey to the Celestial City through, by, or around such areas as the Slough of Despond, Palace Beautiful, Valley of the Shadow of Death, Vanity Fair, or Doubting Castle, he meets many characters with names that clearly indicate their helpfulness or hindrance to his quest: Pliable, Obstinate, Interpreter, Timorous, Charity, Faithful, Hopeful, the dreaded Apollyon, and Giant Despair.

A few years later, Bunyan wrote the story of Christian's wife, Christiana, and their children. The first story is the most famous and beloved, but both are worth reading. Christian's story is the life of a believer who feels the isolation of conversion when he is surrounded by people who are ignorant of spiritual matters. Christiana's story is that of a growing church including women, children, other mature saints, and those who are lame and feeble. These have a different experience of pilgrimage, but in the end, all find the promises are sure.

Few works of literature have had the cultural reach of *The Pilgrim's Progress*. That's pretty amazing—who would have thought an adventure story that pauses every few pages for long discussions of Christian theology would have such a grip on the Western world's imagination? Clearly Bunyan tapped something deep in the human spirit. The analogy of life's journey, with all the struggles and respites along the way, is common to all mankind.

According to Seth Lerer, children's books came into their own as a type of literature partially due to the Puritans who were concerned about their children's souls and invested in publishing books for them. *The Pilgrim's Progress* offered more than moralistic pedagogy.

> *For all its allegorical and pedagogic heft,* [The Pilgrim's Progress] *offered an adventure narrative familiar from old folktales and romances. There remains something childlike about its encounters with such characters as Giant Despair, with his castle and his "grim and surly voice," and his "nasty and stinking" dungeon.*[3]

The development of the printing press a hundred and fifty years earlier made publication easier than it had been for centuries, but home libraries were still sparse. If a family owned one book, it was the Bible. If they owned a second book by the end of the century, it was probably *The Pilgrim's Progress*, which spoke "truth within a fable," as the author himself described his book.[4] Ever since, believers have found themselves encouraged somewhere along the road with Christian, and the story is a hero's journey that was originally intended for a broad audience, including children.

---

3. Seth Lerer, *Children's Literature: A Reader's History from Aesop to Harry Potter* (University of Chicago Press, 2008), 93.

4. John Bunyan, *The Pilgrim's Progress* (Christian Focus Publications, 2007), 13.

References from Bunyan's story have passed into secular culture. When someone speaks of his "Slough of Despond" or mentions her "Celestial City," he or she is hearkening back to one of the seminal quest stories of the Western world. Authors, composers, and artists have taken the allegory as their inspiration for retellings or alluded to it in ways they expect their readers to understand.

Little Women, for example, is full of *The Pilgrim's Progress* references, from the first chapter ("Playing Pilgrims") to "Amy's Valley of Humiliation," "Beth Finds the Palace Beautiful," "Jo Meets Apollyon," and "Meg Goes to Vanity Fair." In "Castles in the Air," the girls dress as pilgrims and hike up the nearest hill, where each one (along with Laurie) describes her ideal castle.

Hind's Feet on High Places, a beloved Christian classic by Hannah Hurnard, enlists the Bunyan character Much-Afraid from Christiana's story as a protagonist and charts her journey from fear to assurance in Christ.

Dangerous Journey, a children's edition vividly illustrated by Oliver Hunkin, uses a shortened version of Bunyan's original text. *Kai'Ro* is an urban retelling by Judah Ben that shows respect for both the original story and a troubled teen audience.

Worthy Retellings

What if, instead of a marketing expert envisioning a bounce house, a curator and an architect bring a different idea to the Biltmore trustees? As much as they love the house and all it represents, they are aware that not every child will be able to visit it in person and that those who do will be overwhelmed.

Maybe they could bring the house to the children.

Imagine a teacher or parent examining a detailed model or intricate pop-up book of the Biltmore with children. "This room holds a suit of armor and a tapestry showing the Triumph of Faith. Here's a copy of the Dürer print that you'll find in this room—do you think you can find it when you're there? The library has a wonderful staircase—wouldn't you love to climb it and read the books on the upper shelves? Here's where you'll find a Monet painting..."

Over time, children would gradually build their own relationships through personal experience on a smaller scale. Those who have the opportunity will be ready to hunt for treasure as in an I Spy book, and each time they go, they will find old "friends" and make new ones.

> *A retelling is an irresistible invitation to the original, not a substitute.*

Have you seen Bible story retellings that look like a bounce house where everyone is smiling, with happy colors and lots of curvy lines? Rather than presenting the glory and the grandeur of the Word of God, the greatest Truth in the most perfect Story ever told, in language that brings you back over and over again, many retellings imply merely that we're all having a great time! Isn't this fun?

A retelling is an irresistible invitation to the original, not a substitute. Adaptations that are designed for education or moral improvement rather than delight are easily spotted and make poor nourishment for the developing imagination. These mediocre or even poor versions are often the result of adults trying to produce high test scores or check a cultural reference box, rather than inviting children to share a beautiful story that brings delight to the adult as well as the child.

Retellings show us how to handle beautiful words and provide a layout, overview, and window into a greater relationship we hope to experience. Reading well-crafted literary versions of Bible stories, Shakespeare's plays, or *The Pilgrim's Progress*, provides an anchor and connection when we finally encounter the original.

Stories and pictures come first; meaning and understanding follow eventually. When children are introduced to excellence in visual form with simple language and given a glimpse into important cultural references, the stories will become more intimate friends as the child matures.

These questions will help evaluate whether a retelling is worthy of introducing young audiences to any classic work.

First, does the author honor the original work as much as he or she respects the child audience? Are the illustrations excellent and beautiful examples of whatever art style appeals to you? Is the text true to the source? Is it simplified without being dumbed down, or is the story compromised to make it "child-friendly"?

Second, does this respect the child and bring delight through both the language and illustrations? Is the story simplified and condescending, or is the language and narrative style literary and pleasant to read aloud with concrete imagery that offers winsome appeal to the imagination?

Not every retelling will excel on every point, but revisiting the story from the perspectives of several different authors will help prepare future audiences to meet the original.

BOOKLIST FOR CHAPTER 6

Further Reading

    Pilgrim's Progress and *Pilgrim's Progress 2* by John Bunyan, Christian Focus, 2013.

For Children/Teens

    The Beginner's Gospel Story Bible, Jared Kennedy
    The Garden, the Curtain, and the Cross, Carl Laferton, illustrated by Catalina Echeverri (and others in the Tales that Tell the Truth series) (Picture Book)
    He Is Risen: Rocks Tell the Story of Easter, Patti Rokus (PB)
    Miracle Man, John Hendrix (PB)
    Something Better Coming, Megan Saben (PB)
    Shakespeare picture books by Bruce Coville (various illustrators) (PB)
    Tales from Shakespeare: Seven Plays, presented by Marcia Williams (PB)
    The Biggest Story Bible, Kevin DeYoung (Middle Grade) (see others in this series)
    Dangerous Journey, illustrated by Oliver Hunkin (MG)[5]
    Little Pilgrim's Progress, Helen L. Taylor, illustrated by Joe Sutphin (MG)
    Shakespeare's First Folio: All the Plays: A Children's Edition, illustrated by Emily Sutton (MG)
    Stratford Zoo Midnight Revue Presents *Macbeth* and *Romeo and Juliet*, Ian Lendler, illustrated by Zack Giallongo (MG)
    Pilgrim's Progress: A Retelling, Gary D. Schmidt, illustrated by Barry Moser (Young Adult)
    Romeo and Juliet, adapted by Gareth Hinds (YA)

---

5. An excellent family introduction; some images may be too intense for sensitive readers.

CHAPTER 7

GRAPHIC NOVELS: ARE THEY LITERATURE?

> The first thing I read are comics about Calvin and Hobbes.
> He is a boy who seems to hate the world as it is
> and love the world that ought to be.
> —Daniel Nayeri, *Everything Sad Is Untrue*[1]

> "Comics!" Freddy interrupted. "Baby stuff!
> No self-respecting animal over two years old looks at that trash....
> I beg your pardon, Sniffy. I don't really mean that, of course.
> It's just that I think these comics are foolish.
> I don't see how anybody can look at them when there are
> so many books around that are more interesting."
> —Walter R. Brooks, *Freddy the Pilot*[2]

It wasn't too long ago that reading comics was frowned upon. Growing up, Hayley's family would joke about cartoons rotting your brain while happily reading *Calvin and Hobbes*. As time passed, a new shelf appeared in libraries; alongside *Garfield* and *Peanuts* were new books in a growing genre called

---

1. Daniel Nayeri, *Everything Sad Is Untrue* (Levine Querido, 2020), 37.
2. Walter R. Brooks, *Freddy the Pilot* (1952; reis., Overlook Press, 1999), 5.

"graphic novels." Many readers have viewed graphic novels with the same skepticism directed at cartoons; yet, at Redeemed Reader, we love introducing readers to graphic novelists like Gareth Hinds, Doug TenNapel, and Ben Hatke. What happened?

A Bit of History

Hayley's city still boasts a comic book store and she lives on the same street where the famous Marvel comic writer, Mark Gruenwald, grew up. Comic books and authors like Gruenwald inspired a generation of young readers and artists to start telling their own stories using illustrations in a new format, the graphic novel.

In the late-twentieth century, a new literary phenomenon was born. Unlike traditional comics, these comics featured new illustrative styles and "were often a hundred or more pages long and because they generally told a story, some people began calling them 'graphic novels.'"[3]

Recent years have brought an uptick in retelling the classics and popular fiction in this format, especially as classics like *The Great Gatsby* arrive in public domain. But are "comic book" versions even literature?

When adapting a work of literature to a graphic novel format, an illustrator is faced with a job like that of a movie producer: using pictures as the primary means of telling a story, with words as secondary. When well-done, graphic novels capture the distinctives that mark works of literature. In addition, they can engage readers to dig deeper, or tell a story without delving as deeply into content that might be problematic for a younger reader.

Literary Graphic Novels ≠ Younger Reader Versions

Sometimes a graphic novel can make a work accessible for a younger reader. In the case of a Shakespeare play, live stage productions are out of the question

---

3. Leonard S. Marcus, *Comics Confidential: Thirteen Graphic Novelists Talk Story, Craft, and Life Outside the Box* (Candlewick Press, 2016), xiii.

for many students. Therefore, a graphic novel adaptation may be the next best option. Shakespeare's original plays were intended for performance; a graphic novel of Shakespeare can help bridge the gap between the stage and the page by offering readers a feel for the visuals of a play.

However, if you find yourself contemplating introducing a classic to a younger reader via graphic novel, remember that many graphic novels are intended for the same maturity level as the original work. Gareth Hinds' adaptations of *Romeo and Juliet*, *Beowulf*, and *The Odyssey* are beautiful, yet also quite violent with some sensuality—just like the original literature. Hinds' collection of *Poe: Stories and Poems* is another example of a well-done adaptation that, like the original, is "gripping, psychological and scary."[4]

Is the Book Always Better?

Several years ago, we discussed graphic novel adaptations of *The Great Gatsby*. K. Woodman-Maynard's adaptation does a particularly excellent job. (We even forgave her for changing Daisy's hair color!) F. Scott Fitzgerald's lavish, tragic tale was brought to life in watercolor panels, with a focus on language and symbolism—two elements that mark the original work of literature. Not all graphic novel adaptations succeed. We read another version of *The Great Gatsby* that fell short. The panels felt like mere illustrations of text, and the graphic novel's format ended up interrupting the story instead of capturing the flow of a novel.

The Giver is another example of a book that loses literary value as a graphic novel because of the color plot twist. Since the graphic novel is in black and white from the beginning, the graphic novelist steals the assumption, and readers miss the shock of realizing Jonas only sees in monochromatic colors before the burst of the red apple.

---

4. Betsy Farquhar, "Poe: Stories and Poems: A Graphic Novel Adaptation by Gareth Hinds," Redeemed Reader, https://redeemedreader.com/2017/12/poe-stories-poems-graphic-novel-adaptation-gareth-hinds/.

Sometimes a graphic novel writer's personal priorities overpower the original work. *Anne Frank's Diary: The Graphic Adaptation* by Ari Folman, illustrated by David Polonsky, focuses far more on Anne's sexuality than the passing sentences in the original text. While the scenes are stylized, the authors' decision to include sensualized artistic images seems to convey far more of a contemporary preoccupation with identity than the adolescent musings of a lonely teenager.

If you're uncertain whether or not a graphic novel is an acceptable form of literature, ask yourself the purpose of giving it to your reader.

If you're uncertain whether or not a graphic novel is an acceptable form of literature, ask yourself the purpose of giving it to your reader.

- Is this for enjoyment?
- Is it to capture a reluctant reader's imagination?

Gareth Hind's *Beowulf* might be just what you need to introduce a reluctant reader to the epic Anglo-Saxon saga. Graphic novel adaptations of *Watership Down* or *Beowulf* could spark an interest that will lead to more reading. Even if it doesn't, your reader now has a deeper knowledge and appreciation of a work of literature. That is no small thing!

- Is it for a school assignment?

Does the illustrator capture and translate the essence of the literary work they are adapting?

If you want to familiarize students with a story line or introduce them to a famous title without taking a deep dive into it—then a literary graphic novel could be a great pick. If this is for a literature class: What do you want students to gain from this story? As Betsy has pointed out, it comes down to your goal: If you want to focus on literary analysis, then you should opt for an original text. If you want to simply expose readers to a story, then pick the graphic novel.[5]

Some graphic novel adaptations like *Watership Down* capture elements of the original story that we might miss. Richard Adams based his story on an actual location, and thanks to Joe Sutphin and James Sturm's marvelous adaptation, readers can glimpse the real Watership Down. Sutphin and Sturm traveled to England to meet Adams's daughters and visited the real locations on which the story was based. But should you read the adaptation? Rosamond Mahoney, reflecting on her father, Richard Adams, summarized: "He just said it was a book that was written for anybody who wanted to read it."[6] Thanks to the new graphic novel the "anybody" Adams envisioned can now be expanded, and even more can enter the world of *Watership Down*.

At Redeemed Reader, we like to remind each other, "Don't overthink it."[7] If you have found a graphic novel adaptation that will spark your reader's imagination and make them love literature more—read it!

Graphic Novels as Standalone Literature

In 2020, for the first time in its history, the John Newbery Medal went to a graphic novel: *New Kid* by Jerry Craft. The Redeemed Reader team, watching the ALA Youth Media Awards remotely, let out excited whoops. *New Kid*, as we summed it up, is "a fresh and funny graphic-novel take on the middle-school blues."[8]

As Betsy said in a discussion leading up to the Newbery Awards, *New*

---

5. "The Great Gatsby in Graphic Novel Form," Redeemed Reader, https://redeemedreader.com/2021/05/the-great-gatsby-in-graphic-novel-form/.
6. Matthew Schuerman, "Watership Down's Latest Iteration Is a Graphic Novel. We Revisit the Enduring Story," NPR, October 29, 2023, https://www.npr.org/2023/10/29/1209313567/watership-downs-latest-iteration-is-a-graphic-novel-we-revisit-the-enduring-stor.
7. This phrase comes from Anne Bogel's book *Don't Overthink It!* (Baker Books, 2020)
8 "New Kid by Jerry Craft," Redeemed Reader, https://redeemedreader.com/2019/03/new-kid-by-jerry-craft/.

Kid is "a near perfect example of what graphic novels do well that a traditional prose novel can't quite achieve."[9] She summed up one of the cardinal strengths of a good graphic novel: Its creator is able to show, not tell. Pressing into this idea, she added, "I think this is one of the ways graphic novels can offer a further perspective on storytelling. The creator has the ability to suggest emotions and scenarios with visual cues and young readers can interpret those in their own words."[10]

Janie observed, "Graphic art should be understood as its own medium, not a dumbed-down version of literature."[11]

As standalone graphic novels have surged in popularity, we have reviewed many and found a number of favorites. They are a great way of catching the imagination of reluctant readers.

However, as the genre continues to grow, it is easy to be overwhelmed by the number of choices. A third grade teacher recently lamented to Hayley how hard it is to get students to read more than just graphic novels. Some graphic novels are just fun for young readers, even if adults dread yet another adventure of Dog Man or Captain Underpants. (We delve more into the "fun" side of graphic novels in chapter 16.) Still, can any of these books be considered literary?

Ethel Heins, an editor of *The Horn Book,* once wrote: "All good illustrations must emanate from the mind, and the quality of the illustration reflects the intensity of the imaginative experience."[12] She then quoted Caldecott winning illustrator, Uri Shulevitz; "The main function of illustration is to

---

9. Betsy Farquhar, "2020 Newbery Buzz #2: New Kid and Guts," Redeemed Reader, https://redeemedreader.com/2020/01/2020-newbery-buzz-2-new-kid-and-guts/.
10. Ibid.
11. Ibid.
12. Ethel Heins, introduction to "Motion and Rest: The Art of Illustration" in *Innocence and Experience: Essays and Conversations on Children's Literature*, comp. and ed. Barbara Harrison and Gregory Maguire (Lothrop, Lee & Shepard Books, 1986), 306.

illuminate the text, to throw light on words."[13] These observations illustrate the power of well-written (and drawn!) graphic novels. Can such works be literary? At Redeemed Reader, we believe they can.

BOOKLIST FOR CHAPTER 7

Further Reading

    Understanding Comics: The Invisible Art, Scott McCloud

For Children/Teens

    Bea Wolf, Zach Weinersmith, illustrated by Boulet (Middle Grade)
    Bolivar, Sean Rubin (MG)
    El Deafo, Cece Bell (MG)
    Family Style, Thien Pham (MG)
    New Kid, Jerry Craft (MG)
    Snow White: a Graphic Novel, Matt Phelan (MG)
    Tommysaurus Rex, Doug TenNapel (MG)
    American Born Chinese, Gene Luen Yang (Young Adult)
    The Great Gatsby, F. Scott Fitzgerald, adapted by
        K. Woodman-Maynard (YA)
    The Iliad: A Graphic Novel, Gareth Hinds (YA)
    Watership Down, Richard Adams, adapted by James Sturm,
        illustrated by Joe Sutphin (YA)

---

13. Uri Shulevitz, *Writing with Words* (Watson-Guptill Publications, 1985), 120.

CHAPTER 8

"SAVAGES" AND "SLAVES": HISTORICAL RACISM IN CHILDREN'S BOOKS

> "Baby, we have no choice of what color we're born
> or who our parents are or whether we're rich or poor.
> What we do have is some choice over
> what we make of our lives once we're here."[1]
>
> Mildred D. Taylor, *Roll of Thunder, Hear My Cry*

In February 2018, the ALA's Association for Library Services to Children (ALSC) appointed a task force to consider changing the name of the Laura Ingalls Wilder Award. The LIW medal was created in 1955 to honor authors who have made significant contributions to children's literature and was first awarded to Wilder herself. Other honorees make up a Who's Who in the field: E. B. White, Maurice Sendak, Dr. Seuss, Eric Carle, and James Marshall, to name a few.

By 2018, concern about racist undertones in the Little House series were making the ALA nervous. The racism was certainly there, evident in Ma's opinion of Native Americans and in Pa's putting on blackface to clownishly

---

1. Mildred D. Taylor, *Roll of Thunder, Hear My Cry* (Puffin, 1991), 129.

imitate African Americans in a minstrel show. Such depictions represented "stereotypical attitudes inconsistent with ALSC's core values of inclusiveness, integrity and respect, and responsiveness."[2] During the association's annual summer conference in New Orleans that June, the ALSC announced Wilder's name had been dropped from what would now be known as the Children's Literature Legacy Award (first recipient: Jacqueline Woodson).

Predictable protests followed, which changed no one's mind. You, the reader, may have strong opinions on the change, pro or con, but let's consider it from the ALA's point of view for a moment. How would you feel, as a black child, about the illustration by Garth Williams from *Little Town on the Prairie* that depicts Pa cavorting on stage in blackface, in deliberate ridicule of "negroes"? Or perhaps as a young member of the Osage Nation reading Ma's harsh judgments?

The website Reading While White (no longer current) dedicated itself to "working for diversity and inclusion in books for children and teens." Reviews pointed out the dreaded "-isms" in classic children's literature: racism, antisemitism, ableism, classism, sexism, and more. A post called "Alongside, Not Despite: Talking About Race and Settler Colonialism in a Children's Literature Graduate Course"[3] challenges the general reader's assumption about "problematic" classic texts.

The post describes an elective graduate course where students (mostly white women) expressed discomfort with rereading the classics of their childhood. They had gained a more critical eye toward current hot-button issues, especially when encountering passages they glossed over uncritically when they were kids. What to think about the "white savior" protagonist of *Maniac McGee*? Or how

---

2. "Welcome to the Children's Literature Legacy Award Home Page!," Association for Library Service to Children (ALSC), archived June 25, 2018 at the Wayback Machine, https://web.archive.org/web/20180625161314/http://www.ala.org/alsc/awardsgrants/bookmedia/wildermedal.

3. Megan Dowd Lambert, "Alongside, Not Despite: Talking About Race and Settler Colonialism in a Children's Literature Graduate Course," Reading While White, April 27, 2017, https://readingwhilewhite.blogspot.com/2017/04/alongside-not-despite-talking-about.html.

Indigenous people are casually smeared as "cannibals" in *Pippi Longstocking*? Is it enough to say we love these books *in spite of* their casual racism?

The writer of the post suggested her students might think about that question another way: Substitute "alongside" for "despite," and rather than racism, propose any other marginal group to which they may relate: "I love this book alongside its misogyny, its antisemitism, its Islamophobia, its homophobia..."' or, we might add, its anti-Christian assumptions.

The Adventures of Huckleberry Finn, to take one example, has frequently been called out for its supposed racism and use of the n-word. Christians can make a case that the novel, in its celebration of human autonomy and negative portraits of pious slave-holding "Christians," is slanted against biblical faith. But we can still benefit from reading it for its indelible characters and insights into the American past, not to mention its sheer entertainment value.

Just because a book is a classic, or even beloved, doesn't mean it's immune to criticism. Society can evolve in healthy ways. In 2021 came news that Dr. Seuss Enterprises, the agency which manages the author's legacy, was removing six Dr. Seuss titles from publication. Many of us who grew up enjoying those books reacted negatively—just another example of political correctness run amok! But after revisiting *If I Ran the Zoo* and *To Think That I Saw It on Mulberry Street*, we have to admit that the stereotypical portrayals of Africans and Asians in those books were truly insulting. What was acceptable in the fifties may be cringeworthy now. Most Americans today, particularly white Americans, rightly feel some degree of shame about certain chapters of our past.

Still, there comes a point when racial and cultural sensitivity ends up working against itself. It can certainly work against literature.

When the discussion of a book circles around its offensiveness, the book becomes an offender rather than a depiction of humanity in historical context. Focusing on offensiveness also demands a reaction. What to do? Censor all the disturbing material? Censor the entire book? And if censorship becomes the recommended practice, wouldn't that mean locking ourselves into the present? Even the most liberal-minded, forward-looking, admirable figures of the past held attitudes we would deem offensive, but we can still learn from them.

When evaluating classic literature, and history itself for that matter, we should keep these considerations in mind:

People are people, in real life and in great literature. We shouldn't make a fictional character stand for an entire history of racial injustice, and a single novel can't reflect everything there is to say about a social issue. Racism may be one factor of a human being's worldview. In some people it may be a dominant one. It's also a sin. We're all sinful individuals with complex lives, acting out our strengths and weaknesses within a cultural context.

When comparing our current era to the past, we seldom consider how we're cushioned by technology. For an entire population to live relatively free of hunger, hard labor, extreme temperatures, discomfort, and the continual threat of fatal disease has only been possible for the last hundred years or so. We have no idea what it might be like to live at the mercy of nature, with little time to explore the world beyond a few square miles. Constant necessity kept noses to grindstones and feet in familiar ruts. There's no leisure for thinking outside the box when all you can do is survive within the box.

We can't overlook the influence of mass communication. When travel was hit-or-miss, print journalism local, and home libraries were limited to two or three volumes (if that), ideas had little room to circulate. Opinions, like property, tended to be handed down through generations.

None of this means that our ancestors never enjoyed life or had meaningful discussions about current issues. The anti-slavery movement of the early nineteenth century was profoundly influential in changing opinions. But enlightenment for the general public comes when the blinders of necessity begin to open up.

There's another *–ism* the critics of our racist, colonialist, paternalist past should consider: "presentism." That is, "An attitude toward the past dominated by present-day attitudes and experiences."[4]

Every generation has its virtues and vices, and acquiring new virtues (and vices) often means letting go of others. We can be critical without being judgmental, and we can appreciate the virtues of the Ingalls family (and others like them) without condoning their colonialist, racist vices. We can do better than that, even—we can love those books for the windows they open to an experience that's now totally alien to us.

The Original Sin

Racism is said to be America's original sin, especially in regard to the African slave trade and all the miseries it produced, from 1619 right up to the present. But our spotted history is much more complicated than contemporary social consciences make it seem.

An original sin, properly understood, is the primary fault from which every other fault stems. Recently, prominent writers have suggested that America was founded on racism, a judgment that fails to take the whole story into account. America was a new world to make a new start, unhindered by the vestiges of serfdom, a permanent underclass, strict inheritance laws, and burdensome taxation.

Unfortunately, the expanded opportunity to succeed meant expanded opportunities to exploit, but exploitation *in itself* is not racism. It is self-centeredness and greed, from which no one is exempt. America's original sin is actually *the* original sin (see *garden of Eden, the*), and racism is an effect, not a cause.

Because of America's unique history as a New World settled by people from all over the globe, racism has taken distinct forms in the United States. People of all races have suffered at various times from prejudice, injustice, and

---

4. *Merriam-Webster*, s.v. "presentism (n.)," https://www.merriam-webster.com/dictionary/presentism.

even violence. But they've responded in their own ways and have contributed to making the United States a more open, welcoming, and generous nation.

American children, of all races and ethnic groups, need to know our country's faults but also our country's virtues. Steering a path through classic literature can make this difficult, especially for children of African, Hispanic, Native American, or Asian heritage. Are there some books they shouldn't read at all? If the central theme of the book (as opposed to a tangential reference) appears to denigrate a class or race of human beings made in God's image, no one needs to read it.

> *We should acknowledge that racist stereotypes and comments encountered in historical literature can still be hurtful, even if they aren't intentional.*

We should acknowledge that racist stereotypes and comments encountered in historical literature can still be hurtful, even if they aren't intentional. For a G. A. Henty adventure tale or a classic romance like *Gone With the Wind*, or even C.S. Lewis's depiction of the dark-skinned Calormenes in *The Last Battle* or *The Horse and His Boy*, some questions are critical to ask:

- When was the book written?
- What do you know about the author?
- What is the author's purpose in writing the book? (e.g., to reminisce, teach, entertain, proselytize?)
- How do the characters express racist attitudes (in words or actions)? Do these attitudes come from active hostility, or carelessness, or lack of empathy?
- Might these characters think differently if they lived today? Might *you* think differently if you lived back then?

- What can you learn from these characters?

It's not necessary to put every Little House or Henty novel under a microscope, but if you're intentional about discussing some classic literature along these lines, your kids will take the hint and begin querying literature for themselves.

Toward a More Positive View

Racism indeed has a traumatic and tragic history, but parents of all races should be wary of an unhealthy focus on trauma and tragedy in literature. Blogger Sarah Hannah Gómez grew up as a biracial (African/White) adoptee in a bicultural (Mexican American/Ashkenazi Jewish) family. In an article in *The Horn Book* she recalls how difficult it was to find balanced representations of her unique heritage in the books she read. When she asked for books about black children at her local library, she got slavery or civil rights narratives. After a while, she "couldn't take any more of it."[5] She found more rounded characters in the Dear America series (historical fiction titles by various authors) and one American Girl protagonist, Cecile Rey, a free black girl living in antebellum New Orleans. But Cecile's shelf life was short; her stories were discontinued after only three years.

Walter Dean Myers, author of over a hundred books for all ages, had a similar complaint: "Black history is usually depicted as folklore about slavery, and then a fast-forward to the civil rights movement. Then I'm told that black children, and boys in particular, don't read. Small wonder."[6]

"For nonwhites," writes Gómez, "the absence of everyday stories and the lack of connection between larger moments of history mean that our collective memory is made up of not just fewer experiences overall but *specifically*

---

5. Sarah Hannah Gómez, "Decolonizing Nostalgia: When Historical Fiction Betrays Children of Color," *The Horn Book*, November/December 2016.
6. Walter Dean Meyers, "Where Are the People of Color in Children's Books?," *New York Times Book Review*, May 15, 2014.

traumatic ones."[7] That is, when children—both white and nonwhite—are fed a steady diet of "traumatic" history, they receive a warped view, inducing negativity, resentment, and guilt.

The ALA neither sanctioned Wilder's Little House books nor officially stated they shouldn't be read. But progressive librarians have been plinking away at classic titles for decades. One popular remedy is *substitution*: Instead of *The Westing Game* with its Asian stereotypes, for example, read *The Mysterious Benedict Society*; instead of the Little House Series, substitute The Birchbark House series.[8]

A better approach is *expansion*: Read the Little House books but expand your children's reading universe to stories about characters of color within their own cultures (the Birchbark House series is a good example). Making literary friends across a wide range of cultures, ethnicities, and backgrounds can expand a young reader's sympathies as well as his knowledge. Along the way, he may just gain an appreciation for the variety of humankind, and of his own place in that splendid mosaic.

---

7. Gómez, "Decolonizing Nostalgia," emphasis added.
8. "Alternatives to Classic Children's Books," New Haven Free Public Library, https://nhfpl.org/wp-content/uploads/2021/03/alternatives-to-childrens-classics.pdf.

BOOKLIST FOR CHAPTER 8

Further Reading

    Steeped in Stories, Mitali Perkins

For Children/Teens

    How Sweet the Sound: The Story of Amazing Grace, Carole Boston Weatherford, illustrated by Frank Morrison (Picture Book)

    How do You Spell Unfair?, Carole Boston Weatherford, illustrated by Frank Morrison (PB)

    Call Me Roberto!, Nathalie Alonso, illustrated by Rudy Gutierrez (PB)

    The Found Boys, S. D. Smith (Chapter Book)

    The Lucky Ones, Linda Williams Jackson (MG)

    My Friend the Enemy, J. B. Cheaney (MG)

    Prairie Lotus, Linda Sue Park (MG)

    When Winter Robeson Came, Brenda Woods (MG)

    One Big Open Sky, Lisa Cline-Ransome (Upper MG/YA)

    All the Days Past, All the Days to Come, Mildred D. Taylor (Young Adult; Logan Family Saga)

    Undefeated, Steve Sheinkin (YA/nonfiction)

    Under a Painted Sky, Stacey Lee (YA)

SECTION 3
Contemporary Issues

CHAPTER 9

"MESSY" BOOKS: WHAT DO WE DO WITH THEM?

> "Where's Papa going with that axe?"[1]
> —E. B. White, *Charlotte's Web*

What are some 'clean' books I can give to my teens?"
At Redeemed Reader, we regularly field questions like this from our readers. Readers of every age can—and will—encounter books that are problematic in some way. We call these "messy books"—books that tend to make readers (and/or their parents) uncomfortable, whether it's a tragic situation or an overly graphic one. Messy books have some issues, but we need not categorically avoid them.

A book is messy when it grapples with sin. Period. Sin is messy—it disrupts God's perfect order, people's lives, and creation. In short, sin messes everything up. Thus, books that honestly reflect the human condition are often messy because sin is messy.

When Adam and Eve sinned, the entire created order, present and future, was impacted. In theological terms, we call this the "fall." In God's great mercy, He provided redemption through His Son, Jesus Christ. Jesus' death on the cross and subsequent resurrection didn't just purchase redemption for God's

---

1. E. B. White, *Charlotte's Web* (HarperCollins, 2012), 1.

people; the effects of the fall will be reversed for the entire earth.

In the meantime, we Christians live in the "now and not yet," the in-between: We're in between Jesus' resurrection and His second coming. Thus, we still grapple with the effects of the fall, both on ourselves and on the world at large. Books portraying the human experience honestly will have to confront this on some level.

Most messy books fall into two broad categories: personal sin and general sin. Personal sin includes individual sinners (characters) and the actions or thoughts they may exhibit. For instance, a character's profanity or habit of lying are particular sins. A younger book character might be rebellious toward parental authority or a downright bully. An older character might sleep with his girlfriend or drink too much.

General sin includes all the many ways this world God made has been negatively affected, or broken, because of the fall: Broken families. Abuse. Racism. Systemic injustice. Religious persecution. The list goes on. These effects certainly make for messy books!

Whether a book portrays a sinful character or wrestles with more general evil, the question we must ask ourselves is *not* "does this book have X kind of content?" (or "is this book 'clean'?"). The real question is "*Why* is this particular content in this book?" *Why* is the main character struggling with alcoholism? *Why* is the book showing the extent of someone's persecution? *Why* is the father divorced?

Equip vs. Protect

As Christian parents and educators who love to read with our children, we must remind ourselves that *discernment*, not comfort, is the goal. Just as an adult human isn't born knowing how to make a mortgage payment or vote intelligently in a presidential election, so young readers aren't born knowing how to read discerningly. We must teach and equip our children and students to do this. Messy books play an important role in this process.

When children are young, in the lap-sitting stage of reading, parents are clearly gatekeepers. After all, the child can't drive herself to the library or order books online. During this phase, parents want to protect and comfort young children, and rightly so. As children grow and begin interacting with the world outside their home, they will see more of sin's effects on the world around them and the people they know. Our gut instinct, as parents, is to continue protecting these precious souls in our care. But growing in discernment includes facing uncomfortable topics. Books provide great avenues for exploring these topics together.

As Christian parents and educators who love to read with our children, we must remind ourselves that discernment, not comfort, is the goal.

So, we bravely dive into *The Great Gilly Hopkins*, *The Bridge to Terabithia*, or even *Charlotte's Web*, knowing what our children will face in the coming pages. It's okay to cry in front of our young readers. Weeping over sin and its effects is a biblical response. We help set the default early on by talking about books, responding biblically to whatever we read (including joy and delight as well as lament and anger).

As children mature, so do the books. Much to our parental dismay, this period coincides with greater independence for our young readers. Now is the time to keep those conversations going, talking about life *and* the books they're reading. Kids, especially as they hit fifth or sixth grade, have lots of opinions. Encourage your children to talk about them. Where are they getting their information? What is troubling to them? We'll suggest some questions later in this chapter.

Middle schoolers are also beginning to think more critically of those around them. Reading books about characters who go through hard things helps our children think of people as subjects, not objects. We cannot love our neighbors well if we have not learned to view them as individuals made in God's image, whether that neighbor is a homeless person on the street, a refugee from another country, someone who looks different from us, or who has a different family structure than ours. We will not seek to share the gospel with those whom we do not love.

When children are choosing more books on their own, whether in third grade or sixth grade, the best tools we can give them as they grow in discernment are the following:

Permission to *not finish* a book, particularly one they picked up for recreational reading. Children grow up assuming all books are read to the end; after all, that has been the norm. Adults know that some books are not worth our time. Sometimes, a book is offensive enough that we need to put it down and read something different. Sometimes a book is too much for a sensitive conscience even if others find it acceptable. Regardless of the reason, ask your child about it. If the book was too hard (i.e., too complex/long), suggest a more suitable title. If the book contained elements in it that were too much for the child's conscience, praise the child for listening to the Holy Spirit and putting the book away. Encourage those baby steps toward discernment!

For example, Betsy's daughter picked up the Wings of Fire series when she was a preteen. Betsy knew the books were popular but hadn't read them yet, so she casually asked her daughter what she thought. The verdict? Her daughter said the books made her uncomfortable and she'd stopped reading them. She told Betsy that the dragons started doing weird things and girls liked girls "in that way." This is a wonderful example of a child listening to the Holy Spirit, and Betsy commended her daughter for heeding her conscience.

People around us will struggle with all manner of sin (as we ourselves will), and we must model how to look to Scripture for guidance and how to pray, confessing our sin to the Lord. It is a sign of maturity when our children demonstrate sensitivity to the Holy Spirit and good discernment.

Permission to talk to Mom or Dad about *anything* in the book without fear of judgment. Our children will not readily come talk to us if they fear retribution. If children concerned about profanity in a book or the level of sexuality or violence want to talk about it, we do well to listen! We can serve them far more by walking side by side through a book rather than overreacting and banning all problematic materials.

Sit with your children and students and acknowledge with them that it's okay to not know how to react. It's an opportunity to lean in with them and wrestle with what God says. Remember, we are training future discerning readers. Books can offer fruitful areas of discussion in a manner that promotes healthy interaction with ideas and issues.

Thorough biblical training. The *best* tool we can give our growing readers is God's Word. The more they know and understand the Bible, the better equipped they will be to think discerningly, to recognize error, and to know how the Bible handles the same issues. The Bible is a "messy book" in its own right: sexuality, witchcraft, rebellious children, broken homes, evil rulers, violence. How does the Bible handle these issues? As our children internalize God's Word, they are better equipped to bring that standard to bear on other messy books.

Evaluating Messy Books

Acknowledging that messy books can lead to productive conversations and growth in maturity is one thing; knowing which books lead to this end and how to handle them is another. There is no one-size-fits-all booklist or specific set of guidelines. Instead, we have a list of points to ponder that will help you decide which books have a place in your own homes and classrooms. They all start with "P" to help you remember, but not every "P" is equally applicable in each situation. Use those that are most helpful at any given time.

Plot Point vs. Political Point

Is the objectionable (or problematic, or messy) content in the book necessary to drive the story, or is there a clear agenda driving the inclusion of this content? For example, in *The Great Gilly Hopkins*, Katherine Paterson includes a lot of profanity, coming straight from the protagonist's mouth.

Paterson defends her choice, admitting she wrote both Maime and Gilly a bit larger than life in order to make readers think.[2] The bad language serves to illustrate just how rough Gilly's life has been, how unlovable a child she was initially, and the lengths to which her foster mother Maime Trotter goes to love this young "neighbor" of hers. In contrast, the volume of profanity in *The Catcher in the Rye* is not necessary, particularly since we do not see Holden Caulfield mature or be rescued out of his deplorable state. Rather, he wallows in his own depravity.

Pleasure or Pain?

Is the messy content a source of pleasure or pain in the book? All sin is pleasurable for the moment (Heb. 11:25). Does the story also show repentance, disgust at sin, or the negative consequences of sin? Or is the sinful act/thought seen to be only pleasurable or desirable? *The Golden Plate* by Bernadette Watts offers a childlike illustration of this concept when a young girl steals something but later repents and makes restitution. In contrast, Junie B. Jones's rampant disrespect is simply presented as funny and entertaining.

Francisco Stork's *Disappeared* illustrates for teens the heavy moral consequences of choosing sin (or not choosing it) in a way that prompts discussion about the painful aftereffects. *13 Reasons Why* offers much content to teen readers that simply feeds their immaturity and gratifies their morbid curiosity.

Preparation

Is the audience prepared for the content, both developmentally and experientially? If the book is a hard (messy) but worthwhile book, like *The Hiding Place* by Corrie ten Boom or *Everything Sad Is Untrue* by Daniel Nayeri, is the audience ready for the book? If readers are too young or immature, they often miss the forest for the trees. That is, they may get caught up in the mess and sinful actions, missing the greater story.

Shock value engages readers, but it can also mask other important points

---

2. Katherine Paterson, "National Book Award Acceptance Speech for *The Great Gilly Hopkins*," in *A Sense of Wonder: On Reading and Writing Books for Children* (Plume, 1995), 120–121.

an author might be trying to make. Perhaps readers are too young for certain types of romantic physical content; a simple kiss might be acceptable in a book for teens, but it carries more weight in a book for third graders. Often, when pondering this "P," the answer might be "not yet," instead of an outright "no."

Proportion

What is the proportion of messy content to the rest of the book? One throwaway line about a character's two moms requires a different response than a book in which the protagonist comes out as a lesbian. We certainly must address the normalization of sin in our culture, but a casual statement in a book can be addressed with a casual correction. A book in which much of the content revolves around a young boy's queer identity, like *King and the Dragonflies*, requires a different response.

Pandering

Is the author simply pandering to a childish audience (remember: teens can be childish!)? Is the content merely titillating the reader? Elizabeth Wein's *The Pearl Thief* adds a romantic physical backstory to two significant characters in this prequel that seems designed to pander to today's publishing trends rather than add depth to the existing story. For middle schoolers, *Goodbye, Stranger* by Rebecca Stead offers a better approach to sexuality gone wrong and the resulting feelings. For older teens, *Forward Me Back to You* by Mitali Perkins is an excellent antidote to the many teen novels that use sexuality more to grab readers' attention than to thoughtfully explore consequences.

Protagonist

Is the *protagonist* promoting or celebrating unbiblical behavior and beliefs with no evidence of repentance or maturation, or is the *villain* the renegade? In the gentle picture book *My Brother Is Away*, the young protagonist mourns the loss of her incarcerated brother. Nowhere does the text indicate that her brother did not commit a crime or his punishment is unjust. Rather, the girl is rightly mourning the effects of sin. In *Disappeared*, the teen protagonists see the "bad guys" using drugs and are rightly warned against it.

Promise

Related to pleasure/pain above, what does the story promise? Explicitly or implicitly, is the story promising redemption and rescue from sin? Or is it promising rewards for sin? Wendelin Van Draanen's *Wild Bird* shows a young drug addict maturing and recovering in a wilderness style rehab program. In this book, sin does not pay, but repentance, restitution, and restoration do.

Problematic or Productive?

Some messy books are productive reads; others are too problematic. Productive messy books illustrate biblical traits like compassion, truth-telling, and repentance. Problematic books do not. *Every Falling Star* by Sungju Lee presents a compelling picture of man's desperate need for redemption, the effects—and lure—of sin, and how broken our world is. The ending offers up hope, a rescue that enters a boy's despair much like Christ enters ours. Does this mean a fourth grader should read this book? No. It will be too much even for young teens. But it is a book worth reading by those ready for it, a book that will offer much productive food for thought and help its readers build empathy toward those in our world who most need it.

The aforementioned *King and the Dragonflies* is more problematic than productive, partly because it tackles too many issues at once to deal with any of them helpfully, but also because it presents unbiblical lifestyles as normal and acceptable.

How to Handle Messy Books

Even if a book is deemed a productive or helpful read, the fact that it's a "messy" book means it will require special handling.

Study God's Word: The world God made is beautiful and amazing, but it is also suffering the effects of sin. How does the Bible handle this? For instance, the Bible does not shy away from sexual indiscretion. Quite the opposite, in fact. But while the Bible shows the consequences of sin, it does not give readers every sordid detail. Meditate on God's Word and pray for wisdom.

Study your children: Before considering the books, know your children and students. Where are they developmentally? What do their consciences need? What will be good for their souls? Their imaginations? Do they need urging to be more courageous or compassionate? What are they prepared for? Where might you help lay a better foundation? Do they need protection in this area? Some children are far more sensitive to violence or abuse or similar content than other children their age might be. Pay more attention to the child/reader than to an arbitrary age-related metric.

Study the books: Do your homework. Read reviews, especially the reviews at Redeemed Reader. Why especially ours? Because we look beyond the surface mess. We do our best to alert you to "considerations" for a given book (i.e., the sort of content you want to know about ahead of time), but we also help you know how to approach that sort of content.[3] Read other sources' reviews as well, so far as they are helpful to you.

Read the book with your child: Whether it is assigned school reading or simply a book you want to read, consider reading it *with* your child (or, at the same time, book-club style). Keep in mind: Audio books are not necessarily the best option here. We remember what we hear a little differently; it is easier to skip crude language or sketchy scenes when reading than it is when listening.

Talk about the books: Talk about what you read with your kids. Not every book is a Lesson About Life, but do strike while the iron is hot, even when children are young or the book is not especially messy. Consider a book club approach with your kids if everyone is reading the same book around the same

---

3. Did you know that you can request Redeemed Reader to review a book? We can't act on every request, but we take them seriously!

time. Perhaps over Friday night pizza, the dinner discussion revolves around *The Giver* and Jonas's new abilities. Or children who might be child soldiers like those in *Bamboo People*. Or when it is okay (if ever) to conceal the truth, like the kids wrestle with in *Code of Silence*. Casually talking about books from the time children are very young will pay rich dividends when a messy book enters the scene later.

Be willing to say "not yet": Some books are amazing . . . for a reader who is fifteen and not five. Be willing to be the authority but consider having some backup options rather than simply "no" (although "no" applies in many situations!). And, depending on your child's age, consider *when* you might let them read *The Hunger Games* or *Okay for Now*. When we review messy books at Redeemed Reader, we try to suggest alternatives at the end of the review.

The Elephant in the Room: Censorship and Banning Books

Banned Books Week has become a signature cause of the American Library Association (ALA). Launched in 1982, it brings together librarians, authors, teachers, and book publishers in one weeklong celebration of anti-censorship. The dates change from year to year, but the week usually falls in September or October.

In the clamor about censorship and "freedom to read," it's easy to get caught up in online "discussions." Some express shock and horror at the sexually explicit books some libraries have for younger readers and cry, "Of course we should ban books!" Others protest the lack of freedom to read, expressing their own shock and horror at censorship. As with most ongoing conversations, it is best to do our homework first.

First, what constitutes a "book ban"? The official definition, from PEN America, is fairly broad: "Any action taken against a book based on its content and as a result of parent or community challenges, administrative decisions, or in response to direct or threatened action by lawmakers or other government officials, that leads to a previously accessible book being either completely removed from availability to students, or where access to a book is restricted or diminished."[4] According to this definition, *any* action, even a request to reshelve a library book for an older audience, constitutes an attempt to "ban" a book.

The Freedom Forum includes the following in its list of the most frequently banned books: *To Kill a Mockingbird*, *The Adventures of Huckleberry Finn*, various Shakespeare plays, and the Harry Potter series (interestingly, this series was first banned by the right, protesting witchcraft in the books, but recently by the left because of the author's supposed anti-trans position).[5] The ALA also keeps a record of attempts to ban or censor books from year to year (based on reporting from libraries). Children's books challenged in the past include *Little Black Sambo* by Helen Bannerman, *The Watsons Go to Birmingham—1963* by Christopher Paul Curtis, *A Wrinkle in Time* by Madeleine L'Engle, *The Giver* by Lois Lowry, *The Sign of the Beaver* by Elizabeth George Speare, *Roll of Thunder, Hear My Cry* by Mildred D. Taylor, and many more.[6]

Certainly, there are also many books on the list that were banned (or requested to be removed) due to sexuality. But the books just listed illustrate that so-called banned books are not automatically "bad" books. They are probably messy, but that does not mean they should necessarily be removed from shelves. The banned book might be a book we most certainly *do* want access to: The Bible has been banned countless times; it is listed as one of the ten most banned books in 2015 according to the ALA.[7]

Headlines about banned books do not give us enough information to make informed decisions. We should handle each "banned" book in the same

---

4. "Frequently Asked Questions," PEN America, https://pen.org/book-bans-frequently-asked-questions/.
5. "Famous Banned Books," Freedom Forum, https://www.freedomforum.org/famous-banned-books/.
6. "Frequently Challenged Books," American Library Association, https://www.ala.org/bbooks/frequentlychallengedbooks/top10/archive.
7. Office for Intellectual Freedom, "Top 10 and Most Frequently Challenged Books Archive," American Library Association. https://www.ala.org/bbooks/frequentlychallengedbooks/top10/archive.

fashion as indicated above for all messy books, evaluating each book for our own audience (our home or classroom). We cannot expect librarians to parent our children and teens. We must be training our children to read discerningly even as we do our own book homework.

Why Books Are Challenged

Often books are challenged for either biblical (moral) reasons or cultural issues. Although anyone can challenge a book, including library patrons, religious groups, and elected officials, parents make up at least 50 percent of challengers.[8]

Books challenged for biblical or moral reasons often relate to concerns over deviant sexuality, graphic sexuality, and the like. Sometimes, the title alone alerts readers to the content; for instance, *Two Boys Kissing* by David Levithan is clear about its subject. Other times, a book simply shows up frequently on banned book lists. *The Absolutely True Diary of a Part-Time Indian* by Sherman Alexie contains plenty of objectionable material (including a young teen's obsession with all things sexual), but the story also presents a picture of life on a modern-day Indian reservation. Seeing it regularly on banned books lists indicates, at minimum, that a parent should read the book or do some homework before casually tossing the book onto a child's nightstand.

Some books are banned for cultural reasons, whether or not the issue is a moral or biblical one. For instance, many conservative groups, in their efforts to keep Critical Race Theory out of their children's schools, have tried to ban books portraying accurate depictions of nonwhite culture. In one example, school boards in Texas pulled the graphic novel *New Kid* by Jerry Craft over CRT concerns.[9] We disagree; the humorous experiences of the protagonist, a black boy at an elite, majority white school, are true to life and gently poke

---

8. "About Banned & Challenged Books," ALA.org, https://www.ala.org/bbooks/aboutbanned-books.
9. David K. Li, "Texas School District Pulls Books by Acclaimed Black Author Amid Critical Race Theory Claims," NBC News, October 6, 2021, https://www.nbcnews.com/news/us-news/texas-school-district-pulls-books-acclaimed-children-s-author-n1280956.

fun at all the ways we misunderstand one another. Attempting to ban books like this counters the full representation of God's creation. He has made all people in all places; contemporary white American culture is merely one area in which He can make His voice known.

What to Do When You Question a Book

What happens if you are the parent or concerned citizen who wants to have a book reshelved or removed? Or what if a teacher assigns a book you do not want your child to read? How should you challenge a book? When should you challenge a book?

Before challenging a book, consider the following:

Build relationships: *Before* you have a concern over a particular title, build relationships with your librarians and your child's teachers. Be friendly. Talk about the books you do like with them. Ask them for their book recommendations or thoughts on the latest award winners.

Read the book: When someone wants to ban a book from a school or public library, read the book yourself (or enough of it to determine whether the challenge is thoughtful and not merely reactionary). Before automatically joining the fray, do your book homework first!

Be respectful: No matter what outcome you would like to see, remember that you are raising this issue with people who are made in God's image, just as you are. Be kind and courteous. Modulate your tone. Consider that the person you are questioning might not be the one who decides which books are in the library, or even which books are taught in his or her classroom.

Ask questions: Why is this book considered a good one for this age group? What is the English class hoping to learn from this book? The more you can discover about why a particular book is in the library collection or in a curriculum list, the better able you will be to address your own concerns with the people involved.

Come with solutions: Whether you are attending a school board meeting, a parent-teacher conference, or casually asking a librarian a question, come with a thoughtful solution to your dilemma. Is the book simply too mature for where it is shelved? Betsy once requested her library to reshelve a book that she and Janie liked (*Ordinary Hazards* by Nikki Grimes); it was in her library's juvenile section and should have been Young Adult at least.

Betsy noted specific content in the book, explaining she did not want the library removing the book from the general collection. Even though her request to relocate the book technically constituted an attempt to ban a book, or "restrict access," her solution was a relocation rather than an outright ban. For issues with assigned school reading, you may need to come with suggested substitutions, such as our list of alternatives for *The Kite Runner* on Redeemed Reader.[10]

Public services reflect the public interest: The American Library Association is no friend to Christians, but most librarians are interested in serving their local public. Many Christian librarians are faithfully attempting to curate collections that will benefit their patrons. Library funding comes partly from "circulation stats," and frequently borrowed books are more likely to stay in the library.

Instead of abandoning your local library,[11] consider telling librarians how glad you are they have certain books in their collection and continue checking out great books. Do not check out the books you do not like. The more people who (respectfully and thoughtfully) voice their concerns over particular titles, the more likely it is that those books will be downgraded because they are not serving the community. Every library has a budget, be it a home library or the New York City Public Library. Every library is bound by shelf space. Think of "selection" vs. "censorship" and encourage your public institutions to

---

10. Betsy Farquhar, "12 Substitutions for The Kite Runner," Redeemed Reader, August 11, 2020, https://redeemedreader.com/2020/08/11-substitutions-for-the-kite-runner/.
11. We recognize that many Christians will conclude that they do, indeed, need to abstain from visiting their local library. We are proposing alternatives to consider first, but know that sometimes, they will not work in a particular situation. We also recommend that you check out the Loving Libraries chapter (#23) later in this book!

purchase the books you would like. Most libraries have options for the public to request books for them to purchase. Take advantage of it!

Pray: Prayer is not a last resort. It is the first step and should be woven throughout. Pray for opportunities to respectfully communicate your concerns. Pray for wisdom about when to speak up and when to stand by. We cannot expect those who do not profess to know Christ to abide by biblical standards. May we pray for those who do not know the Lord before we excoriate them. When we disagree with fellow Christians, let us go to them individually first, following the guidelines in Matthew 18. We live in a fallen world, and we look for our ultimate hope from the Lord.

Prudence Not Panic

Messy books should not cause us to panic, even when our children and teens read content we wish we knew about in advance and would have avoided if we did. The Lord is bigger than that. In any diet, unhealthy and sometimes downright poisonous foods crop up, but if the overall diet is good, the person rarely suffers permanent harm.

Let us be prayerful, thoughtful, and courageous, walking alongside the young imaginations in our care. We can model how to interact with the world, how to read stories of all kinds, and how to love God and our neighbor in the midst. This will serve our children more than all the book-banning we can muster up.

BOOKLIST FOR CHAPTER 9

Further Reading

    Reading Between the Lines, Gene Edward Veith

For Children/Teens

    My Brother Is Away, Sara Greenwood, illustrated by Luisa Uribe (Picture Book)

    The Other Side, Jacqueline Woodson, illustrated by E. B. Lewis (PB)

    Blended, Sharon Draper (Middle Grade)

    Ghost/Patina, Jason Reynolds (MG)

    The Rwendigo Tales, J. A. Myhre (MG)

    Gone to the Woods, Gary Paulsen (YA)

    I Must Betray You, Ruta Sepetys (YA)

    Okay for Now, Gary D. Schmidt (YA)

    Wild Bird, Wendelin Van Draanen (YA)

    Cry, the Beloved Country, Alan Paton (YA/Adult)

CHAPTER 10

DOMINION VS. DEMOLITION: ENVIRONMENTALISM IN CHILDREN'S LITERATURE

> Long ages ago, when the line between good and evil seemed to shift dangerously toward disaster, the Creator began sending a series of Messengers to preserve a remnant of hope on a continent ravaged by injustice from within and without.[1]
>
> J. A. Myhre, *A Forest, A Flood, and an Unlikely Star*

The message that we ought to protect and nurture our environment is not new—it's been around for decades and can be traced back through the conservationist and anti-industrial movements of the last two centuries.[2] But of course, what constitutes "care" for the natural world has changed over the years, as have our cultural messages on the subject.

---

1. J. A. Myhre, *A Forest, A Flood, and an Unlikely Star* (New Growth Press, 2014) 159.
2. Adapted from "Parents' Guide to Environmentalism in Kids' Literature" by Emily Whitten, Redeemed Reader, March 1, 2012, https://redeemedreader.com/2012/03/parents-guide-to-environmentalism-in-kids-literature/. And "A Parent's Guide to Environmentalism in Children's Literature, Part Two" by Janie B. Cheaney, March 10, 2012, https://redeemedreader.com/2012/03/a-parents-guide-to-environmentalism-in-childrens-literature-part-two/.

Today, the landscape of the movement spans quite a range, from Christian to secular conservationists. "Environmentalism" is admittedly a squishy word. For our purposes in this chapter, it is the misguided idea that the environment ought to take precedence over human needs and wants, "particularly actions or advocacy to limit negative human impacts on the environment."[3]

Children's literature is not immune to these changing influences. Publishers gravitate toward books that speak to current issues; if climate change or endangered species are trending, the books will follow suit. Books about caring for the earth speak to God's mandate for human beings to be good stewards of the earth, but many of them contradict biblical teaching.

A chapter on a topic as broad as environmentalism cannot cover the subject in detail. Consider this a primer on a few critical issues likely to appear in contemporary children's literature along with suggestions about maintaining a balance between nature *stewardship* and nature *worship*.

In the Beginning, God

An obvious starting point, but an important one: creation vs. evolution. Who, or what, has brought the earth into being (according to the children's book in question)? Is the earth presented as the product of arbitrary evolutionary and natural forces? Or is the earth portrayed as a marvelous creation by God Himself? We can read books with an evolutionary slant as Christians, and we can even find them helpful, but recognizing the underlying worldview is critical to future discussions with our children.

Both biblical and environmental philosophies affirm the value of the natural world. Both recognize that abusing our natural environment is not right. The natural world (or, "the world God made"[4]) has inherent value; Christians

---

3. Anna R. Davies, "Environmentalism." *International Encyclopedia of Human Geography*, 2nd ed., https://www.sciencedirect.com/science/article/abs/pii/B9780081022955107917.
4. We would like to acknowledge hearing Jonathan Rogers use this phrase in his excellent writing courses. We do not know if it is original to him or not.

know that this is *because God made it*. The authors of *Let Creation Rejoice* write, "All of life is given by God and so derives its value in relation to him; it is not ours merely to do with whatever we please."[5] Repeatedly, Scripture praises God for His magnificent creation. Creation itself will praise the Lord: The rocks will cry out (Luke 19:40), the trees will clap their hands (Isa. 55:12), and the mountains and hills will break forth in song (Isa. 55:12). Together, with our environmentalist neighbors who may not yet recognize the Creator, we can honor and celebrate this beautiful world God made. But we need to recognize the ways in which we differ.

Sustainability vs. Stewardship/Dominion

"Sustainability" is a term that was on the fringes only twenty years ago, but today it is *the* buzzword on how humans should relate to their environment. According to the Environmental Protection Agency, "Everything that we need for our survival and well-being depends, either directly or indirectly, on our natural environment. Sustainability creates and maintains the conditions under which humans and nature can exist in productive harmony."[6] Statements like this encapsulate the view that earth's resources are good but limited, and they must be protected to be maintained. We're all for wise use of resources, but stating that "*everything* we need for our survival" depends on us denies the biblical truth that it is Christ who is upholding and sustaining creation (and, by inference, sustaining us! See Heb. 1:1–4).

External actions may look identical for those seeking to steward God's creation versus those desperately looking for sustainability out of fear of imminent destruction. Books often include internal motivations, though. If the story seems off, consider how it addresses the following two issues:

---

5. Jonathan A. Moo and Robert S. White, *Let Creation Rejoice: Biblical Hope and Ecological Crisis* (IVP Academic, 2014), 83.
6. "Learn About Sustainability," Environmental Protection Agency, https://www.epa.gov/sustainability/learn-about-sustainability#what.

Fall/Redemption: If authors (and readers) do not believe in a real (biblical) fall of man, they will not extrapolate out to a real, coming redemption in which the lion will lie down with the lamb (Isa. 11:6). We know that sin introduced death. It is a terrible intrusion, one that reflects the very real severing of man's relationship with God. The fall also disrupted the natural world. Scripture tells us creation itself is groaning (Rom. 8:22); yet, we have hope because of Christ and His work on the cross.

To quote *Let Creation Rejoice* again:

> *If God is able to give new life to our mortal bodies in a way that we cannot possibly comprehend and yet has been done already in the resurrection of Jesus, he is more than able to give new life to an entire groaning creation—to make everything new (Rev. 21:15).*[7]

So many writers (Christian and non-Christian) have identified and wrestled with man's separation from the natural world. But to see this apart from our separation from God is to look for a very different kind of redemption—one that often involves human agency in the place of God and an unrealistic view of the kind of relationship man can have with the rest of creation before the Lord's return. At its most basic level, "sustainability" often reflects how humanity hopes to restore a right relationship between man and the natural world without God or His redemption.

Stewardship/Dominion: Until creation's redemption, God's people are charged not only with sustaining the earth or finding some "productive harmony," but also with exercising loving, God-honoring dominion (Gen. 1:28). What this looks like in practice is difficult to answer. It is not our calling to redeem all of nature, and to presume we ought to, or even could do so, would be folly and a waste of invaluable time and energy.

Instead, we seek to be faithful in our calling as stewards, not saviors of the earth: faithful tending of our gardens, faithful care for the natural world

---

7. Moo, *Let Creation Rejoice*, 113.

around us, faithful engagement with issues related to stewarding the world God made while we await His return. When children's books start to preach activism for their young audience who has very little agency in the first place, we might want to pay closer attention.

A Negative View of Humanity

Biblically, humanity is the apex of God's creation, the creatures made in His image and who reflect more of His attributes than other created things. Part of reflecting God's image includes human creativity and ingenuity (although we offer a poor imitation of the Creator!). When books begin elevating animals over people, we do well to pay attention.

Extreme environmentalism encourages population control at the expense of human life to promote animals and plants flourishing. Rarely do children's books present this solution, but many present human flourishing in direct opposition to the flourishing of the environment. It's true that many decisions we have made as humans *have* caused harm to the world we are stewarding. Occasionally, that harm to the natural world was necessary for human life (such as the very barley field in which Ruth gleaned—no doubt, some animals lost habitats and some plants were uprooted). But we must humbly admit that far too often, humans have *not* been the best stewards of God's beautiful earth.

Ask yourself (and your children) what the book seems to say about humanity. Are people presented as categorically bad and animals good? Or, are specific decisions presented as harmful, but there is hope ultimately (and, in fact, the people in the book might be one way that hope will be achieved[8])?

These issues are too complex to address in a children's novel, and that is part of the problem. Two recent titles that illustrate the superiority of animals include *Pax* by Sara Pennypacker and *Alice's Farm* by Maryrose Wood. Both

---

8. By saying people are a vehicle of hope in this context, we are not saying humans are solely responsible for sustaining creation. Rather, are the people in the book granted agency to help work toward the solution and not simply presented as the biggest problem or hindrance toward a hopeful future?

are charming tales of animals, but the villains in the story are clearly humans. *Pax* implies that only humans make war, kill for sport, and destroy the environment. *Alice's Farm* implies that animals are better at caring for the land, and that organic farming is the *only* option anyone with any consideration for the land would choose. Children's books like these present simplistic solutions that place nature above humans. At best, they offer hope based upon sustainable practices, not hope in God's work on behalf of His creation (which includes His calling to us to steward it).

A better alternative would be a book like *The Year Money Grew on Trees* by Aaron Hawkins in which a young boy begins caring for a neglected apple orchard. He learns much about teamwork, hard work, and the rich reward of a well-tended orchard. James Herriot's stories reaffirm the benefit caring humans can offer to domesticated animals. In these stories, humans are functioning as stewards, working to protect and care for the earth, not merely destroy it.

Species vs. Individuals

Environmentalism today is based on an evolutionary view of life, and as such, puts a very high value on species. The Center for Biological Diversity reports that something like 30,000 species are dying off every year.[9] This is supposed to tell us that a holocaust is going on in the natural world.

When God made the animals after their kind, the Lord certainly expressed His regard for something akin to species. But Jesus Himself says that not one sparrow falls to the ground apart from the knowledge of God (Matt. 10:29). We ought to care about species, but ultimately, the Christian view of redemption includes individual people and animals. This gives each of us a far greater value than in a purely evolutionary framework.

Incidentally, this is a strength of the many animal stories children love. By forming relationships with specific animal characters, children learn to see

---

9. "Human Population Growth and Extinction," The Center for Biological Diversity, https://www.biologicaldiversity.org/programs/population_and_sustainability/extinction/.

animals as distinct creatures. Those who see creation as the Lord's can use this to encourage children to view each creature the Lord has created as good. Read James Herriot's *Treasury for Children* or *Mishka* by Edward van de Vendel and Anoush Elman or *Toaff's Way* by Cynthia Voigt and marvel that the Lord not only knows each dog, rabbit, and squirrel, He also calls the stars by name.

Hope vs. Despair

Environmentalist writing often centers on a coming apocalypse. Some young couples today even posit this as their reason for not having children.[10] From nuclear war to killer bees to overpopulation, real or imagined threats dominate the news. Behind the sustainability rubric is the implication that life as we know it now is *not* sustainable. In other words, cataclysmic destruction results if we do not figure out a new way to "sustain." The world is falling apart due to some ecological disaster *that humans could have prevented*. Biblically, we can approach this in two ways.

First, literature hinting at a coming apocalypse that results from someone's *sin* or flagrant disregard of stewardship, but which can also be averted due to wise stewardship and recognition of humanity's place in this world, can be helpful to discuss. Works like Kenneth Oppel's *Bloom* illustrate what happens when humanity begins to mess with genetics (not unlike *Jurassic Park*). The Bloom series has some cautions,[11] but the environmental elements are thought-provoking.

Second, literature that acknowledges the brokenness of our world, but which points ahead to a hopeful future, offers an excellent antidote to doom-

---

10. According to Pew Research, 38 percent of adults under the age of fifty who don't want to have children give their reason as "concerns about the state of the world" while 26 percent offer "concerns about the environment" as their reason for not having children. "Reasons Adults Give for Not Having Children," Pew Research Center, July 25, 2024, https://www.pewresearch.org/social-trends/2024/07/25/reasons-adults-give-for-not-having-children/#:~:text=These%20younger%20adults%20are%20also,re%20unlikely%20to%20have%20kids.

11. We recommend reading our website review of this series before handing it to your children. Among other considerations is a gender fluid "creature."

and-gloom titles. The Rwendigo Tales do not shy away from ecological concerns, many of which have been brought on by sinful actions (such as illegal deforestation). However, they offer hope: Work is going on behind the scenes; help is coming, and the world is not lost or given over.

Fuzzy Spirituality, Nature-Worship, and Paganism

Finally, nature often has overtly spiritual dimensions in contemporary children's and teen literature. We easily breeze over these references as metaphor or hyperbole, but occasionally we need to take them seriously. This may look like the healing "magic" of the natural world in *The Secret Garden*, or *Old Turtle* in which rocks and streams are called "God," or something like the Gaia (Earth goddess) girls' novels. Our general culture's openness to stories that include such spiritual content is obviously growing, and kids' books are following that trend. Protagonists now pray to the "universe" or interact with this nebulous force in ways that read as spiritual, whether they identify the universe as a divine being or not.

A throwaway line might be one thing, as when a character mutters, "Thank the Universe!" but look for opportunities to discuss this with your children and teens. For instance, why does the author capitalize "Universe"? To whom, or what, are the characters praying? From where is help expected?

A Better Environmentalism

We can agree with environmentalists that the earth needs care and protection. But we look to Christ for our hope, not humanity's ability to "save the earth." Be alert to the subtext in the books you read with your children and teens, yes, but do not fear. Many excellent titles today help reinforce biblical thinking or offer talking points to that end (whether the author intended it or not).

One of the best tools we have for learning how to honor this world God made is through reading picture books that show us more about the intricacies of creation. The I Can Read/Made by God series for newly independent readers offers information and photographs about many interesting things God has made. Overtly Christian, this well-done series is free of evolutionary content.

Look for good illustrations or photography, text that focuses on the natural world as observed (not how it came to be), and an overall hopeful tone. As long as it celebrates this world instead of preaching evolution, you can gloss over an occasional evolutionary undertone in an otherwise quality picture book. Fear-inducing books will decry the decay and death of this world as we know it; hopeful books will inspire wonder at the world all around us.

Books that present the world God made and people as God made them will awaken us to the needs of the natural world around us without fearmongering or subverting the created order. *Wonder Walkers*, *Sidewalk Flowers*, and *Eye: How It Works* are all good examples of celebrating the beauty of the world around us or marveling at the details God created (although the books are not necessarily from a Christian perspective).

One of the best tools we have for learning how to honor this world God made is through reading picture books that show us more about the intricacies of creation.

Read books about naturalists and scientists who have exemplified good stewardship. Scientists like Wilson Bentley (see *Snowflake Bentley*) spent hours studying the intricacies of God's world. Others, like George Washington Carver (see *The Secret Garden of George Washington Carver*), were professing Christians and eager to learn how this world God made works. Careful studies like those presented in *The Monarchs Are Missing* help us raise good questions about current trends as well as offering suggested actions to be better stewards.

Questions for Discussion

As the need arises, consider the following discussion questions when you read with your children. Note: These questions are for books that primarily focus on environmental concerns, not a "hero's journey" in which the focus is, rightly so, on the character's efforts, or a dystopian novel in which the world has already fallen apart.

- Who, or what, has brought the earth into being (according to the children's book in question)?
- Is the earth presented as the product of arbitrary evolutionary and natural forces? Or is the earth portrayed as a marvelous creation by God Himself?
- If the book does not mention a creator, does it stress evolution as the answer to all questions about the origin of life? Or does it simply focus on the beauty, variety, and wonder of the natural world, leaving Christians to fill in the blanks?
- Are people (readers or the characters) urged to save the world by their actions alone? Or are they encouraged to be responsible citizens and stewards of the earth?
- Are people presented as categorically bad and animals/nature good? Or are specific actions and decisions presented as harmful, but ultimate hope is possible (and, in fact, the people in the book might actually be a vehicle of that hope as opposed to its enemy)?
- If the book is a nonfiction book, is there only emphasis on species or is there a recognition that individuals (animals or humans) matter too? If the book is a fictional story, does it help reinforce that individual creatures are important? Do you find yourself looking at the squirrels in your backyard and now thinking one looks like Squirrel Nutkin?
- Does the author capitalize "Universe"? Or present the universe as an omniscient, sentient being? To whom, or what, are the characters "praying"? From where do they expect help to arrive?

- Is the book "activism" focused or more informational in tone? If activist, can you figure out what the call to action is? Do you agree with it? Is there a way to engage with the recommendation from a biblical perspective?

BOOKLIST FOR CHAPTER 10

Further Reading

Let Creation Rejoice: Biblical Hope and Ecological Crisis, Jonathan H. Moo and Robert S. White

For Children/Teens

Hidden City, Sarah Grace Tuttle (Picture Book)
Jumper: A Day in the Life of a Backyard Jumping Spider, Jessica Lanan (PB)
The Monarchs Are Missing: A Butterfly Mystery, Rebecca Hirsch (PB)
Ribbit! The Truth About Frogs, Annette Whipple (PB)
Water Is Water, Miranda Paul and Jason Chin (PB)
Yellow and Pink, William Steig (PB)
I Can Read/Made by God (Chapter Books)
Saving H'Non: Chang and the Elephant, Tran Nguyễn (Middle Grade graphic novel)
Fuzzy Mud, Louis Sachar (MG)
Tangerine, Edward Bloor (MG)

CHAPTER 11

OF EVERY TRIBE AND NATION: THE BEAUTY AND CHALLENGE OF DIVERSITY

> "You can't run away from who you are,
> but what you can do is run toward who you want to be."[1]
> —Jason Reynolds, *Ghost*

Author Ellen Oh was disgruntled. She had been looking forward to Book Expo America 2014, the largest publishing trade show in the nation—and especially to BookCon, a spinoff event to debut immediately before the expo opened. But now, as she looked over the schedule, her dismay increased. The speaker lineup was overwhelmingly white, and largely male. The signature event was a panel discussion of YA literature featuring James Patterson, John Green, Daniel Handler (aka Lemony Snicket), and Rick Riordan—all bestselling authors. But where were the authors of color?

A few months before, author Walter Dean Myers asked the same question in "Where Are the People of Color in Children's Books?," an opinion piece

---

1. Jason Reynolds, *Ghost* (Atheneum Books for Young Readers, 2016), 155.

for the *New York Times* book review. Myers wrote movingly of how his early reading experience—comic books, classic picture books, Bible stories, and novels—sparked his imagination but did nothing to affirm him as a person of color. He gave up reading altogether during a post-adolescent identity crisis and only returned to it when a story by James Baldwin provided a renaissance: "I was lifted by it, for it took place in Harlem, and it was a story concerned with black people like those I knew. By humanizing the people who were like me, Baldwin's story also humanized me."[2]

Myers was not wrong about the scarcity of children's books for and about minorities. The Cooperative Children's Book Center (CCBC) at the University of Wisconsin/Madison, an organization with a special interest in diversity, reported that the total number of children's books written by black authors was only 69 in 2013 (compared to 82 in 1994).[3] And it got worse: Of the 5,000 children's books published in 2013, 90 were by Asian authors, 48 by Latinos, and 18 by Native Americans. White authors were also overrepresented in the publishing industry as a whole—by over 90 percent. The agents who pitched books to editors, the editors who decided which books to publish, and the art directors who designed jackets and commissioned illustrations shared a similar culture and background.

Ellen Oh began talking to her friends in the publishing world. They formed an organization called We Need Diverse Books and launched a hashtag campaign that took the Twitter social media platform by storm. Authors, celebrities, teachers, and readers of all ages held up signs proclaiming *why* we needed diverse books. And publishers took notice. Clearly, this was a movement whose time had come.

---

2. Walter Dean Meyers, "Where Are the People of Color in Children's Books?," *New York Times Book Review*, May 15, 2014.

3. "Books by and/or About Black, Indigenous and People of Color (All Years)," Cooperative Children's Book Center, May 4, 2023, https://ccbc.education.wisc.edu/literature-resources/ccbc-diversity-statistics/books-by-about-poc-fnn/.

But What Is "Diversity"?

Within a year of its founding, WNDB had established a Diversity Festival, published recommended book lists, and produced classroom materials. Of the Newbery winner and honor books of 2015, two were verse novels about black characters and the other was a graphic novel about a hearing-impaired girl.

At Redeemed Reader we favorably reviewed all three books. *Brown Girl Dreaming* is a heartfelt and mind-expanding memoir; *The Crossover* (winner of the gold medal) portrays a strong, sports-loving black family; and *El Deafo* opens a young reader's understanding to severe disability in an entertaining and relatable way. For us, "diversity" *per se* was not a criterion; these are simply good books. We like diversity because God created it, but a good book is a good book no matter what color the main character is.

That said, an intentional move toward diversity in publishing is welcome and long overdue. Gladys Hunt, author of the long-standing reading guide *Honey for a Child's Heart*, observed, "In the early 1960s when I first began making lists of books that every child should have an opportunity to enjoy, there weren't many picture books showing characters who were not white children. It was shocking."[4] She noted that *The Snowy Day*, published in 1962, was the first full-color picture book to feature a black protagonist.

White readers and writers may not appreciate how pervasive their influence over publishing has been. The publishing world is still notably pale on the agenting, editing, marketing, and designing end, but industry leaders are far more aware and proactive than they were. The number of diverse authors has grown exponentially. As reported by *Publishers Weekly*: "Of the 3,450 books published in 2022 that were received by the CCBC, 40% of the books were by a person of color," defined by the CCBC as having at least one author,

---

4. Gladys Hunt, "Teacher, Do You Have Any Books with Pictures of Kids Who Look Like Me?," blog post archived at Redeemed Reader, May 26, 2023.

illustrator, or compiler of each book being a person of color."[5] We've seen other positive moves toward diversity in the publishing world. Black authors like Angie Thomas and Jason Reynolds have spoken to sellout crowds and served as children's literature ambassadors; novels by Indigenous authors have won top ALA awards; an entire award category for books by or about Asians and Pacific Islanders has been created, as have distinct imprints for books by or about Muslims. Although more work needs to be done, the publishing world has made progress worth celebrating.

But at this point, we should pause and consider "diversity" as its advocates define it. The delineation on the WNDB website isn't limited to race or culture: "We recognize all diverse experiences, including (but not limited to) LGBTQIA+, Native, people of color, gender diversity, people with disabilities, and ethnic, cultural, and religious minorities."[6]

When Diversity Goes Awry

Every positive development has its stumbling blocks. Here are two to keep in mind:

First, diversity as an end in itself can become self-defeating. There are good reasons for greater representation in children's books, such as: 1) Minority children need to see themselves as valuable and productive members of society, and 2) all readers should learn to appreciate other cultures and histories.

So far, so good. Certainly, if I learn more about my Somali neighbors' background I can relate to them better. But even more: I can discover the ways we're alike as well as the ways we're different.

However, instead of seeking ways to affirm different cultural expressions

---

5. Claire Kirch, "Diversity Is on the Rise in Children's Literature," *Publishers Weekly*, June 13, 2023, https://www.publishersweekly.com/pw/by-topic/childrens/childrens-industry-news/article/92543-ccbc-releases-statistics-regarding-diversity-in-children-s-literature-published-in-2022.html.
6. "About WNDB," We Need Diverse Books, February 7, 2019, https://diversebooks.org/about-wndb/.

and ultimately enable us to love one another better, some of the authors and groups that fly the banner of "diversity" can end up widening the gap. An example of this happens when other authors are accused of "cultural appropriation," or writing about racial or cultural identities not their own. Concerned about potential misrepresentation of various groups, publishers have hired sensitivity readers to pore over manuscripts and flag anything that might seem offensive. In some cases, novels on the eve of publication have been abruptly cancelled.[7] The intimidating specter of censorship raised its head, as in this *New York Times* headline: "In an Era of Online Outrage, Do Sensitivity Readers Result in Better Books, or Censorship?"[8] Sensitivity readers can play a helpful role in the editorial process. But when the goal becomes censorship rather than the making of great literature, authors, publishers, and especially readers suffer.

Diversity in literature should be a means to the end of understanding and valuing each other. As an end in itself, it can produce the very antagonism it seeks to remedy.

Diversity in literature should be a means to the end of understanding and valuing each other.

Second, "diversity" in children's books, particularly as related to gender and sexuality, can provide cover for unhealthy questioning and unbiblical practices. "Identities" proliferate: The acronym QUILTBAG enjoyed brief currency for Queer/Questioning, Undecided, Intersex, Lesbian, Transgender, Bisexual, Asexual, Gay. Easy to remember, but it didn't cover all the bases, which is why the cumbersome LBGTQ+ remains the descriptor of choice, with the "plus" standing for all other sexual, gender, and other possible identities.

---

7. Janie B Cheaney, "Age of Outrage," *WORLD* magazine, February 17, 2018, 36.
8. Alexandra Alter, "In an Era of Online Outrage, Do Sensitivity Readers Result in Better Books, or Censorship?," *New York Times*, December 24, 2017, https://www.nytimes.com/2017/12/24/books/in-an-era-of-online-outrage-do-sensitivity-readers-result-in-better-books-or-censorship.html.

The title character of Alex Gino's *Rick* is confronted with a bewildering array of such identities when he wanders into the afterschool Rainbow Club. This happy band of nonconformists is a bright contrast to his best friend, a stereotypical jerk. Through involvement with the Rainbow Club, Rick learns that he is "a-romantic," meaning he has no interest in sex. But is that an identity, or do his feelings simply fall within the normal stage of development for a twelve-year-old boy?

The promotion of transgenderism in children's books—even in picture books marketed to kindergartners—is particularly treacherous for unhappy, confused, or otherwise unsettled kids. Rather than getting help from adults to dig into the reasons for their unhappiness (which is often instability at home), they're confronted with books like *Too Bright to See* or *All Boys Aren't Blue* or *This Book Is Gay*. Books are powerful, and stories like these could steer them down misleading, or even deceitful, paths: *Was I born in the wrong body? I really like that kid who told me he's gay—does that mean I'm gay? Does my disinterest in sex (in fifth grade) identify me as "a-romantic"?*

All humans bear the image of God and are worthy of respect for that reason alone. But sexual and gender "diversities" that contradict biblical teaching are not worthy of affirmation. We can and should sympathize with characters (in literature and in life) who struggle with these identities, even while pointing them toward their primary identity as image bearers.

What About Political Diversity?

"Diversity," as advocated by influential mainstream organizations like the American Library Association, does not apply to political views. Although individual librarians may span the political spectrum, the ALA tilts leftward in its leadership and stated core values.[9] Throughout contemporary culture, progressive causes from abortion to queer advocacy have intensified in the

---

9. About ALA and Our Mission, www.ala.org.aboutala, accessed March 18, 2025.

hothouse atmosphere of partisan politics, extending to children and teens.[10]

After the election of 2016, a series of progressive board books featured titles like *A Is for Activist* and *Feminist Baby*. Here's a sample of the latter: "Feminist Baby loves to dance./ Feminist Baby says NO to pants./ Feminist Baby likes Pink AND Blue./ Sometimes she'll throw up on you."[11] She throws other things, like toys and tantrums. (Why any parent would want to encourage the behavior they're trying to root out otherwise is a mystery.) As much as an activist parent may hope to raise a pint-sized activist, no preschoolers will be recruited to the cause by "N is for No Justice No Peace."[12]

Older children, particularly in the transitional years of middle school, are often preoccupied with changing bodies and peer conflicts. But teens are beginning to look beyond family and home and longing to find their place in the world. They may be easily charmed by the idea of chanting and marching and waving fists as seen on TV and social media. Resistance comes easily enough to a teen already, and for some it may be necessary: One way to discover who we are is to push against previous limits and boundaries. But maturing teens still need guidance in processing new ideas, as well as a place to discuss them from a Christian perspective.

Suppose your politically-minded high school freshman brings home a library book titled *We Rise, We Resist, We Raise Our Voices*.[13] Flipping through the pages, it seems to you that the fifty diverse authors and illustrators who contributed to this compendium lean to the left. If you're politically conservative, your first impulse may be to close the book and take it back to the library.

But what if the content of *We Rise* includes some valuable insights? Kwame Alexander's poem "A Thousand Winters"[14] movingly ruminates on

---

10. For more of our thoughts on activism, see the following posts at RedeemedReader.com: "A Child's Guide to RESISTANCE" and "Little Activists Raising Little Fists."
11. Loryn Brantz, *Feminist Baby* (Little, Brown Books for Young Readers, 2017), n.p.
12. Innosanto Nagara, *A Is for Activist* (Triangle Square, 2013).
13. Wade Hudson and Cheryl Willis Hudson, *We Rise, We Resist, We Raise Our Voices* (Crown Books for Young Readers, 2018).
14. Ibid., 9.

events like the Charleston church shooting of 2015 and the effect of such violence on his daughter. The title of "A Day of Small Things,"[15] by Tonya Bolden, is taken from the Bible and includes Christian imagery. "It Helps to Look at Old Front Page Headlines" by Marilyn Nelson focuses on hope and maybe even God: "Good is, good is in control, and good will win."[16] In her contribution, "Words Have Power," Ellen Oh reminds us that "anger is both a powerful tool and a dangerous weapon. . . You might start with anger, but you need to end up in another place. A better place."[17]

What better place? That's up to the reader because faith is generic. "Some form of the Golden Rule exists in every major world religion," Carole Boston Weatherford informs us. There are "many religions, many traditions, but one world, one yearning—to love and be loved."[18]

Justice, like faith, is another broad concept whose definition is up to the reader. What the authors appear to mean by "justice" is worth examining, as well as how that view stacks up against a biblical view. What a great opportunity to evaluate contemporary concepts of justice in the light of the Ten Commandments and the Sermon on the Mount!

Reading books like *How I Resist: Activism and Hope for a New Generation*[19] with older teens can help both teens and adults sharpen their biblical perspective while discussing the pros and cons of the arguments. Are they rational or irrational? Realistic or Utopian? Might the writers have come to these conclusions through personal experiences of trauma or injustice? What false assumptions might we be harboring? How could we best represent Christ in responding to conclusions that seem unbiblical?

Keep Micah 6:8 in mind: "What does the Lord require of you but to

---

15. Ibid., 47.
16. Ibid., 38,
17. Ibid., 6.
18. Ibid., 7.
19. Maureen Johnson, ed., *How I Resist: Activism and Hope for a New Generation* (Wednesday Books, 2018).

do justice, and love kindness, and to walk humbly with your God?" "Doing justice" is our responsibility toward all mankind, regardless of race or class. "Loving mercy" is extending the grace toward others that God has lavished upon us. And "walking humbly" is the best approach to navigating a politically diverse culture.

Diversity and the Kingdom of Heaven

The Lord loves diversity—no question about it. We come in all colors, all body types and facial features, with all sorts of gifts and talents—also all sorts of sins and evil inclinations. Where can we find unity? How can we relate? There's only one sure way: by looking to Him whose image we all bear. The Lord made every man and woman from one man and woman, and He loves us. Promoting diversity in our reading as well as our interactions is a good thing—even, for Christians, a necessary thing—but as an end in itself it is incomplete. Only as fellow image bearers can we truly understand and appreciate each other. The good news is, that time is coming:

> *After this I looked, and behold, a great multitude that no one could number, from every nation, from all tribes and peoples and languages, standing before the throne and before the Lamb, clothed in white robes, with palm branches in their hands, and crying out with a loud voice, "Salvation belongs to our God who sits on the throne, and to the Lamb!"*
> *(Rev. 7:9–10)*

BOOKLIST FOR CHAPTER 11

Further Reading

    Steeped in Stories, Mitali Perkins

Children/Teens—Cultural Diversity

    Crown: An Ode to the Fresh Cut, Derrick Barnes (Picture Book)
    Vamos! Let's Cross the Bridge, Raul the Third (PB)
    The Magnificent Mya Tibbs series, Crystal Allen (Chapter Book)
    Creative God, Colorful Us, Trillia Newbell (Middle Grade nonfiction)
    Mexikid, Pedro Martin (MG graphic novel)
    The Crossover, Kwame Alexander (MG novel in verse)
    Hereville, Barry Deutsch (MG graphic novel)
    It Ain't So Awful, Falafel, Firoozeh Dumas (YA)

Children/Teens—Disability

    Like Me, Lauren Wifler (PB, younger brother with disabilities)
    Henry, Like Always, Jenn Bailey (ER, neurodivergence)
    Super Jake and the King of Chaos, Naomi Milliner (MG, younger brother with disabilities)
    Out of My Mind, Sharon Draper (MG, cerebral palsy)
    We Could Be Heroes, Margaret Finnegan (MG, neurodiversity)
    All He Knew, Helen Frost (MG verse novel, deafness)
    Calvin, Martine Leavitt (Young Adult, schizophrenia)
    Marcelo in the Real World, Francisco X. Stork (YA, autism)

Children/Teens—Positive Activism

Step Right Up: How Doc and Jim Key Taught the World about Kindness, Donna Janell Bowman (Picture Book)

A Duet for Home, Karina Yan Glaser (Middle Grade)

Hope in the Valley, Mitali Perkins (MG); see also *Rickshaw Girl*

Light Comes to Shadow Mountain, Toni Buzzeo (MG)

Linked, Gordon Korman (MG)

Let Justice Roll Down, John Perkins (Young Adult)

The Promise of Change, JoAnn Boyce (YA)

We Will Not Be Silent: The White Rose Student Resistance Movement That Defied Adolf Hitler, Russell Freedman (YA nonfiction)

CHAPTER 12

WHO AM I? IDENTITY AND REPRESENTATION

> "There's not a belief in the world
> that can save you from doubting."[1]
>
> —R. J. Anderson, *Rebel*

Identity has become a buzzword in recent years. It encapsulates and attempts to define the essence of who we are as individuals existing in the world. As Christians, we can trace this questioning back to the serpent asking Eve in the garden, "Did God actually say?" (Gen. 3:1b). Ever since, we have wrestled with the same question: *Did God really say? What is true? What is false?* Those questions only grow as we look out at the world today and try to make sense of the claimed "identity" that so defines others.

Confusion in defining identity is nothing new. In the book of John, when Jesus' disciples notice a blind beggar, they make a quick assumption. Still, they have a question, so they ask Jesus, "Who sinned, this man or his parents, that he was born blind?" (John 9:2). Jesus' response orients His disciples, and us, to a greater reality: "It was not that this man sinned, or his parents, but that the works of God might be displayed in him" (John 9:3). Jesus goes on to heal the blind man, and we remember the healed man's response, enshrined in a beloved

---

1. R. J. Anderson, *Rebel* (Enclave, 2015), 169.

hymn, "One thing I do know, that though I was blind, now I see" (John 9:25).

The disciples' initial response to the blind beggar mirrors much of the contemporary confusion regarding identity. They notice a man who is blind and a beggar. This is his *identity*: He is known to his neighbors and parents by his disability and social/financial status. If the story continued without comment, this narrative mention of the man's identity would be a *representation*: a reference to identity without engagement. If we look for a worldview in this representation, we are reminded the world is fallen, and we see that truth reflected in the existence of this man's blindness and poverty.

However, the disciples *confuse identity with personal sin*. Like Job's friends, they aren't content to accept the effects of sin in the world without finding a person to blame. Was it the man who brought this on himself? Or something his parents did? Jesus' response reminds His listeners, and us, of the greater truth we should remember when confronted by the identity of sinners in the fallen world. The world, like this man, is caught in darkness. But Jesus is the light of the world. The reality of Jesus and His identity as the Savior lead to the truth of redemption and restoration, as the blind man's sight is restored.

John 9 reminds us we are not the first to struggle as we navigate the place of identity and representation in a fallen world. Praise God for the hope we have in Christ. As we consider issues of identity and representation, let us view them in the light of Christ.

Identity and Representation, Defined

At Redeemed Reader, we consider identity as the features that define or identify an individual. These features can be classified in many ways, but for convenience we will distill them into four broad categories:

- Spiritual (Religion takes up a large portion of this category. It is shared with worldviews held in addition to, or outside of, religious beliefs.)

- Physical (outward appearance and abilities)

- Sexual (transcends mere physicality; impacts and reflects our spiritual being)
- Cultural (encompasses ethnic, racial, and cultural heritage)

Recognizing these components, we often engage with identity in terms of representation, and we aren't the only ones. The publishing industry in recent years has also focused on representation. Some of this has come from activism, such as the #WeNeedDiverseBooks movement. In 2021, #ownvoices joined the conversation. This hashtag "acknowledges the importance of books written by authors who share the culture, ethnicity, disability, etc. as the main character."[2] Redeemed Reader appreciates some of the needed correction this awareness has brought, allowing and encouraging authors to share stories that represent their cultural and physical identities.

To understand representation, it is helpful to use the idea of mirrors and windows.[3] When stories are mirrors, they reflect a reader's own experiences and identity. Stories as windows open a reader's perspective to the world beyond themselves and shed light onto other identities. By reading books that are both mirrors and windows, children can find stories that reflect their own experiences in addition to stories that provide a window into the life of others.

IDENTITY AND IDOLATRY

It is easy to take a good thing too far. An overemphasis on representation and identity in books often occurs to the detriment of the story itself. A story whose author leans heavily on emphasizing worldview may fall short at gripping a child's imagination, since the book's message trumps its story value. Some books blatantly focus on a topic. When we don't agree with the topic, we often use the

---

2. Betsy Farquhar, "Native American Traditional Tales: #Ownvoices," Redeemed Reader, https://redeemedreader.com/2021/03/native-american-traditional-tales-ownvoices/.
3. Emily Style, "National SEED Project - Curriculum as Window and Mirror," National SEED Project, 2013, https://www.nationalseedproject.org/Key-SEED-Texts/curriculum-as-window-and-mirror.

word "agenda." However, if we agree with the book's topic, then we use the more positive descriptor, "worldview." As we look at contemporary children's literature and the idea of identity and representation, it is helpful to discern the difference.

Returning to the idea of representation being a window, there's a difference between being shown a window and having someone on the other side of the window, aggressively trying to invite us into the scene. Representation, taken too far, becomes an advertisement, endorsing an identity. At its worst, it points to a fallen world and invites us to praise it. But what are readers to do when faced with ideology in children's literature?

Let's return to our four categories of identity and explore them further.

Spiritual Identity and Representation

A book that mentions a person of faith offers an example of spiritual identity and representation. At the same time, a book that mentions no belief or faith is in its own way a spiritual reflection. When spiritual references occur in a story, take some time to consider. Is this reference a statement of fact? Is it a moral reflection? Does it imply an absolute truth?

This is not to downplay the role of books focusing on faith. We recognize the importance of books with a biblical worldview and have written about the importance of "church library builders," making sure our church bookshelves aren't just a collection of ragged cast-offs, but beautiful, theologically rich stories.[4]

Books that focus on representing a spiritual worldview as an identity at the expense of story rarely capture a child's imagination. As you consider spiritual identity and representation in a book, here are some questions to guide you.

If a book does not reflect a biblical worldview, consider:

What "truth" is it trying to convey?

How does that truth align with God's truth?

---

4. See chapter 21 for more on this topic.

If a book mentions a character with a different spiritual identity:
How is their faith treated?
Is their faith merely represented, or is it endorsed?

Physical Representation Can Be Good

Since 2004, the Schneider Family Book Awards have been given by the American Library Association annually to "honor an author or illustrator for a book that embodies an artistic expression of the disability experience for child and adolescent audiences."[5] We've reviewed many recent Schneider award-winners that include representations of dyslexia, blindness, prosthetics, and a host of other physical and psychological disabilities and conditions.

These are examples of "good" representation, providing helpful glimpses into the lives of others. Several years ago, Hayley read *Super Jake and the King of Chaos*, often with a lump in her throat. Naomi Milliner poignantly captured everyday life as a big brother to a very at-risk, sick sibling, an experience that mirrored Hayley's own experiences with her brother. Soon after, she found herself discussing the book with a group of readers. She recalls: "I noted the worldview (spiritual identity) since the family is Jewish, and there is no hope reflected for a future beyond this life. However, I also explained that the book is a wonderful example of family and community, reminding me of Romans 12:15, 'Rejoice with those who rejoice, weep with those who weep.'" Hayley related to the physical (and perhaps cultural) identities in the book and connected it to her Christian worldview. Sometimes books, rather than reflecting an experience we know, can shed light on new experiences.

Another recent book shows a little girl preparing for a ballet rehearsal when someone says something unkind. So begins *Big* by Vashti Harrison, which won the 2024 Caldecott medal. Harrison's book succeeds in poignantly

---

5. "Schneider Family Book Award," American Library Association, February 27, 2012, https://www.ala.org/awards/books-media/schneider-family-book-award.

reflecting some of the author's own experiences as a "big" little girl.[6] While *Big* is sweet and thoughtful, not all books handling body positivity are equally helpful. As a movement, body positivity can exemplify identity taken to a point where it glorifies decisions that do not align with a Christian worldview.

In 2021, Janie wrote about the rise of books encouraging fat positivity while noting the movement's Venn diagram overlap with queer theory and transgender ideology.[7] Gone are the days of Wodehousian wit related to width and the fat villains of Roald Dahl and Eva Ibbotson. The problem with body positivity as a movement is that it celebrates something as ultimate, and a person's size becomes a part of their identity as they embrace unhealthy lifestyle choices, dubbing "body sovereignty" the reason. This glorification of unhealthiness and fixation on identity is a far cry from Vashti Harrison's portrayal of a little girl with "big" bone structure.

If you find yourself wondering whether or not physical representation is helpful in a story, here are two questions to consider:

1. Do the physical characteristics in this story tend toward a healthy, positive identity?
2. Or do they embrace physical elements as core to an identity?

Sexual Identity in Words and Pictures

While we love many books that are windows, some may open onto a worldview that is contrary to the Bible. This is especially true in portrayals of sexual identity. From preferred pronouns to relationships outside of male-female marriage, both gender identity and sexual orientation have become common in modern children's literature. The Redeemed Reader team occasionally reviews books by well-known authors and illustrators that don't reflect a

---

6. Vashti Harrison, *Big* (Little, Brown Books for Young Readers, 2023), Author's Note, Kindle.
7. Janie Cheaney, "What Is 'Body Positivity,'" Redeemed Reader, https://redeemedreader.com/2021/04/what-is-body-positivity/.

biblical worldview, such as those about children who have same-sex parents. While we don't necessarily consider a passing reference to same-sex parents (or a similar problematic sexual representation) to be disqualifying in itself, we will mention it in the review.

We recognize some books move from illustrative or background representation to more pointed worldview choices. In these stories, sexual identity is key to the characters' identity. Sometimes this surprises readers. Several years ago, one of our team pulled a chapter book off the shelf at the library and started reading. It featured the imaginative adventures of two siblings, and it was well done with great illustrations and an engaging story. Then she realized that one of the siblings, whom she had mistaken for a dramatic little sister, was actually a cross-dressing little brother. Had she first read the book's Kirkus review, she would have realized that the story's focus was on identity, as the review notes: "Mouse, although he takes the masculine pronoun, wears a pink tutu."[8]

While we love many books that are windows, some may open onto a worldview that is contrary to the Bible.

What are readers to do when faced with such gender ideology in children's literature? At Redeemed Reader we are often urged to warn our readers about these books. However, our mission is to shine a gospel light: We want to bring readers the good and the beautiful. We also want to help our readers engage with books like this if they need to. (All of chapter 9 is about reading messy books!)

If a book only includes a casual reference to gender or sexual orientation, we can consider this under the broader category of representation. In our world, there are a growing number of children whose experiences are mirrored in these books. Twenty-first century culture is different from the one most of

---

8. "Charlie & Mouse from the Charlie & Mouse series" *Kirkus Reviews*, January 31, 2017, https://www.kirkusreviews.com/book-reviews/laurel-snyder/charlie-mouse/.

us grew up in. On the street, in school, and throughout daily life, children are confronted by lifestyles that don't align with the Bible's teaching on gender, sexuality, or marriage. When meeting these topics in books, we must ask: Is the mention a passing reference (the same way one of the team might mention her gay relative) or is it an endorsement of the worldview? Is the story celebrating an alternative lifestyle, or merely referencing something much more commonplace in our day and age? Either way, this can be a good topic for discussion, especially when a child comes across it in their independent reading.

When reviewing the Caldecott honor book, *In Every Life*, we noted at least one depiction of a same-sex couple.[9] Our review of Sophie Blackall's picture book *Ahoy!* mentioned a second adult, who appears at the story's end. We concluded, "Is this a same-sex couple? Probably. Will the charm of the story overshadow that suggestion? You decide."[10]

If you feel a book leans heavily on endorsement versus representation, consider whether it would be helpful for your reader and lead to needed conversations, or whether it would be too confusing and disorienting given their maturity. This comes down to a matter of prayer and discernment.

For example, *Something Like Home*, a middle grade book by Andrea Beatrix Arango, is "a poignant novel-in-verse [that] explores the question: 'What is home when your world turns upside-down?'"[11] We noticed that characters were occasionally introduced with pronouns. Laura, the sixth grade protagonist, does this with a new classmate, making introductions and giving preferred pronouns. The author's choice to emphasize pronouns as part of a polite introduction is something that could spark a discussion with your child about views contrary to the Bible. By subtly showing a therapist in the story as they/

---

9. Janie Cheaney, "2024 Caldecott Honor Books Roundup," Redeemed Reader, https://redeemedreader.com/2024/02/2024-caldecott-honor-books-roundup/.

10. Janie Cheaney, "Four New Picture Books by Caldecott-Winning Illustrators," Redeemed Reader, https://redeemedreader.com/2024/04/four-new-picture-books-by-caldecott-winning-illustrators/.

11. Hayley Morell, "Something Like Home by Andrea Beatrix Arango," Redeemed Reader, https://redeemedreader.com/2024/03/somethinglikehome/.

them, Arango reflects a certain perspective; but what does God say about our gender and identity?

Within the young adult genre, readers find even more boundary pushing as stories intersect with coming of age. While we consider the idea of healthy relationships and romance in chapter 20, it is helpful to note that YA, particularly within the subgenre of sci-fi and fantasy, contains myriad examples of sexual identity and representation. (We've noticed in particular a rise of gender fluidity in alien species.[12]) Ask your readers, are these elements a core part of the story/characters, or are they passing references? How much does the author dwell on divergent sexual identity? Is it normalized by the story's characters?

SEXUAL IDENTITY AND SCIENCE

In recent years, scientists have brought more awareness to sexual variations in nature. This crops up in fiction. For example, a character in the middle grade Wild Robot series is a gobi fish whose gender has changed. It also comes up in picture books such as *And Tango Makes Three*, which tells the story of two male penguins who raised an orphaned penguin chick. In 2023, a Michael L. Printz honor for "a book that exemplifies literary excellence in young adult literature"[13] was given to a nonfiction title: *Queer Ducks (and Other Animals): The Natural World of Animal Sexuality* by Eliot Schrefer.

Confronting questions of sexual identity from a secular worldview, these books and others show various sexual behaviors as "natural." In *Queer Ducks*, Schrefer, a gay man, writes "I really wish I'd had an inkling of all this queer behavior in nature when I was young. . . . Everywhere I looked, *unnatural* was the word that came up again and again."[14] Some of us may relate to Schrefer's

---

12. We have noted this in Kenneth Oppel's Overthrow series and Brandon Sanderson's Skyward series.
13. "Printz Award," American Library Association, February 27, 2012, https://www.ala.org/yalsa/printz-award.
14. Eliot Schrefer, introduction to *Queer Ducks (and Other Animals): The Natural World of Animal Sexuality* (Katherine Tegen Books, 2022), Kindle.

childhood experience of using animal behavior as a litmus for natural (heterosexual) vs. unnatural behavior. Yet, anyone who has spent time on a farm should feel some qualms about looking to nature for lessons on sexual identity. Farm animals are not models of sexual morality. It's important to remember C. S. Lewis's admonition here: "If you take nature as a teacher she will teach you exactly the lessons you had already decided to learn; this is only another way of saying that nature does not teach."[15]

By placing our hope and identity in Scripture, rather than nature, we can engage with sexual identity without being threatened when we find examples in nature that do not align with God's plan for human sexual identity. As people created in the image of God, we have a higher calling than conformance with nature.

As you engage with sexual identity and representation in children's books, endeavor to:

1. **Find books that affirm a Christian worldview and portray men and women as distinct in gender.** This includes books that portray the many opportunities available to both genders. Do you have a boy who loves to tell stories? *John Ronald's Dragons* chronicles the early years of J. R. R. Tolkien. How about a girl who loves science? *Granny Smith Was Not an Apple* is a great place to start.

2. **Learn to read reviews.** Sometimes people lament that a book is not on our website. We don't review every book because we are finite. Also, we trust our readers can identify some books as books that do not match their worldview. This includes recent books that are featured on Pride Month displays. (Recently a YA cover caught our eyes: After a quick scan of the cover, we searched for reviews online. It was a Shakespeare historical adventure with gender-queer characters and polyamory. We did not check out that book or review it.)

---

15. C. S. Lewis, *The Four Loves* (Harcourt, Brace and Company, 1960), 37.

God created gender. We live in a fallen world. The conversation about gender isn't just in children's books, it is everywhere. Can a story be an opportunity for a conversation? Will it portray someone like a relative your child knows? Will it spark a conversation, or is this something that will normalize unbiblical behavior?

In *Parenting Without Panic in an LGBT-Affirming World*, Rachel Gilson provides parents with a wise, thoughtful guide to engaging with culture within our family conversations. She navigates how to talk about sexuality and later, how to have conversations if your child shares that he or she is struggling with same-sex attraction. Gilson observes, "While we cannot guarantee that our children will confide in us, if we speak early and often about sexuality in ways that are calm, confident, and respectful, we will greatly increase the odds that they will."[16] Stories are one such calm, confident, respectful way we can model engaging with sexual identity in discussions with children.

Cultural Identity

Multiculturalism has been a buzzword for decades. In 1980, Peter Spier published *People*. The picture book is a celebration, illustrating diversity in the world. There's a reason it's still in print today as it cheerfully pictures people in all their glorious individuality. (It also pictures people around the world in their normal dress, which in some places features partial nudity.) Spier observes, "People are funny. Some with straight hair want theirs to be wavy, and others with little curls want theirs to be straight."[17] We find ourselves nodding along to the sentiment!

At Redeemed Reader, we love finding books that reflect God's multiethnic creation. We recognize the many current authors, including Daniel Nayeri, Mitali Perkins, and Gene Luen Yang, who thoughtfully engage with and portray cultural identity in their stories. Positive cultural representation is

---

16. Rachel Gilson, *Parenting Without Panic in an LGBT-Affirming World* (Good Book Company, 2024), 98.
17. Peter Spier, *People* (Doubleday Books for Young Readers, 1980), n.p.

wonderful and needed. While cultural forces shape each one of us, our identity in Christ brings us together. We know that one day every tribe, tongue, and people will gather around the throne and worship the King.[18]

To Read, or Not to Read?

As we think about identity and representation, what are the stories that encourage us to celebrate or mourn? Do books lead us to rejoice over something that God says is good ... or do they affirm something that goes against our Christian faith?

Some recent changes to children's literature are positive. They reflect more of God's creation and encourage us to notice and understand the world. Some books, embracing a worldview contrary to God's good plan, reflect the truth of sin, that this world is fallen. While this might mean not reading some books to a toddler, reading such books with a tween or teen could provide an excellent chance for a conversation.

Whether reflecting creation, fall, redemption, or restoration, children's stories can provide excellent discussion starters. When you and your readers discover wonderful stories that reflect God's good creation, redemption, or restoration—praise God! When facing questions of identity and representation in children's literature, let us not fall into the same mistake as Jesus' disciples and lose sight of God's truth and design. Rather, let us read in light of the hope of Christ, our Savior. He can, and does, redeem us from all sin.

In picture books, chapter books, middle grade novels, and young adult fiction, may we delight in stories that remind us of the world God has made. Most importantly, may stories spark reminders of our ultimate identity in Christ.

---

18. See previous chapter for a further discussion of diversity.

BOOKLIST FOR CHAPTER 12

Further Reading

   Parenting Without Panic in an LGBT-Affirming World, Rachel Gilson

For Children/Teens

   God's Very Good Idea, Trillia Newbell and Catalina Echeverri (Picture Book)
   Creative God, Colorful Us, Trillia Newbell (Middle Grade nonfiction)
   Lizzie Bright and the Buckminster Boy, Gary D. Schmidt (Upper MG)
   Insignificant Events in the Life of a Cactus, Dusti Bowling (MG)
   Ugly: A Memoir, Robert Hoge (MG)
   American Born Chinese, Gene Luen Yang (Young Adult)
   Everything Sad Is Untrue, Daniel Nayeri (YA)
   Flygirl, Sherri L. Smith (YA)
   The Ranger's Apprentice series, John Flanagan (YA)
   Road to Memphis, Mildred D. Taylor (YA)
   You Bring the Distant Near, Mitali Perkins (YA)

CHAPTER 13

TURN ON THE LIGHT: "DARK" YA FICTION

> Trauma is a memory hog,
> It gobbles up all available space
> in the brain,
> leaves little room to mark
> daily happenstances,
> or even routine injuries
> which are less than
> life-threatening.[1]
>
> —Nikki Grimes, *Ordinary Hazards*

Once upon a time there was no such thing as "Young Adult" in the publishing world. Even earlier than that, there was no such thing as teenhood. A "youth" began taking on adult responsibilities somewhere between the ages of twelve and eighteen, and adults young and old read the same books. Robert Louis Stevenson, Mark Twain, and Booth Tarkington were considered "youth" authors only because their protagonists were young: Their readers ranged from eight to eighty.

Around the 1950s, children's librarians began stocking series novels with teen protagonists: nurses and "sleuths" and high school girls seeking Mr. Right. These were okay for passing a summer afternoon when the only alternative

---

1. Nikki Grimes, *Ordinary Hazards: A Memoir* (Astra Publishing House, 2022), 109.

was daytime TV, but by the time children reached their teens, they were either serious readers or they weren't. Serious readers from the age of twelve found their way to the adult stacks, where they began to develop a permanent literary taste. To read *A Separate Peace*, *Lord of the Flies*, and *The Catcher in the Rye* (all of which were written for adults, though they featured young characters) was almost a rite of passage for baby boomers.

The landscape began to shift in the 1970s, owing in part to Robert Cormier and *The Chocolate War* (1972). Cormier intended the story for adults but because of the setting (a parochial boys' school) his agent urged him to consider marketing it as "young adult." Cormier had his qualms, because *The Chocolate War* is unremittingly dark. But it's also compelling in plot and characterization, and readers debate its merits to this day.

Judy Blume, a popular middle grade author, broke another barrier in the mid-seventies with *Forever*, an explicit novel about teens experimenting with sex. The more "mature" theme didn't belong on the same shelf with Blume's earlier titles like *Tales of a Fourth-Grade Nothing* and *Freckle Juice*. Teen content was definitely getting edgier, making it advisable for public libraries to carve out separate YA spaces—even though the term "Young Adult" was a bit misleading because serious teen readers were still going for adult books. The actual target for YA was mostly twelve to fifteen years old.

In the 1990s, YA was overrun by "problem" books: neglected boys, abused girls. *Speak* (Laurie Halse Anderson, 2001), about a fourteen-year-old victim of rape, was emblematic of the trend. Just about every problem a teen could have was relentlessly explored, with corresponding parental challenges. Even though other YA genres have surpassed realistic fiction in popularity since then, problem books still feature prominently on the ALA's Michael L. Printz Award roster.[2]

In the early 2000s, paranormal romance (Twilight, etc.) swept the field,

---

2. The Printz medal was created to honor excellence in YA literature, first awarded to Walter Dean Myers in 2000 for *Monster*, a novel about a sixteen-year-old black teen on trial for murder.

just before *The Hunger Games* sparked a stampede for dystopian science fiction. Supernatural and futuristic titles now dominate the market. Another factor makes YA one of the most dynamic areas in publishing today: the bestselling Young Adult titles attract almost as many grown-up readers as teens.[3] Why is this? One reason may be that they're plot-driven—focused on the story rather than psychological analysis or literary flourishes. Also, no matter how depressing, most YA novels end with at least an intimation of better things ahead. Hope deferred indefinitely makes the heart sick (Prov. 13:12), and there's only so much hopelessness we can take.

With more adults reading YA (and more adult fiction authors writing it), the limit of what's appropriate for young readers has stretched beyond definition. In 2002, the ALA introduced the Alex Award, recognizing "ten books written for adults that have special appeal to young adults ages 12 through 18." Many Alex titles feature teenage protagonists, but the premises are often grim: dystopias and domestic abuse and rough upbringings in dysfunctional families. *GenderQueer* and *Lawn Boy*, two of the most challenged books of the last decade, found their way to high school libraries through the Alex list.

In June 2014, the *Wall Street Journal* published an article by Meghan Cox Gurdon titled "Darkness Too Visible."[4] Ms. Gurdon was experiencing culture shock over the amount of gloom and doom on YA fiction shelves. Rape, incest, self-mutilation, and more were showing up in teen novels, and the language used to tell about it was in some cases as graphic and profane as anything on the adult shelves. Is this, Ms. Gurdon asked, what we should be offering our kids to read?

Immediately the knives came out—not against the literature, but against

---

3. E.g., Entangled Publishing is introducing two new imprints to appeal to different levels of teen development: "Empyrean Series Publisher Announces Two New YA Imprints Truly Crafted with Teens in Mind," *People*, February 7, 2025, https://people.com/empyrean-series-publisher-announces-two-new-ya-imprints-truly-crafted-with-teens-in-mind-exclusive-8788145.
4. Meghan Cox Gurden, "Darkness Too Visible," *Wall Street Journal*, June 11, 2014.

Meghan Cox Gurdon. Hundreds if not thousands of authors, librarians, and bloggers chimed in. Many of them wondered if Ms. Gurdon supposed that all children are raised on Sunnybrook Farm. Others asked how teens in desperate situations were going to feel seen and heard if they didn't have fictional protagonists to identify with. Sherman Alexie's post on the WSJ arts blog was typical of the histrionic tone: "Why the Best Kids Books Are Written in Blood."[5]

The hashtag "YA Saves" enjoyed a heyday, with dozens of authors citing letters from grateful fans who finally realized they were not alone. Book bloggers contributed their own experiences of literary vindication. As author Laurie Halse Anderson put it: "Books open hearts and minds, and help teenagers make sense of a dark and confusing world. YA literature saves lives. Every. Single. Day."[6]

Pushback was more muted. Writing in *The New Atlantis*, Alan Jacobs challenged the notion that grim fiction was a net positive: "Salvific power, no danger. Even penicillin is dangerous for some people, but not YA fiction!"[7] Ms. Gurdon denied that she was advocating censorship. She was only raising valid questions, such as: What view of the world might impressionable teens receive from an abundance of depressing stories? And might reading too many novels about perverse behavior have the effect of normalizing pathology?

Today, with record levels of youth depression and suicidal ideation—not to mention actual suicide—it might be time to revisit those questions. Realistic "problem" fiction no longer dominates the YA bestseller list, but authors still emphatically wave the emails they received from readers, all testifying to the value of seeing themselves in print. "You gave me hope," they say. Or even "You saved my life."

---

5. Sherman Alexie, "Why the Best Kids Books Are Written in Blood," *Wall Street Journal*, June 9, 2011, https://www.wsj.com/articles/BL-SEB-65604.
6. "Teen Fiction Accused of Being 'Rife with Depravity'," *The Guardian*, June 7, 2011, https://www.theguardian.com/books/2011/jun/07/teen-fiction-accused.
7. Alan Jacobs, "YA Saves!," The New Atlantis, June 8, 2011, https://www.thenewatlantis.com/text-patterns/ya-saves.

The abused victims, the terminal teens, and the rape survivors of the last two decades of problem fiction have receded a bit; many of today's traumas are about sexual or gender identities. In nonfiction memoirs such as *GenderQueer* and *All Boys Aren't Blue*—#1 and #2 on the ALA's list of Most Challenged Books for 2023—the authors come to recognize their nonbinary or transgender identity after extensive sexual experimentation. *This Book Is Gay*, #3 on the list, is a self-help guide to locating oneself on the LGBTQIA+ spectrum. *Flamer* (#5) is a YA graphic novel about the author's coming out as gay. The cover blurb by novelist Jarrett Krosoczka is literally, "This book will save lives."

But how? How will those lives be saved? Where does that hope come from? In a Redeemed Reader post titled "The Lord Saves," Emily Whitten wrote, "We look to our authors to save us from a thousand secret sins, to lay their characters on the altar and sacrifice them in ways that will break our loneliness and hardness of heart and bring us again into communion with each other. We are a culture looking for YA and other literature to save us."[8] Defenders of dark YA fiction insist that merely being seen and affirmed in their suffering is salvation enough.

Some readers may indeed feel seen and affirmed and temporarily reassured. But nobody mentions the others, the teens from intact families who were never seriously abused or traumatized. They are bright, well-liked, and personable. How much dark fiction is too much for them? Are there lines that shouldn't be crossed?

In another Redeemed Reader post, Emily Whitten explored the reading lists recommended to high school college-bound seniors. Almost all the books on the list she surveyed featured themes of abandonment, despair, alienation, and, of particular concern, suicide. Literature can romanticize suicide, like it once romanticized the ugly throes of tuberculosis (all those pale dying heroines of yore). To a teen, death itself can seem romantic, as a statement or a protest against

---

8. Emily Whitten, "The Lord Saves," Redeemed Reader, https://redeemedreader.com/2011/09/22the-lord-saves/.

the evils of this world. The effect on loved ones left behind is seldom explored.

How much is too much? Robert Cormier said that no topic was off-limits for young readers; what mattered was the way it was handled.[9] Life had its tragic side and teens already suspected that. Good literature was a way of helping them accept tragedy along with joy.

True, as far as it goes, but something is missing. We hear of some college students who need counseling and teddy bears when an election goes the wrong way or their youthful assumptions meet serious pushback. Did those collegians read *The Chocolate War*, *Speak*, *The Bluest Eye*[10] or *The Fault in Our Stars*[11] in high school? If so, how odd is it that seniors who supposedly plowed through an AP reading list of tough topics can't handle real-life challenges when they get to college?

> *Grown-ups can appreciate a message of accepting life's tragedies along with its joys, but readers who haven't gained an adult perspective first need some idea of joy.*

Grown-ups can appreciate a message of accepting life's tragedies along with its joys, but readers who haven't gained an adult perspective first need some idea of joy. The evil, the false, and the ugly are possible to bear only if one knows something of the true, the good, and the beautiful. That's the main objection to these grim fairy tales and traumatic memoirs: no grounding in transcendent truth. YA literature usually (but not always) ends with some uptick of hope at the end: the identity is affirmed, hidden reserves of courage are discovered, new relationships are forged on the ashes of broken relationships. But the default mainspring of that "hope" must be found within. A supportive friend or relative

---

9. Lyn Gardner, "Dead Bodies in Suburbia," *The Guardian*, August 18, 2000, https://www.theguardian.com/books/2000/aug/19/booksforchildrenandteenagers.
10. By Toni Morrison, a novel written for adults featuring rape and incest, #6 on the ALA's Most Challenged list.
11. By John Green, a novel about teens dying from cancer.

may play a key role, but in the end, the protagonist, whether fictional or factual, must pull strength from his or her own hidden reserves.

Not many young people have developed those reserves. They are typically self-dramatizing and self-absorbed. That's not a criticism; for most of us, it's a stage on the way to maturity. Nobody denies that many young people face serious problems, and a literary avatar may help some of them deal. Also, a certain degree of darkness in literature can also help develop sympathy in those who don't have to grapple with it in real life.

But there are times and seasons. Children mature at different levels, and some are more sensitive than others. Parents and teachers need to be aware of what their kids can handle and how they react. Ideally, parents should read some of these books themselves and discuss them along the lines suggested in chapter 4 (Worldview) or chapter 9 (Messy Books). Those conversations can have a lasting effect on a young person's attitude. Above all, teens need to realize that they can weather any trauma or trial if they are grounded in capital-T Truth. And we know the ultimate source of that.

Someone once said, "I have read in Plato and Cicero sayings that are wise and beautiful; but I have never read in either of them, 'Come unto me all ye that labor and are heavy laden.'"[12] We know where true rest from the burdens of this world can be found. Only Christ can save.

---

12. Josiah H. Gilbert, *Dictionary of Burning Words of Brilliant Writers: A Cyclopaedia of Quotations from the Literature of All Ages* (Wilbur B. Ketcham, 1895), 62. This source attributes the quote to St. Augustine.

BOOKLIST FOR CHAPTER 13

Further Reading

    The Secret Thoughts of an Unlikely Convert, Rosaria Butterfield

For Teens

    Butterfly Yellow, Thanhhà Lai
    Disappeared, Francisco X. Stork
    Enter the Body, Joy McCullough
    Forward Me Back to You, Mitali Perkins
    Gone to the Woods, Gary Paulsen
    The Life and Crimes of Hoodie Rosen, Isaac Blum
    Nearer My Freedom, Monica Edinger and Lesley Younge
    Offsides, Lori Z. Scott
    Ordinary Hazards, Nikki Grimes
    The Passion of Dolssa, Julie Berry
    Ugly, Robert Hoge
    When I Was the Greatest, Jason Reynolds

SECTION 4
Ages, Stages, and Genres

CHAPTER 14

THE PICTURES MATTER! HOW TO ENJOY PICTURE BOOKS

> "What is the use of a book," thought Alice,
> "without pictures or conversations?"[1]
> —Lewis Caroll, *Alice in Wonderland*

As you enjoy picture books with your children, you are introducing them to an author—someone beyond themselves—who understands them and who knows how to tell a story they will love. A picture book story is a profoundly different kind of communication from daily household conversations.

We long to be known. We long to be understood. Reading picture books that recognize and reach that longing—that say, "I see you, and I know you, and let me tell you a story" are some of the best preparation for introducing your children to the ultimate Story, written by a sovereign God who sees and loves and understands, and who has given us a book to know Him more.

The glory of picture books is that, like poetry, every word matters, and more isn't necessarily better. A good picture book story may be longer or

---

1. Lewis Carroll, *Alice in Wonderland* (Peter Pauper Press, 1984), 9.

shorter, rhyming or not, using words that interact with the illustrations.

Like fine works of art, the pictures are an essential part of appreciating the story. The length of the text varies widely, but because it is meant to be read aloud, the best picture books are almost lyrical with carefully chosen words and each scene portrayed theatrically. These books form a child's first exposure to both art and literature, whetting the appetite for more.

Parents who seek quality picture books as a matter of delight rather than duty, who do not compromise their own pleasure in loving the illustrations for the sake of adding a mediocre title to their shelves, show children that art is worthy of being received, not simply accepted.

Picture Book Standards

When we choose picture books, we look at the illustrations first. Of course we judge the book by its cover because no matter how lovely the story might be, if the illustrations make no attempt at excellence, our pleasure is compromised.

Sometimes picture books settle for perky but static characters with shallow emotions, who appear to be posed in a tableau or acting in a commercial. The pictures are cluttered and complicated rather than thoughtful and complex. There is nowhere to rest your eyes, and the details add nothing to the story beyond what the text says.

Thankfully, having a class in art appreciation is not a prerequisite for enjoying certain pictures or being turned off by others. The watercolors in *A Visitor for Bear* and the cartoony style of the stories about George and Martha (the hippos, not the presidential couple) are both excellent. A wide range of artistic styles can reveal the harmonization of a well-written narrative with talented expression.

Is a reader's enjoyment purely subjective, or can they objectively judge the book based on qualities inherent in the work? Trained artists understand elements of design including composition, perspective, and palette (the colors). The best picture book illustrations follow the same principles, but with a key difference: The text and the art are mutually dependent. Picture book writers leave a gap in the narration for the illustrator to fill, and the best illustrators not only show what is being told, they also add to it.

Children love to hunt for a recurring character who appears on every page, like Gold Bug in Richard Scarry's *Cars and Trucks and Things That Go*, or to share a joke with the artist as in *A Pinecone!* by Helen Yoon or *Rosie's Walk* by Pat Hutchins. Perhaps emotion is expressed more deeply than the words imply, as in Paul O. Zelinsky's *Rapunzel* when the sorceress tenderly takes the child and raises her as her own, then later shows the anguish of betrayal in her stricken face. Perhaps the illustrations provide clues to the outcome, as in *One Cool Friend* by David Small.

Drawing pictures realistically is not the same as creating *real* characters on the page. Realism is an artistic style that may or may not show personality; real characters offer an emotional connection with the reader. If there is no opportunity for the child to connect with unique, individual characters who show real emotions (joy instead of generic happiness, grief instead of a frowny face, anxiety or curiosity in response to events in the story), there is no relationship to return to in future readings.

The Frances books by Russell Hoban are detailed, with line drawings and pastel highlighting, and the characters have real personalities. Frances sulks as Mother buttons her dress and explains that there are no raisins for the oatmeal because she was busy with the baby, which is something children can relate to. Frances's expression is a small, yet effective detail.

Condescending illustrations assume that children lack maturity to appreciate fine art, thus depriving them of interesting details to notice. Excellent stories and illustrations respect the reader, expecting the child to enter into the story and bring it to life. Children and adults will appreciate the same excellent book differently, based on their personal experiences.

In *Show Me a Story! Why Picture Books Matter*, twenty-one great picture book illustrators reveal what goes on behind the scenes in a single page of illustration. Like the best writers of literary retellings,[2] these illustrators not only have high regard for the story they are bringing to life, but also for their child audiences.

Some of these award-winning illustrators have a background in film or theater. These artists understand that each page is merely a snapshot of action, assuming that there is more going on "backstage" and outside the page than what the reader sees. Others compared their work to music, stand-up comedy, painting murals, or creating cartoons or graphic design for prestigious magazines. Such experiences provided breadth to their later work illustrating picture books for children.

James Marshall, known for the George and Martha books and the Miss Nelson trilogy, likes to think more of what might be going on backstage and all around the scene he's illustrating, explaining that "no matter what the style, there are certain principles that underlie the picture book as a genre. How to move it. When to stop it. How to pace it. What to leave out. A picture book becomes a whole world if it's done properly."[3]

Robert McCloskey, creator of such favorites as *Make Way for Ducklings* and *Blueberries for Sal*, understood how much children enjoy poring over pictures. He treated his work like painting murals and experimented with pacing and different viewpoints to "create a sense of space and movement and a feeling of something going on."[4]

Helen Oxenbury, illustrator of *The Three Little Wolves and the Big Bad Pig*, *We're Going on a Bear Hunt*, and the Tom and Pippo books, among many other titles, is a great example of an honest illustrator who shows parents and children in unguarded, messy, realistic situations. In her words: "It's almost opposite to the television commercial, where everything is perfect and the mother produces white clothes out of the washing machine. I find that awful because

---

2. See chapter 6.
3. Leonard Marcus, *Show Me a Story! Why Picture Books Matter* (Candlewick, 2012), 124.
4. Ibid., 148.

it's not true, and because it makes people dissatisfied and feel inadequate."[5]

Children have no trouble accepting imaginary, unrealistic scenarios portrayed in the illustrations. They are discerning enough about the world around them to recognize that life isn't sterile and they aren't fooled by books in which everything seems blissfully flawless. Speaking truth to them means offering them books that are artistically honest because the world we live in is broken, and we're pilgrims wondering what will happen next on our journey.

Picture Book Progression

Good board books are an early gateway to falling in love with picture books and reading. Babies get their first taste of reading by gnawing on the corners. Board books are an interactive conduit to how books work as objects, with thick pages that allow children to use (and abuse!) them. Board books fit nicely in a diaper bag, whereas picture books are more likely to be bent and are harder to pass into the back seat to placate a bored child (and then be thrown on the floor).

Some are produced with adults in mind, such as the educational *Quantum Physics for Babies* or "first classics" type that try to condense *Pride and Prejudice* or *The Lion, the Witch and the Wardrobe* into a concept book. (Don't bother with these.) Others function less as books intended for a child's reading pleasure and more as toys with sounds or activities (touch and feel the farm animals, pat the bunny, and press the buttons to hear recorded sounds). Many board books are quickly laid aside as children get older and move on to other interests, but books with well-crafted text and clever rhymes introduce delight and eventually become part of family culture. Sandra Boynton's *Belly Button Book* and *The Going to Bed Book* are excellent examples of this. (Go ahead—make up a tune in celebration of the belly button!) A child who has enjoyed *Ten Little Fingers and Ten Little Toes*, illustrated by Helen Oxenbury, will enjoy going on a bear hunt with similar characters.

---

5. Ibid., 159-60.

Some stories, such as *One Big Pair of Underwear* by Laura Gehl, may be available in both board book and traditional picture book format; this is a matter of discretion. If your child loves the story but is still rambunctious and learning to be gentle with pages, then favoring the thicker format might be a practical bridge. Remember as you transition from one stage to another that your child will still want to enjoy the board books they've come to love.

How and when does that adjustment occur? When your child is consistently sitting through multiple readings of board books, begin to introduce a picture book. (You might also be getting tired of multiple rereadings of favorite titles ... it is okay to say no to a second or third or fourth reading in favor of a new picture book: "I'll read that again *after* we read this new book!")

> *When your child is consistently sitting through multiple readings of board books, begin to introduce a picture book.*

Picture books provide a transitional introduction to longer sentences and stories in the world of myths, legends, fairy tales, folklore, biographies, and science. Some are simpler, like *Simon and the Better Bone* or *Kitten's First Full Moon* (read both of these and see what they have in common). The sophisticated vocabulary of *Peter Rabbit* and the imaginative irony of Maurice Sendak's stories invite children toward deeper engagement with books, which becomes more fully manifested later when they start reading on their own. *The Spider and the Fly* is a captivating film noir version of Mary Howitt's familiar Victorian-era poem. *The Lion's Share* by Matthew McElligott shows the consequences of greed and honors humility while teaching fractions and the significance of doubling. There are so many wonderful titles to choose from!

Fine motor skills are something to take into account as you introduce picture books, and it is appropriate to expect gentle handling. You and your child will both enjoy them more if you practice patience and forgiveness when pages are bent or torn. Teach children to practice lifting pages properly at the corner rather than close to the gutter down the middle of the book, and embrace the convenience of repairs with tape during this season.

While we prefer hardcovers, paperbacks are cheaper and can be a bit more forgiving under rough handling. Save the special copies (like that gift edition inscribed from grandparents or the hardcover with a dust jacket that is signed by the author) until children have learned how to handle this format.

Megan covers all her dust jackets library-style, which not only protects them from tearing and getting sticky, but also reinforces the strength of the book. Hayley checks out copies of books from the library rather than introduce special copies she doesn't want damaged because library bound editions are often reinforced and intended for heavier use.

READ IT AGAIN!

Do those words from your children fill you with dread? Or do you have a shelf of well-loved stories? It can be hard to find a picture book that you and your child both enjoy, one that is fresh, though not yet a favorite. While going to the library or bookstore in times past would yield a plethora of desirable, engaging picture books, today they can be harder to find. Here are three categories to avoid in your quest:

1. Resist sermonizing feel-good bibliotherapy. These books might look beautiful and sound sweet, but their shallow encouragement to be [insert virtue] and feel [insert desirable trait] are going to bore everyone. Moralistic picture books do not change a child's heart or behavior, either in Christian or mainstream titles.

2. Beware the celebrity picture book. These are often ghostwritten and rely on a name for selling a trite, simplistic story.

3. Flee the branded spin-offs. These lack both substance and creativity as they rely on flat cardboard stereotypes instead of the dynamic characters that made these brands well known. Mater the tow truck in the movie *Cars* is funny as a cartoon, but he falls flat as a picture book character.

Sample reading a few pages aloud and see how the sentences flow. Do the words bounce energetically? Roll smoothly off the tongue? The best ones are crafted in such a way that even the prose is almost poetic, sometimes onomatopoetic. *Bartholomew and the Oobleck* by Dr. Seuss is a great example of a picture book that demonstrates both Truth and Story. Although the author is best known for his clever, tightly rhyming easy readers, the same skill with the sound of words overflows into his prose writing. Onomatopoeia (words that sound like what they mean) are fun to read and to hear. In Robert McCloskey's *Blueberries for Sal*, there is an almost musical refrain as the berries fall "kerplink, kerplank, kerplunk" into the bucket.[6]

Children who have a hard time sitting still or who are not yet accustomed to the joy of picture books will find funny ones more appealing. *Shark vs. Train* by Chris Barton, *A Visitor for Bear* by Bonny Becker, *Do Like a Duck Does!* by Judy Hindley, *My Little Sister Ate One Hare* by Bill Grossman, and *Mr. Fox's Game of "No!"* by David LaRochelle bring plenty of giggles.

Alphabet books are remarkably creative, clever, and contrary. From the classic *Chicka-Chicka-Boom-Boom* by Bill Martin to *A Apple Pie* by Gennady Spirin and the remake *Apple Pie ABC* by Alison Murray, to *LMNO Peas* by Keith Baker, to *The Met ABC: An Alphabet Book of Art* or *A is for Artist* or *Museum ABC*, to *A is for Musk Ox* by Erin Cabatingan and *Z is for Moose* by Kelly Bingham, you will be amazed at the versatility of twenty-six letters.

Wordless picture books can be studied independently or shared and talked about. Turn the pages together and talk about what you notice in the illustrations. Try adding your own narration, simply state what's on the page, or ask your listeners to find things on each page. There is no one way to enjoy a wordless book!

Nonfiction picture books include the same genres that nonfiction for older readers do: interactive books, fact books, and books about science or math or history. Picture book biographies are outstanding uses of the format.

Math, science, and biographies come alive when the author takes a

---

6. Marcus, *Show Me the Story!*, 150.

narrative and crafts a story accompanied by high-quality photographs or excellent illustrations. These include books like *Mysterious Patterns: Finding Fractals in Nature* by Sarah C. Campbell, the Adventures of Sir Cumference series by Cindy Neuschwander, *Life After Whale: The Amazing Ecosystem of a Whale Fall* by Lynn Brunelle, *Ribbit! The Truth About Frogs* by Annette Whipple, and *Whoosh! Lonnie Johnson's Super-Soaking Stream of Inventions* by Chris Barton.

I Spy books and *Can You See What I See?* by Walter Wick are like playing hide-and-seek and solving puzzles, and children never seem to tire of rediscovering what they saw or might have missed last time. Joan Steiner's *Look-Alikes* books are similar.

Bible story retellings and Christian picture books should be richly illustrated, and the text beautifully written. Some of our favorites are illustrated by John Hendrix, Catalina Echeverri, Khoa Le, Kevin and Kristen Howdeshell, and Patty Rokus.[7]

What kind of rigors and artistic qualities should we expect to find in picture book illustrations? Next time you read a picture book, consider some of these questions:

- Who is the author? Who is the illustrator? Have you read any of their other books?
- Do the pictures add anything original besides what is described in the text?
- Are the pictures merely decorations, or do they contribute artistic interest, meaning, and depth?
- Are the pictures detailed or not? What kind of colors did the artist choose (soft or bright)?
- Do the characters seem real? Do they show expression?
- Is there a subtle side story in the details?

---

7. See further thoughts in chapters 6 and 21.

- Can you imagine movement before and after the page, or does everyone seem to be waiting to be told where to go next?
- Is your eye always viewing from the same perspective?
- Is the scene full of visual noise, or is there a place to rest your eyes or focus on what is important to the story?
- Is everyone happy and artificially clean, or is there a sense of realism and imperfection that you can relate to?
- Are there any details you didn't notice last time you read the book?

How to Read a Picture Book

Begin with an appealing stack, including a variety of topics and illustration styles (cartoon, realistic, different cultural settings, watercolor, line drawings, bold, soft, etc.). Introduce books you loved as a child. If you didn't grow up with much experience or aren't sure where to begin, *Honey for a Child's Heart* is one of our favorite resources for classics.

Pay attention to the endpapers and title page. Where does the story actually begin? Do you notice any connections with the rest of the book? Read the story. Compare the illustrations with the text. Don't spend too long the first time through; you can further discuss the details another time.

Next time you read the story, consider using creative voices for the characters, either suited to the story or something quite contrary, like a strong accent where it doesn't belong. Your child will either strongly object or find it hilarious! Keep reading picture books aloud as your child is learning to read; some books are particularly suited to a more sophisticated audience.

All great picture books invite repeated perusals of their art. Perhaps it's time to note some of the techniques the illustrator has used to make the story pop. Ask yourselves, "Why did the illustrator do it this way?"

- Palette: What colors does the illustrator use? Just one or two or a whole rainbow? Is there one color that is used for added punch? *The Napping House* is a classic that uses color to tremendous effect. Jerry Pinkney often adds pops of red.

- Perspective: Are the pictures far away? Close up? Bird's-eye view? A mix? Where is your eye drawn when you look at a page? Frank Morrison is a fun illustrator to study for his use of perspective.

- Composition: What's in the picture? What's left out? How much white space is there? *One Cool Friend* leverages composition in very fun ways!

- Details: (Related to the above ideas!) What are the faces like? Can you see leaves on the trees? Are there recurring background details that enrich the story? *Mr. Squirrel and the Moon* is a lively story with plenty of hilarious details. Conversely, a well-placed eyebrow might be all the detail needed, such as in the Elephant and Piggie books.

A successful reading results in growth, richness, and joy, all of which are good gifts that could only come from God. Isn't it wonderful that even enjoying a book together reminds us of God, the giver of every perfect gift? Remember that thought the next time you enjoy an especially wonderful picture book, no matter what the story is about. When you, the reader, are delighted, there are whispers of Truth and Story, and praise is due to the One who opened your heart to receive them.

BOOKLIST FOR CHAPTER 14

Further Reading

    Picture This!, Molly Bang

For Children/Teens

    Belly Button Book; *The Going to Bed Book*; others, Sandra Boynton (Board Book)
    I Kissed the Baby!, Mary Murphy (BB)
    Peek-a-boo, Janet & Allan Ahlberg (BB)
    Ten Little Fingers and Ten Little Toes, Mem Fox, illustrated by Helen Oxenbury (BB)
    Heckedy Peg, Audrey Wood; illlustrated by Don Wood (Picture book)
    Kitten Red, Yellow, Blue, Peter Catalanotto (PB)
    Knight Owl, Christopher Denise (PB)
    The Monkey and the Crocodile, Paul Galdone (PB)
    My Lucky Day, Keiko Kasza (PB)
    Room for Everyone, Naaz Khan, illustrated by Mercè López (PB)
    Sam and Dave Dig a Hole, Mac Barnett, illustrated by Jon Klassen (PB)
    The Seven Silly Eaters, Mary Ann Hoberman, illustrated by Marla Frazee (PB)
    The Spider and the Fly, Mary Howitt, illustrated by Tony DiTerlizzi (PB)
    A Visitor for Bear, Bonny Becker, illustrated by Kady MacDonald Denton (PB)

CHAPTER 15

THE EMERGING READER: NURTURING A LOVE OF STORIES AND READING

> "A reader is *reading us!*"[1]
> —Elephant and Piggie in *We Are in a Book!* by Mo Willems

After board books and picture books, the next season of reading comes when a child is motivated to learn to read, not because it is a subject taught in school, but because the imagination has been designed to desire its own relationship with stories.

A child who watches friends or an older sibling enjoy riding a bike can't help but put on a helmet and beg to ride through the park. Would you first explain how a bicycle works and require a completed worksheet identifying the parts? No, you'd buckle on a helmet, roll out a coaster bike or training wheels, and send the child on his way to have fun while gaining confidence and learning independence.

---

1. Mo Willems, *We Are in a Book!* (Hyperion Books for Children, 2010), 13.

Learning to read should be a quest, not a task, with just enough knowledge to provide the skills to overcome the obstacles for the sake of treasure at the end. When the child isn't laboring through the technical process, developing the skill happens efficiently and effortlessly. It's like playing another math game instead of going through a deck of flash cards a dozen times.

Developing Readers

The best easy readers work the same way. These books are generally geared toward kids ages four to seven. Using simpler language and a larger font size to help children who are learning to decipher words independently, books known as "easy readers" (sometimes "early readers") encourage progress among children who are laboring through the process. They may be written by specialists using formulaic controlled vocabulary measure levels, but the true joy of reading happens when a child reads outside of the requirement. Handing a child the next book prescribed in the curriculum because she has covered the vocabulary can make reading feel like a task rather than a delight; the story is presented as secondary to the "assignment."

Irresistible easy readers are more than instructive. They can be as literary as picture books, are often funny, and are written with words that are tantalizing to the ear.

These are books with controlled/precise vocabularies designed for new readers (did you know that *The Cat in the Hat* only has 236 different words in the whole book?) and plots that are simple enough for them to grasp. Illustrations still play a prominent role in helping young readers decode the words. And there are some truly great pieces of literature in this category. Almost without exception, easy readers also work well as read-alouds for younger children, especially those on the brink of reading.

Easy readers are often assigned a reading level by a publisher (Level 1-2-3 or A-B-C). You should know two things: These levels are not consistent from publisher to publisher, so your child might be comfortable reading Level 1 in I Can Read books but perhaps move up a level in a category from another early reader publisher. Also, your child might be comfortable reading selections from multiple levels. The levels work best as a rough guideline when you're just starting to choose easy reader books. Your child's comfort/ease/interest should be your primary guide.

A child's first attempts will be made in stories with only a few words on each page, simple enough for the child to sound out, with hints in the illustrations to help him decode unfamiliar text. *Go, Dog, Go!* by P. D. Eastman is an excellent example. The ongoing exchange between a girl dog and a boy dog who is unimpressed with her hat provides a side plot with a satisfactory resolution.

There are quite a few pages, so the child may not make it through *Go, Dog, Go!* on the first try, but that's okay. Eventually, finishing a book that has a lot of pages feels like an accomplishment, no matter how many words the child has actually read in a single sitting. A child gaining confidence will move on to stories with more words on the page that still maintain generous font size and restful white space. Books may be divided into chapters, or the stories may simply be longer.

COMMON CHARACTERISTICS OF EASY READERS

A common theme in easy readers is friendship, and one of our favorite examples is found in the Elephant and Piggie series in which no eyebrow is wasted. Elephant and Piggie are actors on a minimalist stage, using nothing more than props, costume changes, and perhaps dramatic lighting for special effects. Because the text is also minimal and the stories are humorous, these are popular with readers who are emerging into confidence. Thankfully, there are plenty of titles in the series.

More best friends duos include Frog and Toad, Minnie and Moo, and Mr. and Mrs. Green, as well as "character plus pet" stories such as the Fly Guy books, Henry and Mudge, and the Cowgirl Kate and Cocoa series.

Another type of easy reader centers around a lovable or quirky main character: *Little Bear* by Else Holmelund Minarik, *Dodsworth* by Tim Egan, *See the Cat: Three Stories About a Dog* by David LaRochelle, and *You Are (Not) Small!* by Anna Kang fall under this category.

Children who enjoy nonfiction may be more interested in informational books such as the DK readers, Kids Guides by Edge books, and *Eye: How It Works* (and others by David Macauley). These are often mixed in with regular juvenile nonfiction; check out hot topics such as weather, natural disasters, wild animals, ocean animals, dinosaurs (read with discretion), space, and robots.

Some of the best illustrations are those that make the characters and setting seem real. The palette in the Frog and Toad books is limited to the greens and browns of frogs and toads, and yet the characters are lively and relatable. Although real frogs and toads don't wear pants or eat cookies, both the characters and the illustrations show us things that are true about the world God has made and about genuine friendship.

Don't assume that your child who is learning to read is ready for the challenge of deciphering all the words right away. Read *Green Eggs and Ham* and *The Cat in the Hat* aloud a few times with the child beside you, occasionally inviting him to point out a word he recognizes. You can also alternate reading pages, building both confidence and stamina. Make the experience fun, not stressful, and eventually the child will be surprised and proud to discover how many words he can read.

What could be better to keep a child reading than a good mystery? Short chapter books like King and Kayla (a series about a dog and his girl), Nate the Great (a young sleuth who is very fond of pancakes), and Mercy Watson (a porcine wonder who loves buttered toast) are a lot of fun. A little longer than easy readers, but not yet middle grade length, these books have plenty of white space and engaging illustrations.

Billy and Blaze is a series of picture books about the adventures of a boy and his horse with larger text and white space that is easier to read. Beginning-level comic books and graphic novels with action clearly depicted in the illustrated story panels also help children progress further as deciphering the words comes more naturally.

This season is short, but vital. Because children develop fluent reading skills at different ages, it's worth finding books that resonate with them with characters they can relate to and fall in love with more than plot-driven stories. Visit the library regularly because each progressive stage is relatively short and the library is likely to hold most of the volumes in a favorite series.

A Bridge to Beyond

When should your child stop reading easy readers? There's no official timeline, but there will be a natural transition to more advanced books, with less frequent visits to the Frog and Toad collection on your shelf. The kids will develop opinions about what they like, and they may not prefer the books you loved as a child.

The good news is, you don't have to get tired of reading the same book over and over because your child will be able to do it himself. The best easy readers will become part of your family culture, just like favorite board books and picture books because they'll be cherished and quoted from now on.

When your child moves from easy readers into beginner chapter books with longer chapters, fewer pictures and somewhat smaller font, characters are more likely to be children (rather than animals) near your child's age. Some will be fun and relatable, like neighborhood playmates, but others will be so annoying you'll just want to send them home until they learn better manners. What makes the difference?

As you read more children's books with your kids, you'll notice that some stories are simply childish while others are delightfully childlike. One way to discern between the two is through the characters. There is an enormous difference between characters in a childish story and those in a childlike story.

Childlike and childish are both aspects of childhood. The first is a positive expression of childhood, the qualities that we don't want to outgrow as adults: innocence (about worldly concerns), delight in make-believe, enjoyment of a rollicking good adventure, the suspension of disbelief, the reliance on one's family. On the other hand, childishness consists of the negative aspects of childhood, traits we want children to outgrow as they mature: an attitude of selfishness and exaggerated dependency, a demand for things or privileges that have been withheld, or pretending helplessness instead of confidence developed through practicing skills imperfectly.

When grown-ups still read The Chronicles of Narnia or Edith Nesbit's books with delight, that helps explain the meaning of "childlike." Having a childlike quality is part of the reason easy reader series such as Mo Willems' Elephant and Piggie books are so popular. In Scripture, Jesus encourages us to have faith like a child, so we know that there is something inherent in a child's approach to the world that should stay with us into adulthood.

To illustrate the difference between "childlike" and "childish," let's explore two chapter book series for emerging readers: the Junie B. Jones series and the Jasper John Dooley series. On the surface, they have several things in common. Both title characters are early elementary students and only children and . . .

. . . well, that's about it. Junie B. Jones books appear on numerous suggested reading lists—including those from Christian schools—and the inclusion of these books is puzzling. Junie B. Jones is a classic example of a childish protagonist. She has a bad attitude, is terribly disrespectful to her parents, and tries to be funny at the expense of others—in short, she is a perfect example of the terrible twos. We expect children to grow out of these behaviors (and, hopefully, our parenting reflects that goal); we do *not* find these traits admirable, nor do we desire them to continue on in our children into first grade. Why, then, do we give books featuring protagonists like this to our children?

In contrast, Jasper John Dooley is childlike. He is funny, endearing, lovable, and makes plenty of mistakes. But his mistakes are childlike and the logical outworkings of a busy, energetic, and creative elementary student. He is not disrespectful, he does not laugh at others' expense, and he has a pretty good attitude even when things don't go his way. *This* is the kind of kid we want our children to enjoy "getting to know."

Books that are helpful in this later stage include the Imagination Station series, Deckawoo Drive, Anna Hibiscus, Clementine, the My Father's Dragon trilogy, Encyclopedia Brown, and Tree Street Kids series. These books are a little shorter in length, which feels more doable for an emerging reader.

It's worth helping your children pick their book friends the same way they pick their real-life friends. If there are traits in book friends that you wouldn't want in real-life friends, it's time to break off the relationship and find better friends. Easy readers provide some of the first book friends children meet on their own. Seek out the easy readers that offer good book friend choices. In other words, use the same criteria for those books with short, predictable words that you do for longer, complex novels.[2]

---

2. Some of this content first appeared on Redeemed Reader.com: https://redeemedreader.com/2014/03/librarians-list-easy-leveled-reader-part-1/, https://redeemedreader.com/2014/03/librarians-list-easyleveled-readers-part-2/, https://redeemedreader.com/2015/04/finding-good-chapter-book-friends-junie-b-jones-v-jasper-john-dooley/.

BOOKLIST FOR CHAPTER 15
THE EMERGING READER

Further Reading

    The Read-Aloud Family, Sarah Mackenzie

For Children/Teens

    Elephant and Piggie books, Mo Willems (Easy Reader)
    Fly Guy series, Tedd Arnold (ER)
    Fox Plays Ball, Corey Tabor (ER)
    Ling and Ting series, Grace Lin (ER)
    Makeda Makes a Home for Subway, Olugbemisola Rhuday-Perkovich (ER)
    See the Cat: Three Stories About a Dog, David LaRochelle
    Anna Hibiscus series, Atinuke (Chapter Book)
    Imagination Station series, Marianne Hering and Paul McCusker (CB)
    The King's Cadets and Little Joe, Joe Sutphin and Kevan Chandler (CB)
    Lulu series, Hilary McKay (CB)
    Orris and Timble: The Beginning, Kate DiCamillo (CB)

CHAPTER 16

JUST FOR LAUGHS: KID HUMOR

> Q: What do you get when sheep do karate?
> A: Lamb chops.[1]
> —Rob Elliott, *Laugh-Out-Loud Jokes for Kids*

Do you remember giggling at Amelia Bedelia's obtuse literalness? Did you devour Garfield the Cat or Calvin and Hobbes comics? Or laugh out loud when your mother read Sid Fleischman's McBroom books? Humor is a quality unique to humans (and not to angels, as far as we know), owing largely to our tendency to trip over our own feet and fall on our faces.

"Life is a comedy to those who think, and a tragedy to those who feel." That's a line from Horace Walpole, British philosopher and politician. Or from the French playwright Racine. (It was somebody in the eighteenth century, who said something profound.) Feelings come easily; we were born with them. That's why babies cry—they are overwhelmed with feelings of hunger, displacement, loneliness, discomfort, or sometimes actual pain. These things come at them before they have the capacity to think about them, and crying is their only means of making themselves heard. That wail at 2 a.m. means, "Hey! I'm feeling something!"

But when they aren't crying, they are looking—learning to recognize faces and places. Learning how a certain configuration of the face gets a smile in

---

1. Rob Elliott, *Laugh-Out-Loud Jokes for Kids* (Revell, 2010), 76.

return, and how certain sounds, like "ma-ma" and "da-da," earn the attention of important people. And sometime between three and four months, a baby makes a sound she's never made before. She laughs.

There she is, minding her own business of observation. All of a sudden, a head pops up in front of her. She startles, and blinks, and realizes this is not the way Mom and Dad appear. She smiles, uncertain. Her brother wags his head back and forth and makes a ridiculous face. A chuckle rises from Baby's chest. Encouraged, big brother ducks down and pops up again. This time the chuckle rolls up with a little shriek of surprise. "She's laughing!" Mom says. Big brother does it again and again, each time rewarded with the involuntary gasps and rumbles of laughter, until the joke gets old.

What happened? Something *funny*. Humor depends on the unexpected: the banana-peel slip, the proud brought low, or the misunderstood situation. For a joke to work, the audience must already understand what's normal and expected, so they can appreciate the abnormal and unexpected. By three or four months, a baby is beginning to understand "normal." The surprising abnormal, if it isn't scary, defaults to funny. Laughter is one of the first signs that a baby is beginning to think.

Trying to explain funny is never funny; suffice it to say that kids not only love to laugh, they *need* to laugh. It's no wonder that the two bestselling book series for children are humor books—both of which may raise red flags for Christian parents. But both say a lot about the kind of humor that appeals to second through seventh grade readers.

Middle School "Losers"

It all started with a web comic.

Jeff Kinney's ambition from boyhood was to write a comic strip for syndication, but his artistic talent didn't match his limitless imagination. While working as a developer of video games for Pearson, a leading educational publisher, he began posting a strip called "Diary of a Wimpy Kid" on

FunBrain.com, Pearson's website arm. The web comic was originally designed for adults who remembered their middle school years (or "the Pits," as some recall that time in their lives). But seventh grade hero Greg Heffley struck such a nerve with younger readers that by the time *Diary of a Wimpy Kid* was published as a hardcover MG novel, it already had thousands of seventh grade (and much younger) fans.

The "Diary" is written in block letters and liberally illustrated with Greg's cartoony, snarky, and often hilarious drawings. The protagonist who emerges in book #1 is an anti-hero who casually double-crosses the "losers," including his friend Rowley, and still comes out worse for it. That's because Greg is also a loser, though he resolutely believes in his own cleverness.

Storylines are thin and rambling. For example, in book #7 (*The Third Wheel*, 2012), Greg begins with a twelve-page recollection of himself as a pre-born infant and baby. Then to the central storyline, the Valentine's Dance: finding a date, shelling out bucks, arranging transportation, etc. The meandering plot takes us through the school assembly diversion, the toilet-paper diversion (toilet paper being a WK standby), and the mad pantser diversion. The dance itself, like every Wimpy Kid scenario, is an exposition of Murphy's Law, from running up an outrageous bill at Corny's Family Restaurant to senior citizens crashing the dance.

Is it funny? Yes. When Kinney plans a new novel in the series, he writes the jokes and pratfalls first, then a first-person narrative strung between the jokes, and finally the primitive cartoons. It's all about funny, but are there any other positives?

Greg belongs to an intact family, goes to church, doesn't use bad language, and appears to know right from wrong. He just doesn't always—okay, he almost never—lets it get in the way of personal advantage. The saving grace is that none of his schemes work out as planned. Cheating and lying do not pay in Greg's world. Typical of preadolescent boys? Typical of all of us, deep down. He's instructive in a negative way: "There is none righteous" (Rom. 3:10 NKJV).

The great thing about humor—especially the self-mocking kind—is that it offers perspective. While Greg mercilessly ridicules other kids, the author subtly or not-so-subtly makes him the butt of the jokes. Readers younger than ten may not get the irony, but for preteens a few thoughtful questions might be in order, such as: Would you like to have Greg as a friend? Would you trust him to take care of the family dog for a weekend? Do you share any character traits with him, good or bad?

Self-consciousness is painfully evident in the preteen and early teen years, and some readers may be reaching for WK to reassure themselves that however dorky they are, there's always somebody dorkier. Imitators such as Timmy Failure, Big Nate, The Odd Squad, and Nikki Maxwell of The Dork Diaries (for girls) are all misfits to some degree, some more likeable than others. Kids can laugh at them, but if they're also learning to laugh at themselves, that's healthy, refreshing, and thoroughly human.

Potty Humor

The other bestselling author who has turned kid humor into comedy gold is Dav Pilkey, who writes for the third through fifth grade set. Younger humor tends toward the scatological, personified in Pilkey's Captain Underpants, who made his debut in 1997. The title character is the not-so-secret identity of Mr. Krupp, every kid's idea of the pompous, dictatorial school principal. Fourth graders George and Harold, aspiring comic-book creators, imagine Mr. Krupp as an anti-superhero who does his superpower thing dressed only in briefs and a polka-dot cape. Imagination becomes real when Mr. Krupp is hypnotized into becoming Captain Underpants. Book titles in the series tell us all we need to know about the humor: *The Attack of the Talking Toilets*, *The Perilous Plot of Professor Poopypants*, etc.

Captain Underpants has thankfully retired, but not before those two pranksters, George and Harold, happened upon a stash of comics they wrote before creating their undie-clad superhero. They decided to share these with loyal readers, and thus: Dog Man. The title character is the result of a dastardly trick played by Petey, the World's Most Evilest Cat, who planted a bomb for the police. Officer Knight and Greg the Dog discovered it, and in the ensuing explosion, Knight's head and Greg's body were damaged beyond repair. Loyal & true Nurse Lady suggested joining the man's body and the dog's head, which worked out brilliantly because Greg was the smart one anyway. Petey's evil plot backfired as Dog Man became his implacable foe.

Over the course of thirteen volumes (and counting), Petey reforms and tries to become a better version of himself. But other villains are always waiting in the wings, along with explosions, monsters, robots, and monstrous robots.

Pilkey has a lot of fun with subtitles, as in *A Tale of Two Kitties*, *Lord of the Fleas*, *Fetch-22*, and *Mothering Heights*. Readers who don't get the literary references can expect plenty of bathroom humor and behavior of which grown-ups don't approve. *Mothering Heights*, for example, features song parodies about diarrhea, which is probably typical—parents be warned about what they might hear their seven-year-old belting out in the shower.

On the positive side, Dog Man is sweet-tempered and true blue (as well as a *very* sloppy kisser), and Petey's struggles to be a better cat are both touching and commendable. Love and kindness win out over dastardly schemes every time. Parents can make up their own minds about potty jokes, but most readers know what's acceptable at the dinner table. Or, if not, this is one way to learn.

Potty humor is a stage most kids go through, and (mostly) grow out of. Immature and unfunny as it may seem to adults, it's a clue to something profoundly human: This creature is "a little lower than the angels" and crowned "with glory and honor" (Ps. 8:5 NKJV) who is nonetheless subject to all kinds of undignified bodily functions. Perhaps God is keeping us humble. C. S. Lewis wrote that much of theology could be deduced from the fact that humans "make coarse jokes" and "feel the dead to be uncanny."[2] That is, we subconsciously know we are immortal beings created in a divine image, and the particulars of death, digestion, and reproduction strike us as incongruous. Incongruity is the essence of laughter.

---

2. C. S. Lewis, *Miracles: A Preliminary Study* (MacMillian, 1958), 206.

The Serious Side of Humor

Not all kid humor is of the Wimpy Kid/Dog Man variety. Janie laughed along with her kids at *The Cricket in Times Square* and *Stuart Little*, as well as the outlandish characters and plots cooked up by Roald Dahl. More recently the Ben Washington series by Jasmine Mullen introduces a twelve-year-old whose narrative voice is often hilarious as he meets the challenges of a black kid in a white-bread community. *Mooses with Bazookas* by S. D. Smith aims straight for the funny bone in a collection of letters from a desert island castaway.

> *Gentle jabs, riddles and puns, well-meaning goofballs, and simple silliness all have their place, even in the most serious novels.*

Gentle jabs, riddles and puns, well-meaning goofballs, and simple silliness all have their place, even in the most serious novels. In *Everything Sad Is Untrue*, Daniel Nayeri uses a middle grade voice and humorous observations (including scatological ones) to leaven intense subject matter. Gary Schmidt also tackles difficult topics with comical touches.

Still, not all varieties of laughter are wholesome, and kids may need discernment to see the thin line between healthy and toxic. Watch out for the scornful, mocking, sarcastic, and disdainful kinds. Watch out for narrators who assume a position of superiority while making others the butt of their ridicule, thus inviting readers to laugh along. Be careful with history series and picture books that poke fun at respected historical figures. Humorous touches are certainly appropriate, as long as these characters are treated as real people, not caricatures.

The best kind of laughter comes at the expense of our own frailties and pomposities. Life is not a joke, but in a way, *we* are: created in dust but destined for glory, with countless pratfalls along the way.

The opportunity to laugh will introduce many a book-shy child to the joys of reading, but choices are up to parental discretion. Answering these questions may help them decide which books are appropriate:

1. Are the subject matter, vocabulary, and/or character qualities without any redeeming features?

2. Is humor snarky, mean, sarcastic, or gross?

3. Can I laugh along with my kids, but also talk about the content?

Christian parents should be teaching their children to exercise discernment for themselves, but in the process of developing a palate for excellence, children are bound to waste some time and devour a few stinkers. As long as they can talk it over with a wise teacher or parent, even that can be a learning experience.

BOOKLIST FOR CHAPTER 16

Further Reading

    Ha! A Christian Philosophy of Humor, Peter Kreeft

For Children/Teens

    Battle Bunny, Jon Scieszka and Mac Barnett (Picture Book)
    Church Mice series, Graham Oakley (PB, out of print but worth tracking down)
    Noodleheads series, Tedd Arnold (Easy Reader)
    Fly Guy series, Tedd Arnold (ER)
    The Chicken Squad series, Doreen Cronin (Chapter Book)
    Detective Sweet Pea series, Sara Varon (CB Graphic Novel)
    The Asterix series, René Goscinny and Albert Uderzo (Middle Grade graphic novel)
    Brixton Brothers, Mac Barnett (MG)
    Chronicles of a Lizard Nobody, Patrick Ness (MG)
    Maple's Theory of Fun, Kate McMillan (MG)
    The Strange Case of Origami Yoda, Tom Angleberger (MG)
    The Terrible Two, Mac Barnett and Jory John (MG)

CHAPTER 17

DELIGHT AND WISDOM: THE JOY OF POETRY

> Even the silence
> Has a story to tell you.
> Just listen. Listen.[1]
>
> —Jacqueline Woodson, *Brown Girl Dreaming*

P oetry is one of the oldest literary genres in the world. Homer's great epics were written in verse. Shakespeare wrote primarily in poetic form. *Beowulf, The Canterbury Tales, Paradise Lost*, the original Arthurian legends—all were written as poetry. A third of the Bible is poetry. And yet, many readers tell us they do not understand, enjoy, or have time to bother with poetry.

Those readers are missing out. If you do not seek to appreciate poetry, you will lack a fundamental understanding of some of the greatest works of literature, including God's Word. Literature professor Gene Edward Veith, Jr., argues:

> *Modern poetry as well as classic poetry and Biblical poetry deserve the attention of contemporary Christians. If poets are the unacknowledged legislators of the world as Shelley says . . . then Christians dare not*

---

1. Jacqueline Woodson, *Brown Girl Dreaming* (Puffin Books, 2014), 278.

surrender poetry's influence on the whole mind to the rock musicians or to avant garde nihilists. Christians should think of poetry as well as music when they are enjoined to "speak to one another with psalms, hymns, and spiritual songs" (Ephesians 5:19).[2]

Author Ruth Sawyer urges:

In this modern world of slipshod education, of incessant hurry, of space rockets and of threatened destruction, children need to hear the singing heart of the world. Poetry brings to the growing years something nothing else can bring, whether it be the psalm-poetry of David, the fairy songs of Shakespeare, or the sea poems of John Masefield.[3]

Poetry requires us to slow down and listen. The further students advance in their schooling, the more we pile onto their plates, which leaves less room for the slow, meditative practice of poetry. It is true that the pleasure of poetry may not generate measurable results on comprehension tests the way novels do, but the overall rewards for both mind and heart make reading poetry worth the time. Veith highlights the rewards for Christians in particular:

Poetry has been called "a trap for meditation." When we read a poem about a little star or God battering the heart or a Grecian urn or the wrath of Achilles, the language and the form of the poem cause us to respond with our minds and feelings, concentrating and reflecting on some aspect of life. This sort of meditation can be a valuable discipline for a Christian.[4]

Christians should cultivate poetry appreciation in their homes and classrooms because poetry helps us creatively use words to communicate, both with

---

2. Gene Edward Veith, Jr., *Reading Between the Lines: A Christian Guide to Literature* (Crossway, 1990), 97.
3. Ruth Sawyer, *The Way of the Storyteller: A Great Storyteller Shares Her Rich Experience and Joy in Her Art and Tells Eleven of Her Best-Loved Stories* (Penguin, 1977), 201.
4. Veith, *Reading Between the Lines*, 85.

God and our neighbor. Poetry marries delight with wisdom[5] and need not be difficult to understand. You just might find that you like it. Bonus: Once you begin to enjoy poetry, you are ready to read the richest works of literature.

5 Steps to Cultivating Poetry Appreciation

Since poetry is important for Christians, and we want to encourage delight as well as build discernment in our children, how do we begin?

Step 1: Lay a Foundation of Delight

We lay a foundation of delighting in words and build on this foundation by keeping poetry in the mix of what we read to and with our children. In *Honey for a Child's Heart*, Gladys Hunt writes, "Poems, like good seasonings, should be sprinkled lightly on the life of a child. One here, another delightful one there."[6] If poetry is the seasoning for a rich reading life, then read it alongside fairy tales, easy readers, classics, and picture books. Think of poetry like cinnamon: no one wants to eat cinnamon plain, but no one wants to eat pumpkin bread, apple pie, or a cinnamon roll without it!

When your children sit in your lap for stories, include nursery rhymes and rhyming books. Babies and toddlers love them! All rhyming books are not created equal; pay attention to the text. Does it "sing"? Or is it only singsongy? Look for Mother Goose collections in your local library. Invest in a good children's poetry anthology (or two), complete with illustrations and poems on a wide variety of subjects that children enjoy, such as animals and seasons. Pick poems at random; sprinkle them in at night when you read a bedtime story or

> *We lay a foundation of delighting in words and build on this foundation by keeping poetry in the mix of what we read to and with our children.*

---

5. Robert Frost: An oft-quoted line is "Poetry begins in delight and ends in wisdom."
6. Gladys Hunt, *Honey for a Child's Heart Updated and Expanded* (Zondervan, 2021), 53.

read one at breakfast each morning.

Soon, children will start to request their favorites. Do not be surprised when they start reciting simple poems back to you. Encourage them to find new poems to share with you. National "Poem-in-Your-Pocket" Day happens every April (National Poetry Month), but you can reward children any day of the year for having a poem in their pocket to share with you. Hugs, chocolate, and exuberant recitation can all serve as rewards.

Step 2: Memorize Poetry

When children are around age four or five, consider memorizing poetry more intentionally. Very short poems such as nursery rhymes work just as well as longer works. Your children may already know them by heart. Be sure to include some psalms as well; Psalms 23 and 100 are excellent starting points.

As children enter elementary school and have a better grasp of language, they begin to enjoy funny poems (such as those by Shel Silverstein or from Chris Harris's hilarious *I'm Just No Good at Rhyming*). A Redeemed Reader favorite includes the very silly: "The vulture eats between his meals/ And that's the reason why/ He very rarely feels/ As well as you or I."[7] Edward Lear's limericks are also favorites.

Poems by Robert Louis Stevenson and A. A. Milne are perfect for kids ready for slightly longer works. As children grow, consider having them memorize dramatic works such as "Charge of the Light Brigade" by Tennyson, word-play poems such as "Jabberwocky" by Lewis Carroll, or longer portions of Scripture (like Job 38).

A poetry recitation at the end of a season or semester is fun for all and offers a little performance reward for the hard work of memorizing. Serve some snacks, invite some friends, and make an evening of it. Grown-ups should recite too!

---

7. Hilaire Belloc, "The Vulture," Poetry.com.

Step 3: Understand Poets and Poetry

How do we start understanding poetry, not merely enjoying the sound of the words? In elementary school, introduce poets as authors, reading selections by one poet over a few weeks or months. Read one poem a day or every few days without worrying whether you cover every poem by a poet. Good poets for this age group include Robert Frost, Christina Rossetti, Paul Laurence Dunbar,[8] and Henry Wadsworth Longfellow.

Picture book versions of longer, narrative poems (such as Longfellow's patriotic poetry) offer excellent entry points. The Poetry for Young People series collects a poet's best works into convenient picture book form. Explore more contemporary poets for children (such as Douglas Florian, Valerie Worth, and others) alongside these more classic authors.

By middle school, children who have grown up listening to and delighting in poetry will be ready to learn about basic poetic techniques and terminology (such as identifying the meter of a poem), but it's better to enjoy poetry than to dissect it. Adult readers of poetry do not explicate each poem they read; they simply read it and let the poem settle. Discuss the terms casually as you come across them in the poetry you read. If you do not know what a sonnet is, then learn alongside your children and students. Any good language arts textbook will include a glossary of terms such as "simile" or "sonnet." Understanding some basics will help you and your children appreciate the skill demonstrated by a poet and discuss his or her work intelligently.

Step 4: Bridge the Gap—Verse Novels

Children on the verge of puberty—that upheaval wreaking havoc in middle schools and families across the country—are ready to grapple with more emotionally resonant texts. Add in some verse novels along with your prose

---

8. Look for the book *Jump Back, Honey*, illustrated by Brian Collier, for a terrific introduction to Dunbar.

novels. Verse novels are simply stories told in verse (poetry). They provide more immediate windows into the protagonist's thoughts and feelings than traditional prose narratives, but this does not mean they are "fluffy" or sentimental. Good options for both girls and boys are available, such as *The Crossover* by Kwame Alexander (about a basketball-loving boy) or *Inside Out and Back Again* by Thanhhà Lai (about a young girl refugee).

Verse novels are quick reads and help train the eye and brain to read a story smoothly, despite frequent line breaks and white space. This is excellent preparation for the great epic poems of Homer and Virgil or Shakespeare's plays. In addition, verse novels help children talk about big ideas and abstract feelings.

Middle school is also an ideal time to try reading a longer narrative poem aloud, in short bits. It may take a while, but children will enjoy the story. Do practice reading the work aloud before you dive into a lengthy poem like *The Rime of the Ancient Mariner*! Not only do you need to know how to pronounce names, but you need to learn the poet's rhythm. Let children draw stick figure comics or stage a scene with LEGO building blocks while you read one section at a time. Offer short summaries ahead of time and/or encourage your children to retell what happened afterward. Some children may need plot "hooks" ahead of time to help them keep up with the story.

Step 5: Read Epic Poetry and More

When teens enter high school with an interest in words, an appreciation for poetic language, and a few verse novels in mind, then *Beowulf* or Homer's *Odyssey* is the logical next step. Don't bother with workbooks or reading guides; just plunge in and allow readers to get caught up in the action. Will Beowulf slay the dragon? Will Odysseus make it home? Read one section at a time, slowly, and let the story sink in.

A word on translations here: Older translations are more elegant and elevated. Newer translations offer more immediate access for contemporary readers.[9] Both have their place. Read a portion of several and choose the one you think is the best fit for your readers.

Teens are ready for more sophisticated poets and analysis. Try reading John Donne, George Herbert, Anne Bradstreet, or Malcolm Guite with them as devotional reading. Dive into the rich prophetic works of the Old Testament. Parts of Isaiah are simply breathtaking (try Isaiah 11, or 25, or 40, or 53).

Do not try to figure out each word's precise meaning. As you continue to read poetry and God's Word over and over, you will understand them better. And you can remind your teens when they read Homer that he was probably writing down his stories when the Israelites were taken into captivity in Assyria! What biblical poetry do we have from that same period? How does the picture of hospitality in the *Odyssey* inform our understanding of similar biblical commands? Let the texts talk to one another and worry less about "analyzing" correctly.

What if your teens (or you) do not have a foundation in poetry appreciation? Instead of beginning with John Donne, try Robert Frost. Read the aforementioned picture book versions of Longfellow's poetry before tackling John Milton. Novels in verse are excellent precursors to Homer's *Iliad*. In fact, learning to enjoy poetry and demystifying those strange line breaks will do far more to prepare them to read Homer than dumbed-down prose summaries of the *Iliad* on repeat.

Betsy's three teens still launch into impromptu poetry recitations when they see "whirlygig beetles,"[10] feel sick,[11] or it's too quiet.[12] Why? Because they read, reread, and listened to poetry together as children. They recited poetry and listened to their friends recite. After a lifetime of delighting in words,

---

9. Please note that older translations will handle sexuality much like the King James Bible, veiled. New translations can be far more blunt!
10. Paul Fleischman, *Joyful Noise: Poems for Two Voices* (Harper Trophy, 1988), 32.
11. Shel Silverstein, "Sick," in *Where the Sidewalk Ends* (HarperCollins Children's Books, 2003).
12. Chris Harris, "I Love Quiet," in *I'm Just No Good at Rhyming* (Little Brown and Company, 2017), 122.

they appreciate a wide range of verse, including Shakespeare and Homer. The simple layering of poetic language year after year yields fruit. It is not hard, but it does require consistent perseverance.

"Poetry begins with delight and ends with wisdom," wrote Robert Frost. If we want to raise readers who delight in words and can bring wisdom to bear, then poetry should have its place in the canon, especially for Christians.

BOOKLIST FOR CHAPTER 17

Further Reading

Soul in Paraphrase, Leland Ryken

For Children/Teens

Joyful Noise, Paul Fleischman (Picture Book; must be read aloud by two or more people)
Kyoshi's Walk, Mark Karlins (PB)
My Daddy Rules the World, Hope Anita Smith (PB)
When Green Becomes Tomatoes, Julie Fogliano (PB)
All the Small Poems and Fourteen More, Valerie Worth (anthology)
I'm Just No Good at Rhyming: And Other Nonsense for Mischievous Kids and Immature Grown-Ups, Chris Harris and Lane Smith (anthology)
The Random House Book of Poetry for Children (anthology)
Sing a Song of Seasons: A Nature Poem for Each Day of the Year, Fiona Waters, illustrated by Franna Preston-Gannon (anthology)
Brown Girl Dreaming, Jacqueline Woodson (Middle Grade novel in verse)
Inside Out and Back Again, Thanhhà Lai (MG novel in verse)
One Last Word, Nikki Grimes (MG)

CHAPTER 18

WEIRD NEW WORLDS: SCI-FI AND DYSTOPIA

"It was a dark and stormy night."[1]
—Madeleine L'Engle, *A Wrinkle in Time*

Science fiction movies are big business: epic stories played out on the big screen with equally epic special effects.[2] Consider the longevity of the Jurassic Park and Star Trek franchises. At its broadest, science fiction is a fantasy story in which the fantastic elements (that is, the ones that, strictly speaking, cannot currently happen) are driven by science instead of magic. Some sci-fi stories zero in on laboratory science, experimentation, and "real world" consequences. Jurassic Park is a clear example. Others capitalize on space and extraterrestrial activity (and creatures). In addition to Star Trek, stories like *Independence Day* or *The War of the Worlds* cater to this niche.

Dystopian movies and literature are another subset, often bringing together scientific elements from one with the outer space element of the other to create a frightening and unjust futuristic society that functions more as a critique of our world than merely an escape from it. Common elements

---

1. Madeleine L'Engle, *A Wrinkle in Time* (Square Fish, 2007), 7.
2. Much of the first part of this chapter is based on (and quoted from) a Redeemed Reader blog post: "Science, Ethics, and Philosophy: The Need for Science Fiction," https://redeemedreader.com/2018/06/philosophy-science-ethics-the-need-for-science-fiction/.

include "oppressive societal control and the illusion of a perfect society."[3]

As our society's technological capabilities increase, our science fiction stories grow ever more elaborate with ever more astounding special effects; our dystopian literature presents eerily possible scenarios. But sci-fi is more than blockbuster specials and quirky, niche reads. Science fiction, including dystopian fiction, kindles discussion of big ideas more effectively than many other genres. Why? It asks big questions and poses potential solutions, particularly regarding the nature of humanity itself. For instance, *The Giver* brings young readers face to face with heavy issues like abortion and euthanasia, asking essentially: What makes us human? What is the value of human life? What does it mean to be made in God's image—to be an image bearer? Good science fiction poses answers that could happen, and that almost-but-not-yet quality is what really gets readers thinking.

Science Fiction as a Genre

Science fiction in its present guise is directly tied to the nineteenth century, sparked by Darwin's theory of evolution, the Industrial Revolution and the resulting mechanization of our world, and the increasing emphasis on science in general (as opposed to religion or philosophy). As such, it is distinctly Western and modern. *Frankenstein*, written in 1818 by Mary Shelley, is widely regarded as one of the first science fiction novels.

A little over two hundred years have passed, and many science fiction works are still asking the same questions that Victor Frankenstein did in his lab: *Can I create life? If I do, what will happen?* For contemporary answers to that, look no further than *Jurassic Park* (it was a book before it was a movie!). Kenneth Oppel's Bloom trilogy asks similar questions as does the Above

---

3. Read Write Think, "Dystopias: Definition and Characteristics," NCTE, 2006, https://www.readwritethink.org/sites/default/files/resources/lesson_images/lesson926/DefinitionCharacteristics.pdf.

World series by Jenn Reese.[4] Both Reese and Oppel dive into genetic manipulation in their works. If this sounds eerily familiar to current headlines, that's because it is. In fact, the 2024 Nobel Prize in Chemistry went to three scientists, one of whom "succeeded with the almost impossible feat of building entirely new kinds of proteins."[5] Scientists are currently working on resurrecting the woolly mammoth, beginning with "woolly mice."[6]

M. T. Anderson's novel *Feed*, published in 2002, raises interesting questions related to the intersection of human nature with a "feed" directly implanted in the brain. This feed functions much like our smartphones do today, although the book predates smartphones by several years. The conclusion of the book: People are essentially cyborgs after living long enough with the "feed." Prescient about the future of a culture consumed with their smartphones? Due to foul language and crude comments, this is a book best reserved for mature teens, but it is an outstanding discussion starter. We are blind to our own idiosyncrasies, but we notice these issues in a book. May we ask ourselves, "Am I becoming more like my machine? Or more like Christ?"

Stories like *Dune* show us epic battles of good vs. evil and the ways in which societies use technology to further their own, often selfish, ends. When contemporary world powers start discussing their nuclear arsenals in similar fashion, we begin to wonder: To what end?

Why does sci-fi bring up big issues so effectively? American science fiction author Ursula Le Guin sums it up well:

---

4. As mentioned earlier, the Bloom Trilogy has some considerations parents may wish to review before reading; our website review contains details. The Above World trilogy is an example, not necessarily a recommendation.
5. Royal Swedish Academy of Sciences, Press Release, October 9, 2024, https://www.nobelprize.org/prizes/chemistry/2024/press-release/.
6. Katie Hunt, "Scientists Created a 'Woolly Mouse' with Mammoth Traits. Is It a Step Toward Bringing Back the Extinct Giant?," CNN Science, March 5, 2025, https://www.cnn.com/2025/03/04/science/woolly-mouse-mammoth-resurrection-colossal/index.html.

> *We who hobnob with hobbits and tell tall tales about little green men are quite used to being dismissed as mere entertainers, or sternly disapproved as escapists. But I think that perhaps the categories are changing, like the times. Sophisticated readers are accepting the fact that an improbable and unmanageable world is going to produce an improbable and hypothetical art. At this point, realism is perhaps the least adequate means of understanding or portraying the incredible realities of our existence. A scientist who creates a monster in his laboratory; a librarian in the library of Babel; a wizard unable to cast a spell; a space ship having trouble in getting to Alpha Centauri: all these may be precise and profound metaphors of the human condition. The fantasist, whether he uses the ancient archetypes of myth and legend or the younger ones of science and technology, may be talking as seriously as any sociologist—and a good deal more directly—about human life as it is lived, and as it might be lived, and as it ought to be lived.*[7]

Science fiction is modern fantasy that presents the human condition "as it is lived, and as it might be lived, and as it ought to be lived." It shows us our potential if science and technology continue to progress: What might we, as a human race, accomplish? (And, as in the case of *Feed*, do we *want* to accomplish that?) What sorts of issues should we consider? (Malcolm, in *Jurassic Park*, would remind us that life cannot be controlled.) Where does the line between human and machine/artificial life begin and end? (Jonas, in *The Giver*, is beginning to learn some of that. So, too, does Victor Frankenstein.)

We could read current events articles about these issues. But science fiction removes the discussion to a weird new world, a world that (currently) doesn't, and (probably) cannot, exist. Thus, our discussion happens in abstract terms. We aren't as emotionally invested or politically divided. A serious, intellectual book discussion can occur in which readers wrestle with big ideas in the book without hiding behind politically correct answers.

---

7. Ursula K. LeGuin, "National Book Award Acceptance Speech," in *The Language of the Night: Essays on Fantasy and Science Fiction* (Perigee Books, 1979), 57–58.

Dystopian Fiction as a (Sub-) Genre

Dystopian fiction uses elements of science fiction to portray a degenerate world recognizable as our own, populated with beings recognizable as us.[8] It often takes the form of a cautionary tale: If present trends continue, something like this could happen. The two great classic examples of dystopian fiction, *1984* and *Brave New World*, are often required reading in high school. Dystopian literature has won a respectable place in the literary pantheon, especially for a form so relatively new.

In science fiction's early days, futuristic projections emanated optimism, such as the astonishing inventions and conveniences in Jules Verne's work. But something happened between now and then, not least of which is two world wars, numerous instances of genocide, countless petty dictatorships, weapons of mass destruction and mass weapons of destruction. Those events might have affected our current less-than-cheery outlook. But the explosion of dystopian fiction in children's literature—especially YA—is both troubling and intriguing. What distinguishes youth dystopias from the adult variety? Why now? And what is the Christian response?

Besides being uniformly grim, dystopian novels typically share:

- A post-apocalyptic future—The story opens after an event of universal destruction so huge that humanity must reorganize itself along new principles, usually some variation of survival of the fittest.

- A young hero trapped in circumstances seemingly beyond his/her control—Most have accepted the status quo or don't realize there might be anything better, until something happens to shake up their complacence.

---

8. Much of the dystopian section of this chapter was taken from Janie's three-part series at Redeemed Reader: "Dystopia: Dead Ahead," December 23, 2010, https://redeemedreader.com/2010/12/dystopia-dead-ahead/; "Dystopia, Part Two," January 25, 2011, https://redeemedreader.com/2011/01/dystopia-part-two/; "Dystopia, Part Three," January 25, 2011, https://redeemedreader.com/2011/01/dystopia-part-three/.

- A "quest" plot usually involving escape and sometimes a journey.
- Pretentious statements about how this story is "eerily relevant" to modern-day events.

But what does it all mean? A few possibilities exist for why some young adults are drawn to grim futurist fiction.

First, over the last several years, there's been a general degradation of leadership, or at least how we view leadership. Recent presidential elections have not seen a return to civil public discourse. Bad temper tends to beget more bad temper, and rhetoric has escalated in a way that undoubtedly affects teens. One common characteristic of all dystopias is terrible leaders, so it's no stretch to suppose that smashmouth politics has influenced YA writers and readers.

Second, we live under the shadow of actual nuclear holocaust. Janie's generation was the first to grow up with the possibility of destroying the planet. She remembers backyard bomb shelters and air raid drills at school and lying awake at night during the Cuban Missile Crisis, wondering if her hometown was a big enough population center for the Communists to attack. Subsequent generations have lived with their own visions of hell-in-a-handbasket: nuclear war, environmental disaster, economic collapse. Teens these days have been indoctrinated from elementary school with doom-and-gloom predictions of climate change (some version of which haunts the post-apocalypses of *Ship Breaker* and *The Hunger Games*, among others).

Third, teenagers tend to be natural self-dramatizers. It is the logical result of gaining the appearance of adulthood without its perspective, when every (perceived) slight is a game-changer and every flaw dooms one's chances of success forever. Laura Miller, writing in the *New Yorker*, proposes that most teens live in a real dystopia known as high school, a hothouse of unbridled ambition and supercharged inspection, magnified on social media. Surveillance cameras (also known as peers) are everywhere, and no misstep will go unpunished.[9] It's always been so, but perhaps today more than ever, and readers see in the adventures of a Jonas or a Katniss a metaphor for real life. Their social media reels don't feel all that different from the latest blockbuster dystopian reality.

Fourth, every generation needs a narrative, an organizing principle to shape their idea of destiny. Are we pioneers or the last of our breed? Is the future ours or someone else's? Can we look forward to expanding or shrinking opportunity? Many young readers today seem to lean more toward the idea of a diminished future, which dystopian novels reinforce as do many news headlines. But that's where the fifth reason comes in:

Fifth, there's always a hero who joins forces with one or two others to buck the tide. Going it alone is the most reliable element of dystopian fiction, and it hits teens at a time in their lives when individual determination is crucial. Until the age of twelve or so, they're defined by family; in early adolescence they look to their peers. Now, they have to figure out who they are individually, the precise dilemma faced by the protagonists of these novels they're reading. Todd Hewett of the Chaos Walking series must find out if he's capable of killing. Katniss Everdeen of *The Hunger Games* trilogy must discover if she's capable of loving. They all must navigate perilous environments where one mistake could cost their lives. That's what getting to independent adulthood can look like to a thoughtful, introspective teen. These young people in extremity are characters to relate to and copy; one thing they all share is courage.

How to Read Sci-Fi and Dystopian Literature

What's the problem with a glut of grim, futurist fiction on the YA bookshelves?

Maybe nothing. Youth is resilient, and most young people are smart enough to know that fiction is fiction. If their reading is balanced, and they get out in the fresh air often enough, no harm done. Too much of anything

---

9. Laura Miller, "Fresh Hell," *New Yorker*, June 7, 2010, https://www.newyorker.com/magazine/2010/06/14/fresh-hell-laura-miller.

has its effect, though, whether good or bad. A teen whose homelife is rather dystopian probably doesn't need any more depressing stories. What better way to reinforce the view that life holds little good for him? A steady diet of grim fiction might convince a young person that death, struggle, strife, and dissatisfaction are "reality," while happy families, lasting marriages, and easily solvable problems are the stuff of old sitcoms.[10] Remember, C. S. Lewis's character Screwtape advised his nephew to convince his human that war and destruction are "real," while children playing on a green hillside is cheap sentimentality.

There's also a theological "problem" with post-apocalyptic scenarios. All's fair in fiction, to a point, but could there really be life after the apocalypse? When Jesus returns, isn't that the end? Yes, we realize that Christians disagree as to exactly what happens when, but if Jesus' death and resurrection is the turning point of history, His return would seem to close the door. Can there be a future where civilization is utterly destroyed but the Lord still tarries?

C. S. Lewis solved the problem this way: *That Hideous Strength*, the third in his space trilogy, is a pre-apocalyptic dystopian novel, so to speak. The action takes place shortly after World War II, when the British government has been taken over by visionaries, utopians, and outright scoundrels who negotiate with supernatural forces in their quest for power. Catastrophe comes perilously near but is averted in the nick of time by a small resistance group with God on their side. *That Hideous Strength* is a bit didactic and wordy and may be hard for teens to get into. But it is well worth reading and actually *is* "eerily relevant" to modern-day events!

Both science fiction and its dystopian child raise thought-provoking issues and questions we do well to discuss with our teens (and preteens). As with all genres, considering the maturity level of young readers is important, but it is especially important with these genres because the lines get blurry regarding what is real (i.e., "actually possible *and* probable") and what is not

---

10. We addressed this in chapter 13, on Dark YA literature, as well.

(i.e., "interesting thought experiment but not probable"). Good science fiction leaves readers pondering abstract, big ideas that some young readers simply aren't ready to think about. If your child is struggling with pre-algebra, perhaps wait on sci-fi and dystopian literature. Why? Because pre-algebra is when students really begin to leverage abstract reasoning in their schoolwork. Science fiction demands similar levels of thinking! We've intentionally referred to "teens" in this chapter for a reason.

When you and your children or students are ready to dive into science fiction, keep the following classic worldview questions in mind. The better you can deduce what the novel is proposing in these areas, the easier it is to tease out the nuances lurking behind cyborgs, authoritarian governments militating against fairy tales, the Thought Police requiring citizens to report on neighbors, and what the feed is actually doing to society.

Both science fiction and its dystopian child raise thought-provoking issues and questions we do well to discuss with our teens (and preteens).

- **Is there a higher power? What is it?** A godlike figure? A machine? A vague nebulous "center"? How would the characters in the book describe it/him/her?

- **Who or what determines morality?** The good of society? The ability to do something mechanically? The absence of strife? An overlord or council of autocratic elders? Vague tradition from before the apocalypse? A follow-up question: Who or what administers consequences? Is there any grace apparent in the system?

- **What is the nature of humanity?** Perhaps the primary consideration in science fiction, what is humanity like? What is it capable of? What determines its limits? (scientific ability? God?)

- **What happens when humans die?** Do they "die" or has some other term replaced this word to indicate a different sort of understanding? Has most of humanity already died and a small remnant is left picking up the pieces? Is death wielded clinically as a solution to society's ills (like in *Scythe* or *The Giver*)? Do humans die but robots survive?

- **Is there an afterlife? What is it like?** If the book is apocalyptic, this answer is easier. What is presented as the ideal world? When people are creating a new society, how do they envision it? If humanity is engaged in a desperate struggle against alien bugs (such as in *Starship Troopers*), for what are they ultimately fighting? God and country? A frantic push to save civilization because there is nothing else?

That said, don't make every science fiction or dystopian story an opportunity for sermonizing. Do take opportunities when they present themselves to engage with your teens and with these ideas. Teens themselves are wrestling with these questions in their own lives. Helping them parse the ideas present in a popular book trains them to be discerning.

Readers, we have a tremendous opportunity to raise Christian thinkers—and scientists and technicians who are willing to grapple with the big ideas present in the work they do in their laboratories. Don't spend all your reading time in the worlds of realistic and historical fiction. Be willing to engage with science fiction and dystopian literature even when the aliens make you roll your eyes or the scenario presented horrifies you.[11] Some of the best discussions we've had with our children have been in relation to science fiction.

---

11. "Horrifies you" simply means a world such as presented in *The Giver*. We are not advocating for readers to engage with books like *The Handmaid's Tale* or other works that flagrantly use sexuality and violence to shock readers even more than encouraging them to think.

BOOKLIST FOR CHAPTER 18

Further Reading

    Of Other Worlds: Essays and Stories, C. S. Lewis

For Children/Teens

SCIENCE FICTION

    A Rover's Story, Jasmine Warga (Middle Grade)

    Wake Up Missing, Kate Messner (MG)

    The Mutant Mushroom Takeover, Summer Rachel Short (MG)

    Cinder, Marissa Meyer (Young Adult)

    Ultraviolet, R. J. Anderson (YA)

    The Man Who Was Thursday, G. K. Chesterton (YA/Adult)

DYSTOPIAN

    The Giver, Lois Lowry (MG)

    Mysteries of Cove series, Scott Savage (MG)

    Scythe, Neal Shusterman (YA; only first in series is recommended and comes with cautions)

    MindWar, Andrew Klavan (YA)

    Landscape with Invisible Hand, M. T. Anderson (see also *Feed* by M. T. Anderson; both are YA with significant cautions)

CHAPTER 19

THE HORNS OF ELFLAND: ON READING FANTASY

> Ella fetched the milk from the doorstep. Just as she stepped out
> a strange lady stepped in, carrying a fancy umbrella.
> "I am your Fairy Godmother," she told Ella, briskly peeling off her gloves.
> "It's my job to see that you go to the ball, so let's not waste time."[1]
>
> —Shirley Hughes, *Ella's Big Chance*

> You'll have to make up your own mind, but I, for one,
> like Cinderella and elves and talking animals and even Santa Claus.
> Children don't take life as seriously as adults and are more inclined
> to read for pleasure without theorizing until all the fun is wrung out.[2]
>
> —Gladys Hunt, *Honey for a Child's Heart*

The very mention of fantasy and characters like Santa Claus can spark lively discussions, debates, and arguments. So, before we proceed further, let us center this discussion with a reminder: God is sovereign. He is sovereign over creation. He is sovereign over every story ever written. He is sovereign over the reading of stories.

---

1. Shirley Hughes, *Ella's Big Chance: A Jazz-Age Cinderella* (Simon & Schuster Books for Young Readers, 2004), n. p.
2. Gladys Hunt, *Honey for a Child's Heart* (Zondervan, 2010), 32.

In God's goodness, we are given a responsibility to exercise discernment in the stories we read. Due to certain factors, the fantasy genre of children's literature requires discernment. There are many compelling arguments for reading fantasy, so we are going to approach this topic from the other direction and explore three reasons why *not* to read fantasy.

The X Factor

Whether in a picture book retelling of Cinderella or a novel like those in the Harry Potter series, readers of fantasy will encounter the idea of magic and the supernatural. Sometimes these elements are overt with witches, spells, curses, and elves. Sometimes they are more muted within a subgenre of fantasy: talking animals, a time machine, or unexplained magic without any source.

Because of supernatural elements, not all readers are comfortable with fantasy. Some readers choose not to read fantasy, interpreting the injunction of Leviticus 19:31, "Do not turn to mediums or necromancers; do not seek them out, and so make yourselves unclean by them: I am the Lord your God," as a binding command not to read fantasy. We respect their belief and see this decision as a matter of conscience. In this case, it is important to remember, in the words of Gladys Hunt, author of the classic *Honey for a Child's Heart*, "When we do not choose a book, we make that decision for *ourselves*, not for another family, a school, or the population in general."[3]

At Redeemed Reader, as readers of fantasy, we look to the apostle Paul's conclusion concerning interactions with the pagan supernatural, "yet for us there is one God, the Father, from whom are all things and for whom we exist, and one Lord, Jesus Christ, through whom are all things and through whom we exist" (1 Cor. 8:6). We believe fantasy, with its magic, falls within this understanding. We also believe that fantasy and fairy tales provide glimpses of the greater Story. Tolkien, in his essay "On Fairy-Stories," points to this truth:

---

3. Gladys Hunt, *Honey for a Child's Heart Updated and Expanded* (Zondervan, 2021), 23.

It is the mark of a good fairy-story, of the higher or more complete kind, that however wild its events, however fantastic or terrible the adventures, it can give to child or man that hears it, when the "turn" comes, a catch of the breath, a beat and lifting of the heart, near to (or indeed accompanied by) tears, as keen as that given by any form of literary art, and having a peculiar quality.[4]

Tolkien continues, "The peculiar quality of the 'joy' in successful Fantasy can thus be explained as a sudden glimpse of the underlying reality or truth."[5] Tolkien catalogs these glimpses, noting the prohibition evident even in a story like Peter Rabbit: "you shall not" (go into the garden) lest you die (be put in a pie.)[6] He likens these prohibitions to echoes, or "horns of elfland" that point back to the greater Truth.[7]

Indeed, fantasy lends itself to both Truth and the encouragement of wonder. C. S. Lewis realized such a connection in nature, writing: "Nature never taught me that there exists a God of glory and of infinite majesty. I had to learn that in other ways. But nature gave the word glory a meaning for me."[8] Fantasy, in its wonder and prohibitions, can also give the word *glory* a meaning. But what about when fantasy turns dark?

> *Fantasy lends itself to both Truth and the encouragement of wonder.*

Unbiblical Fantasy

Nikabrik, the black dwarf in *Prince Caspian* muses, "The stories tell of other powers besides the ancient Kings and Queens. How if we could call *them* up?"[9] At first his listeners think he is referring to the great lion, Aslan. But

---

4. J. R. R. Tolkien, *A Tolkien Miscellany* (Quality Paperback Book Club, 2002), 136.
5. Ibid., 137.
6. Ibid., 115.
7. Ibid., 135.
8. C. S. Lewis, *The Four Loves* (Harcourt, Brace and Company, 1960), 37.
9. C. S. Lewis, *Prince Caspian: The Return to Narnia* (HarperCollins, 1994), 167.

no, Nikabrik has someone else in mind—"We want power: and we want a power that will be on our side." When Caspian realizes Nikabrik's plan is to call on the White Witch, he is appalled at the prospect of "black sorcery and the calling up of an accursed ghost."[10] This exchange captures the difference between magic as a story construct, and magic associated with darkness.

Thankfully, most children's fantasy does not portray necromancy as a good thing. However, as we are discussing magic in stories, it is worth noting this is an issue in children's nonfiction. We have noticed a growing collection of supernatural "nonfiction" targeting young readers. Books like *The Junior Witch's Handbook* purport to be "a kid's guide to white magic, spells, and rituals."[11] Meanwhile, *The Little Witch's Book of Spells* is a beautifully illustrated guide that assures readers, "You are a witch if you feel somehow different or special, and believe that within your uniqueness lies your power."[12] The library puts these books in the children's section under 133 in the Dewey Decimal System: nonfiction dealing in the occult. While these books might appeal to a young reader on the hunt for a new fantasy novel, this is an example of unbiblical magic to avoid. Inviting a reader's active participation in magic is different from describing magic in a fictional narrative such as Harry Potter.

The apostle Paul writes, "For we do not wrestle against flesh and blood, but against the rulers, against the authorities, against the cosmic powers over this present darkness, against the spiritual forces of evil in the heavenly places" (Eph. 6:12). We recognize that our world is one that contains good and evil, angels and demons, light and darkness. Sometimes in stories, the supernatural power portrayed overtly subverts what Scripture teaches. What the Bible calls evil is shown as good. Heroes use "black sorcery" with impunity. The use of magic is enlightened while faith/religion is repressive. Magical power is used with an "ends-justify-the-means" attitude. While we live in a fallen world

---

10. Ibid., 170–71.
11. This is the book's subtitle.
12. Ariel Kusby, introduction to *The Little Witch's Book of Spells* (Chronicle Books, 2020).

where the wicked sometimes prosper, fantasy that endorses and glamorizes such narratives is problematic.

Another troubling element of fantasy for some readers is the presence of supernatural elements with real world parallels. Pentagrams occur in Jonathan Stroud's Bartimaeus Trilogy as well as in the world of Diana Wynne Jones's middle grade fiction. Possession crops up in the Bartimaeus Trilogy, too, as well as in Angie Sage's Septimus Heap series. We often note such supernatural elements in our reviews since some readers feel they are too closely linked to biblical prohibitions. However, we ultimately recommended the above titles to our readers because of our final metric for reviewing fantasy. This involves asking the following question:

How Does the Story End?

We recognize the existence of evil. Yet, as Christians, we do not live in fear of it. With the Puritan writer of *Valley of Vision* we can say:

> Calvary broke the dragon's head,
> and I contend with a vanquished foe,
> who with all his subtlety and strength
> has already been overcome.[13]

When good triumphs over evil in fantasy, we are reminded of this gospel truth. Gene Edward Veith writes in his essay on Christianity and fantasy: "By definition, fantasy is wholly imaginary. It is not reality, but it can provide a way to think about reality."[14] A young student who sat in on Tolkien's lectures, Diana Wynne Jones, went on to write magical, whimsical fantasy. Though not a person of faith, Jones recognized the power of fantasy to shape a child's worldview. Reflecting on this, she wrote, "You make clear that it is make-believe. And by

---

13. *The Valley of Vision* (Banner of Truth Trust, 2003), 328.
14. Gene Edward Veith, "Good Fantasy & Bad Fantasy | Christian Research Institute," www.equip.org, April 20, 2009, https://www.equip.org/articles/good-fantasy-and-bad-fantasy-2-article/.

showing it applies to nobody, you show that it applies to everyone. It is the way all fairy tales work."[15]

Discernment involves more than just the ending of the story.

Q. In your fantasy, what virtues are being exemplified?

E.g., In the adventures of Bilbo Baggins, an ordinary hobbit, we see perseverance, courage, and loyalty.

Q. As you read, consider: Is authority something respected or something to be defied? Does disobedience have consequences?

E.g., Although we have greatly enjoyed Harry Potter, we deplore all the sneaking about after hours that keeps getting "rewarded" with house cups!

Q. Are there wise, older characters, or are the young the only ones who can fix the problem and save the world?

E.g., The "chosen one" motif can be particularly problematic. In the first book of the popular Keeper of the Lost Cities series, we've noted this particular theme causes some overall concern as it glorifies youth and removes adults and authority figures from the character's decision-making.[16]

Reading fantasy in light of such questions led us to recommend books by Jonathan Stroud, Diana Wynne Jones, and Angie Sage. We believe the books' overall messages and worldview can remind children of the greater Truth and the truest Story. In the words of another Christian fantasy author, Madeleine L'Engle, "Fantasy gives you options. It's an attempt to touch on reality, in a way that can't be done better otherwise."[17]

---

15. Diana Wynne Jones in "Children in the Wood," in *Reflections: On the Magic of Writing* (Greenwillow Books, 2012), Kindle.

16. Betsy Farquhar, "Keeper of the Lost Cities: Is It Safe? Is It Good?," Redeemed Reader, September 19, 2022, https://redeemedreader.com/2022/09/keeper-of-the-lost-cities-is-it-safe-is-it-good/.

17. Madeline L'Engle, interview by Leonard Marcus, *The Wand in the Word: Conversations with Writers of Fantasy* (Candlewick Press, 2006), 114.

For this reason, we are comfortable with plot elements like the ghost in *Ferris* by Kate DiCamillo. Why? Because the ghost is not serving the purpose of encouraging mediums. Rather, the ghost points to a truth running through the book: "Every story is a love story. Or every good story is a love story."[18] *Ferris* ends with hope despite sorrow and encourages readers to wonder and joy. This ending reflects the ending that we, as believers, look forward to one day when we will join a heavenly feast and sorrow will be no more.

Considering the story, themes, and endings of fantasy makes it easier to differentiate the good from the problematic.

What Then Shall We Read?

For some readers, the existence of magic and/or supernatural elements is enough reason to avoid the fantasy genre and its sub-genres. For others, it is something to be weighed and considered. It is a continuum with room for conscience and conscious consideration. Still, at the end of the day, we believe the underlying truth and story is the most important weight to consider when reading fantasy. Tolkien understood this when he mused:

> *Fairy-stories deal largely, or (the better ones) mainly, with simple or fundamental things, untouched by Fantasy, but these simplicities are made all the more luminous by their setting... It was in fairy-stories that I first divined the potency of the words, and the wonder of the things, such as stone, and wood, and iron; tree and grass; house and fire; bread and wine.*[19]

When written and read rightly, fantasy can invite us to wonder, and it can remind us of our own "assurance of things hoped for, the conviction of things not seen" (Heb. 11:1).

---

18. Kate DiCamillo, *Ferris* (Candlewick Press, 2024), 6.
19. Tolkien, *A Tolkien Miscellany*, 130.

BOOKLIST FOR CHAPTER 19

Further Reading

"On Fairy-Stories," J. R. R. Tolkien

For Children/Teens

DragonQuest, Allan Baillie (Picture Book)
Three Tales of My Father's Dragon, Ruth Stiles Gannet (Chapter Book)
Inkling, Kenneth Oppel (Middle Grade)
Tuesday at the Castle series, Jessica Day George (MG)
Circus Mirandus, Cassie Beasley (MG)
Sweep, Jonathan Auxier (MG)
100 Cupboards series, N. D. Wilson (Young Adult)
No Ordinary Fairytales series, R. J. Anderson (YA)
Monster Blood Tattoo trilogy, D. M. Cornish (YA)
Mythmakers, John Hendrix (YA nonfiction, excellent exploration of fantasy)
The Song That Moves The Sun, Anna Bright (YA)
Thorn, Intisar Khanani (YA)

CHAPTER 20

BEYOND EVER AFTER: A VISION FOR CHRISTIAN ROMANCE

> "If ever two were one, then we," he whispered.
> "If ever man were loved by wife, then thee," I said, answering the words from Mistress Anne Bradstreet with the following line of the poem.
> —Marly Youmans, *Charis in the World of Wonders*[1]

What is the appeal of romance? While Hayley was in college, in her early twenties, she wrote an essay, "Reading About Romance," for Redeemed Reader. Looking back, she sees part of it as rather naïve, but still agrees with her younger self in the conclusion:

> *Whether in classics, mystery, humor, historical or general fiction, romance shares many of the same appealing elements. Why do we love good romance in books? Because, unlike life around us, we can read the last page and find a happy ending.*
>
> *We have eternity written in our hearts. We know that really, once upon a time, a prince came to his country in disguise, ready to give his life to win an undeserving bride. We know that the bride, despite her faults, is loved, valued, and cherished by Him, made beautiful in His sight.*

---

1. Marly Youmans, *Charis in the World of Wonders* (Ignatius Press, 2020), 191.

And we know, deep within us, that stories were meant to conclude with "... and they all lived happily ever after." As Christians, we can hold to the hope that someday that is just what each of our stories will do, and the end will be but a better beginning. All this is romance![2]

Why read about romance? Because romance echoes a deeper story. As humans, we long to be known, and romance offers a glimpse into deeper knowing. Romance also captures our longing for redemption and restoration. Good romances reckon with sin and have characters who struggle yet ultimately show grace, forgiveness, and love.

A good love story doesn't end with happily ever after. Instead, it shows a couple continuing to grow in love for each other. It is hopeful, but doesn't shy away from the messiness of life or marriage. This kind of romance can kindle the romantic imagination of young readers while keeping their feet grounded in the reality of this world.

Where Is the Line?

Over the years, we've fielded many questions about the topic of romance in fiction for young readers: *Should my thirteen-year-old daughter be reading clean romance novels? What do you think about closed door romance novels? Where is the line? Do you have a zero-romance booklist for my son? What books can you recommend for adults?*

Often, the questions boil down to where the line should be drawn for physical expressions of intimacy or an appeal for books that fall within a set boundary. If the phrases above left you bewildered, let's take a look at some current terms used to describe romance novels.

- Clean/Sweet: no sex, possibly no kissing, varying degrees of actual romance

---

2. Hayley Morell, "Romance + Reading = Love," Redeemed Reader, February 12, 2016, https://redeemedreader.com/2016/02/romance-reading-love/.

- Closed door: implies sexual relations but does not portray sex explicitly
- Open door: contains explicit sex scenes with varying degrees of "steam"

From these terms, one can extrapolate a zero-romance in which characters interact with each other and have absolutely no physical or emotional intimacy aside from platonic friendship.

Within clean/sweet romance exists a realm of imaginative stories where heroines fall into love (or loathing that turns out to be, goodness, love?!) and that rely on nebulous emotions versus physical butterflies to explain how romance works.

Unfortunately, not all books come with accompanying romance tags. Charlie Holmberg, a fantasy/romance author, has a diagram on her Instagram profile that digs into the romance question. Holmberg clarifies that none of her books are "steamy," and she rates her novels' romance levels by fire emoji(s): 1 - Super Chaste, 2 - Getting Saucy, 3 - Sexy times ahead.[3]

As book reviewers, we wish that all young adult authors and children's books were so transparent! Still, terms like these can help as you navigate books suitable for your readers. Using the Holmberg scale we would recommend avoiding romance levels 2 and 3 for middle grade readers. For older teenage/YA readers, romance levels 1-2 may be appropriate, but while Holmberg's #3s do not include open door sex, we would be cautious of this level since the implications are more overt. A recent popular term marketed toward YA and adult readers is "romantasy." While seemingly just a combination of "romance" and "fantasy," romantasy can often include graphic and/or deviant sexuality with "spice." Such content is not appropriate for teens.

At Redeemed Reader, we come to the idea of romance with a biblical worldview that sees sex as a gift given for marriage between one man and one woman. We enjoy romances that are clean, yet we are not against closed-door moments if the couple in question is married. We believe it is good to show

---

3. Charlie Holmberg, "Heat Levels for My Books," October 5, 2022, https://www.instagram.com/p/CjVwUPirFyg/?img_index=1.

a positive view of sex within marriage.

We also understand that sex can be horribly abused, and so we sometimes review and recommend books that are messier than these neat categories. (See chapter 9 on messy books.)

Safe, but Is It Good?

Some authors go too far down the "clean" road of romance. In these books, when marriage happens, nothing changes. The characters continue their clean banter, share kisses ... the only difference is the adventures now start from the same house. This portrayal of romance is problematic because it doesn't show a realistic "leaving and cleaving."

The problem with clean romance is that, when done poorly, these stories end up like a Thomas Kinkade painting: cozy looking and utterly unrealistic. A steady diet of this type of romance is unhealthy and will provide imaginative young readers with unhealthy expectations.

Reading and longing for romance isn't wrong, but what do we do with those feelings? It is hard to find a good romance that realistically portrays the deepening relationship between a man and a woman.

R. J. Anderson, a Christian author who writes middle grade and young adult fantasy, once told Hayley: "My conviction has become that if Christian writers refuse to talk positively about sex in a right and holy context, then the only depictions of sex in media will be unChristian and unholy (as indeed they are). I don't think there's a need for explicit details, but I also don't think we should be more conservative about sex than the Bible itself is!" She continued, "However I know that some of my Christian readers may find it offensive that I talk about it at all."[4]

We sympathize! We remember talking books one day with a homeschool mom and mentioning a good author who shared our faith. The mom said she

---

4. R. J. Anderson, Instagram DM conversation with author, 2023. Permission granted to quote August 28, 2024.

had been disappointed by that author ever since reading a YA novel that contained kissing. Hayley's husband has a rather unconventional view of kissing when talking about books that contain hints of romance. He asks, "Could they get married?" If the readers are twelve, of course not! This is a good litmus test for the helpfulness of romance in a book. Still, in the twenty-first century, one must remember we have extended adolescence. Could an eighteen-year-old get married? For most of human history the answer would be a definite yes.

A book with teenage kissing—but nothing more—could be a good discussion starter, or create space for a young teen, particularly a girl, who is starting to daydream about romance to have a conversation about romance. Young Christian teens can be encouraged to see that romance is a good thing. Reading a story like *Emily of Deep Valley* (1950) shows that, unlike the interactions in some romantic novels, it is possible to kiss a person and then say goodnight and walk away. Old books aren't the only books that contain such restraint: R. J. Anderson, Joanna Ruth Meyer, Mitali Perkins, and Andrew Klavan[5] are all recent authors who have written appropriate YA romance.

Without Christian authors reflecting that sexuality and romance are good gifts to be stewarded, young readers are just going to get the world's side that insists romance and sex are primarily for individual pleasure and fulfillment. A phrase we use at Redeemed Reader that encompasses a Christian view of romance is "beyond ever after." In one of our online discussions, Betsy recalled her younger self's

> *Without Christian authors reflecting that sexuality and romance are good gifts to be stewarded, young readers are just going to get the world's side that insists romance and sex are primarily for individual pleasure and fulfillment.*

---

5. While we recommend Andrew Klavan's young adult books, his adult books are decidedly adult when it comes to sex, and we do not recommend them for teens.

desire for something that portrayed love, courtship, and all its excitement *along with* the maturing of love in a married relationship with all its struggles and benefits. True love in a marriage is so much richer than its flashy, youthful counterpart. It's worth knowing what the reward can look like for those who continue to mature and practice self-control![6]

Janie added: "Some of the best love stories are folded into a much larger context. Romantic love is only part of the big picture, and humans err when we move it to the center. That's why it's important to nudge our kids toward healthier romantic reading and never leave the impression that romantic love conquers all, justifies all, and lasts forever. Only one kind of love does that. If our kids are graciously oriented toward the greatest love of all, they can't go wrong!"[7]

Toward a Positive, Hopeful Approach to Romance

Do you have a young reader who is drawn to romance? At Redeemed Reader, some of us were (and still are) incorrigible romantics. This looked different at different stages of our reading lives. Before the age of ten, it meant devouring every single Andrew Lang fairy tale involving a princess. The concept of romance was distant, an ideal found in fairy tales.

As a shy middle grade reader, Hayley read historical fiction and biographies, hoping to find romances within the pages. She delighted in the quiet, sweet, faithful romances she discovered. What's more, she thrilled at the passionate characters who fell in love. Hayley is not the only member of the team who promptly thinks of Elizabeth George Speare's *Calico Captive* as an example of this latter category. Janie has reflected: "That's the love story I remember loving the best, and I could have done worse. It introduced me to the idea that romantic attraction isn't enough; a suitable match also includes

---

6. Janie Cheaney, "Those Love Stories We Loved," Redeemed Reader, February 20, 2018, https://redeemedreader.com/2018/02/love-stories-loved/.
7. Ibid.

shared values and culture."[8] Notice, romance in this realm is creeping from the abstract into real life scenarios.

Love stories and romance novels do not always occupy the same space. Love stories occur within "the context of a larger story or genre," but romances are about "boy-meets-girl and what happens after that."[9] As a middle grade reader, Hayley also discovered Jane Austen and read and reread her novels. While proudly "enjoying" British literature, it was really the romance that drew her to Austen's work.

Romance in Children's Literature

Romance manifests in different ways in children's literature. A modern fairy tale like Shirley Hughes's Jazz-age retelling of Cinderella, titled *Ella's Big Chance*, is an excellent example of overt romance. Hughes's Ella, faced with the dreamy prospect of marrying a handsome duke she's spent the night dancing with, remembers her faithful friend Buttons . . . and she tells the Duke (very politely, mind you!), "No thank you . . . I'm in love with someone else."[10]

Chapter books tend toward easy, uncomplicated, platonic friendships.[11] Some middle grade stories maintain the simplicity of chapter book friendships. In *Ferris* by Kate DiCamillo (2024) Ferris's best friend is Billy Jackson. She remembers their meeting in kindergarten and Billy's request, "Can I hold your hand?"[12] However, in other middle grade books, the question begins to shift from "Can I hold your hand" to "Can I kiss you?" (as R. J. Anderson's heroine is asked in her middle grade murder mystery). Friendships between the sexes can be complicated in middle grade fiction.

---

8. Ibid.
9. Ibid.
10. Shirley Hughes, *Ella's Big Chance: A Fairy Tale Retold* (Red Fox, 2005) n. p.
11. Reading about some chapter book authors can complicate a reading of their books, but regardless of an author's personal romantic life, a good chapter book focuses on friendship above all.
12. Kate DiCamillo, *Ferris* (Candlewick Press, 2024), 2.

Middle grade novels that appeal to young teens sometimes contain romantic elements. Still, friendship tends to be the focus, with occasional awkward crush moments. Some middle grade books, like *Swallow's Flight* or *The Penderwicks* series, portray characters growing up and beginning to experience attraction toward the opposite sex. Since many middle grade readers are beginning to imagine a future involving a hazy Prince Charming, these stories might be considered "healthy" expressions of romance.

Puberty adds a whole new element of angst and is the focus of many middle grade plots. Sometimes books introduce puberty and layer in additional sexual identity issues with an occasional side of tweenage romance.

Is it wrong to want love stories? No! But some ways are healthier than others.

Redeeming Love?

By the time we reach young adult fiction, the topic of sex has become something referenced, referred to, rejected, embraced, or ignored. In recent years, the paranormal romance genre has risen in popularity within the young adult category, bringing with it some problematic tropes. Janie calls one trope, "a variation of the tortured-hero-whom-only-true-love-can-save prototype."[13] Even when dealing with a vampire or the stereotypical bad boy, young adult stories often focus on our very human, God-given desire to be loved.

However, in both real life and fiction, this desire can be warped and twisted into a powerful commodity. For girls, romance (or, put bluntly, sex) becomes a power to be wielded; while for boys, sex becomes a hook that influences all actions. Such confusion reflects a deeper truth. We are made to love and be loved. But love, apart from the love of our Savior Jesus Christ, cannot save. Until teenagers can learn to love and be loved by the Savior, their hearts will be restless.

How does one engage with such longing? As we've observed on the website: Some Christian parents won't let their teenage girls read *Twilight*. That's

---

13. "Those Love Stories We Loved," Redeemed Reader.

their prerogative, but they need to know that the desire comes from within; paranormal romances that scale the juvenile heights of passion and self-sacrifice only speak to what's already there. Showing the idolatry in *Twilight* for what it is would be no bad thing. Parents could also talk about how *Jane Eyre* managed her passion for Mr. Rochester, how romantic fantasies burn to ashes in *Les Miserables*, and how sweet love is when it waits the proper time for consummation (Song of Solomon 2:7; 3:5; 8:4).[14]

Faced with the probable messiness of young adult romance, it is tempting to turn toward the apparent safety of Christian or "clean" romances. Still, as Janie has wryly observed: "When you think about it, 'Christian fiction' is itself something of an oxymoron, splicing absolute truth with an art form that stops being art as soon as it starts stating absolutes."[15]

Hayley remembers working at a Christian camp one summer. A battered copy of *Redeeming Love* by Francine Rivers made its way around the female staff cabin, eagerly devoured by the young Christian women, many still in their teens. Later, she helped organize the church library and was appalled by the number of "Christian" romances that took up shelf space. (Especially when she flipped one open and read the dramatic prose!)

One look at the highly lucrative genre of Christian romance shows that many Christians are happy to read love stories. Unfortunately, many Christian romances offer an unhealthy paradigm. Grace Livingston Hill, a classic Christian romance novelist, portrays missionary dating as always working out; the unsaved party always gets saved by the end. The implication for a young reader? Go ahead and date unbelievers. The Stonewycke Trilogy by Michael Phillips and Judith Pella features a young woman blatantly defying her father

---

14. Janie Cheaney, "Looking for Love: The Paranormal Teen Romance," Redeemed Reader, April 12, 2011, https://redeemedreader.com/2011/04/looking-for-love-the-paranormal-teen-romance/.
15. Janie Cheaney, "Five Red Flags to Watch for in YA Christian Romance Fiction," Redeemed Reader, February 16, 2018, https://redeemedreader.com/2018/02/all-for-love-five-red-flags-to-watch-for-in-ya-christian-romance-fiction/.

to follow her true love. Does this occasionally happen? Sure. Is it the paradigm we want to promote for impressionable young readers? Absolutely not!

There is a time and place for romance. Unlike some topics, it is not something that could always be considered helpful for young readers; but when well done, it is perfectly suitable for its intended audience.

Beyond Ever After: A Vision for Christian Romance

Let us not forget the idea of "beyond ever after." If all the romances children encounter end, like a Disney movie, with beautiful dresses, flowers, and sunsets, young readers will not receive an accurate view of love in a sinful world. If, on the other hand, readers are given good, hopeful books that portray love as a gift to be enjoyed between a man and a woman who are both flawed, unique sinners, they will learn to see romance as a good gift within God's plan.

Let us strive for books that encourage this view of romance. It is all right to love happily ever afters, but let's not forget that our "ever after" will not occur on this side of eternity, no matter how much romance we experience.

BOOKLIST FOR CHAPTER 20

Further Reading

    The Meaning of Marriage, Tim and Kathy Keller

For Children/Teens

    Calico Captive, Elizabeth George Speare (Middle Grade/Young Adult)
    Emily of Deep Valley, Maud Hart Lovelace (MG/YA)
    Echo North, Joanna Ruth Meyer (YA)
    Lovely War, Julie Berry (YA)
    Mara, Daughter of the Nile, Eloise Jarvis McGraw (YA)
    No Ordinary Fairytale + Flight and Flame series, R. J. Anderson (YA)
    The Perilous Gard, Elizabeth Marie Pope
    The Red Palace, June Hur (YA)
    Seeds of America Trilogy, Laurie Halse Anderson (YA)
    The Queen's Thief series, Megan Whalen Turner (particularly books 1–3, see our review of the last title; YA)

SECTION 5
Practical Application

CHAPTER 21

BIBLES AND BEYOND: CHOOSING CHRISTIAN RESOURCES

> The grass withers, the flower fades,
> but the word of our God will stand forever.
> —Isaiah 40:8

Every Christian parent longs for their children to follow Christ. When the apostle John wrote, "I have no greater joy than to hear that my children are walking in the truth" (3 John 4), he was thinking of the spiritual children he had discipled during his long ministry. But we parents are also disciplers, not just caregivers, and we participate in the same great joy when our babies mature into followers of Christ. We live in a world of boundless resources to help toward that end, but our main resource must be the Word of God.

In 1989, the first edition of the *NIV Adventure Bible* was published by Zondervan: a full-text, richly annotated edition of the Word of God for children ages six to twelve. By 2020, the brand had sold over ten million copies. Its kid-friendly, easily relatable features included book introductions, interesting facts, key verses, applications, and more—a pattern copied by other Bible publishers in every popular translation. The

Before purchasing a children's Bible, it's worth taking the time to dig into the Bible market.

Adventure Bible has stood the test of time and still outsells its many imitators; but it's not the only option and might not even be the best for your family or your child. Before purchasing a children's Bible, it's worth taking the time to dig into the Bible market.[1]

Let's Consider . . .

Suppose your second grader has outgrown the sturdy family Bible storybook and wants a real Bible to read along in family devotions—should you go for a children's translation at third grade level, or a standard translation for a beginning reader to grow into? Does she like to pore over illustrations and talk about moral issues? Is he interested in details and maps?

If you're the average Christian household you already have multiple translations and editions on your shelves, perhaps even that early edition of the NIV *Adventure Bible* you owned as a child. Churches and Sunday schools once gave away copies of the "Good Book" as a reward for attendance or memory work. Basic "reading texts" can be had for a few dollars plus postage.

Still, you wonder if there's something out there that will not only present the text but also encourage both reading *and understanding* of the text. Christian publishers are continually rolling out brand-new editions of the Bible for kids, some with superhero or comic book themes, others with glitter and bling. Are they all the same under those eye-popping covers, or might there be hidden treasures inside that will stimulate interest and love for the Word?

Before facing the bewildering array of Bibles at the local Christian bookstore, parents should consider what they want from a children's Bible for their own, one-of-a-kind child. Probably the first priority should be cultivating a love for the Word that will last a lifetime. Here are several things to keep in mind:

- **Substance**—an accurate, but also readable, translation. We will cover translation choice in more detail later in this chapter.

---

1. The following section on Bibles is adapted, with some text previously published in "Children's Bible Guide: a Redeemed Reader Guide."

- **Reading level** matters, particularly for beginners. If your third grader is already a voracious reader, you can easily skip the children's versions and go right to a standard translation. But not all children learn to read easily or quickly. If you feel they need a little extra encouragement, one of the two main children's translations might be worthwhile. Please see sample texts from each of these below in the translation section.

- **Supplementary material**, such as book introductions and sidebars, can overwhelm the text, but study helps that actually help are a plus. Every children's Bible should include a basic dictionary and maps (bonus points if it's more than the standard eight!). Other valuable aids are charts, book summaries, and lists (the kings, parables, miracles, etc.). Introductions might also feature timelines and some sense of where the book fits in the overall storyline.

- **Physical details** include type size, weight, and binding. Be wary of paperback editions; soft, flexible covers usually indicate a long-lasting binding, while books with stiff covers will start shedding pages within a few years.

- **Speaking of covers** . . . leather or leatherette is nice, but expensive for a volume your child may not be using very long. Plain or abstract cover designs are preferable to gaudy bling or cartoonish characters a six-year-old will soon outgrow. Look down from the top edge of the Bible, next to the spine. You should see distinct folded sections (known as "quires"), indicating that the pages are sewn. Many newer editions with soft, flexible covers also have sewn binding, so they can be a good investment.

- **Font:** The younger the child, the larger the font should be. For example, 8-point is standard for children's Bibles, but many are printed in 9- or 10-point. Small type (letter) size can also be an issue. Generally, the larger the type, the larger the book, so weight can be as great a consideration as reading ease.

- **Layout** includes elements such as one column or two, chapter/verse number arrangement and color, and location of the supplemental material—preface, sidebars and boxes, full-color inserts, appendix, or all those.

  Most modern Bible translations arrange the text in paragraph form with two notable exceptions—the NASB and some NKJV editions, which stick to the traditional format of beginning each verse on a new line, headed by the verse number. The paragraph format makes it easier to see related thoughts and concepts and how they are developed; but the lineup of verse numbers on one side of the column makes verses much easier for children to find.

  Children's editions often use a contrasting color for chapter numbers and sometimes even verse numbers. That can be helpful when kids are learning to look up Bible passages for themselves.

- **In-text features** throughout the text might include memory verses, interesting facts, and personal applications. These *can* be more distracting than helpful for your young reader.[2]

- **Personal taste** is a consideration, but probably the one of least importance. We're thinking about your children's taste, although you should be aware how your own preferences determine your choices. Just because your son is into superheroes is not the best reason to pick the *Super Hero Bible* for him, and your little girl's princess preference doesn't mean you should get her a *Precious Princess Bible* with a glitzy cover. God calls us to adapt to Him; He doesn't adapt Himself to our latest interest. So, in general, avoid trendy, and focus on the basics.

---

2. See Janie Cheaney, "To 'Study the Bible' Means What?," Redeemed Reader, April 13, 2020, https://redeemedreader.com/2020/04/to-study-the-bible-means-what/.

- **Pictures of Jesus**—Some parents object to picturing Jesus in a children's Bible, based on the second commandment. Illustrated Bibles will almost always include such pictures, although some may represent Him as an outstretched hand or from a back view only.

- **Reading Bible, study Bible, or devotional Bible**—What's the difference? See "the Five General Classifications of the Bible Market," below.

A Word About Translations

If you ever searched for a passage on BibleHub.com, you were confronted with a bewildering array of translations. The market boils down to around ten standard translations (see the reading-level list below). Just remember that every major *translation* appears in many *editions*. Consider what version is used in your church, but don't feel limited by that. Some children enjoy having different versions to read from, and they can be helpful. These editions may be study Bibles annotated by popular preachers; devotional Bibles for bikers, cowboys, professional women, teen girls, etc.; journaling Bibles with designer covers; presentation Bibles and gift Bibles; paperback copies for a few dollars, as well as bedstand-sized heirlooms that could double as doorstops.

- New International Readers Version (NIrV), International Children's Bible (ICB)—3rd grade (more about these translations below)
- Contemporary English Version (CEV)—between 4th and 5th grade
- New Living Translation (NLT) and God's Word—5th grade
- New Internation Version (NIV), and Christian Standard Bible (CSB)—7th grade
- English Standard Version (ESV)—8th grade
- New King James Version (NKJV)—between 8th and 9th grade
- King James Version (KJV)—10th grade

The two major children's translations are the NIrV and the International Children's Bible (ICB). The former first appeared as the text for Zondervan's *Kid's Bible* in 1996. The latter, appearing in 1985, evolved out of an effort by the Church of Christ to translate Scripture into English that the deaf could understand—greatly simplified and almost entirely devoid of idiom.

In comparison, the NIrV reads a bit more smoothly than the ICB, with more of a dramatic tone. Opening at random, here's Jeremiah 22:10 from the ICB:

> *Don't cry for the king who has died. Don't cry loudly for him.*
> *But cry painfully for the king who is being taken away from here.*
> *Cry for him because he will never come back again.*
> *He will never see his homeland again.*[3]

And from the NIrV:

> *Don't sob over dead King Josiah. Don't be sad because he's gone.*
> *Instead, sob bitterly over King Johoahaz. He was forced to leave his country.*
> *He will never return. He'll never see his own land again.*[4]

The ICB is typically sold without a lot of bells and whistles—just the basic Bible with brief book introductions. Perhaps for that reason, the type is usually bigger than the NIrV—10-11 point as compared to 8 or 9, which is no small factor with beginning readers.

Whether to buy a children's translation is a judgment call; in general, they aren't needed for competent young readers who can transition quickly enough into one of the leading English translations for grown-ups. A children's translation can still be helpful as a supplement, for reading aloud, for comparison,

---

3. Scripture taken from the International Children's Bible®. Copyright © 1986, 1988, 1999 by Thomas Nelson. Used by permission. All rights reserved.

4. Scripture quotations marked (NIrV) are taken from the Holy Bible, New International Reader's Version®, NIrV® Copyright © 1995, 1996, 1998, 2014 by Biblica, Inc.™ Used by permission of Zondervan. All rights reserved worldwide. www.zondervan.com The "NIrV" and "New International Reader's Version" are trademarks registered in the United States Patent and Trademark Office by Biblica, Inc.™

and for encouraging a slow or reluctant reader.

One thing to note about these two young reader versions (NIrV and ICB) that might be worth mentioning: They are surprisingly more direct about sex than the adult versions. For example, instead of figurative expressions like "knew" or "lay with," ICB commonly uses the clunky and clinical "had sexual relations with." The NIrV varies: For lawful relations between husband and wife it says "made love to." For the other kind, it's usually "had sex with." Be aware lest you get awkward questions from your five-year-old.

Most of us have memorized from more than one translation. That's not a big problem, as long as the translation is both accurate and stylistically pleasing. But if you decide to start with a simplified, early reader translation, such as the New International Readers Version (NIrV) or the International Children's Bible (ICB), you may want to assign memory verses from an adult version. Finally, if you have a reluctant reader, *The Action Bible* is a graphic novel form that shows high regard for Scripture. It doesn't contain every chapter and verse, but it is certainly engaging.

Five General Classifications of the Bible Market

Almost all Bibles published today can be sorted into categories. There's often some overlap: Many devotional Bibles will contain some study helps, study Bibles may include significant application, and resource Bibles will include useful information for individuals.

Study Bibles

Every major translation has its flagship study Bible: a hefty chunk packed with charts, theological articles, maps, and tons of notes, sometimes taking up more of a given page than the text. In the children's publishing world, the "study" part usually takes the form of in-text features like word definitions, Bible facts, book summaries, and lists of characters, themes, events, etc. The NKJV *Early Reader's Bible* and NIV *Kids' Visual Study Bible* are good examples.

Devotional Bibles

Devotional Bibles feature brief meditations scattered throughout the text, along with prayer suggestions, application questions, and sometimes journaling space. Zondervan has specialized in NIV editions tailored for women, dads, armed forces members, homeschool moms, policemen, first-responders, etc.

Children's devotional Bibles are not that specific, but often gendered, such as the NIV *Bible for Teen Girls* and *NIV Revolution* for boys. More generic is the NIrV *Love Letters from God*. The features lean toward application and often include sketches of major Bible characters.

Reading Bibles

These are light on additional features but may add brief book introductions and full-color inserts. The inserts contain basic information such as books of the Bible arranged by classification, lists of kings, miracles of Jesus, the Ten Commandments, and hints on how to study the Bible or how to pray. Popular themes (like Minecraft, Star Wars, or LEGO) usually fall into this category.

Resource Bibles

These are highly specialized editions with features that could be useful for teachers, children's church leaders, or Child Evangelism Fellowship organizers. The features are geared more toward activities than quiet reading or study. The *NIV Kids' Quiz*, *NLT Hands On*, and *NIrV Seek & Explore* are good examples.

Interactive Bibles

These became popular in the mid-2020s, first for grown-ups and teens and then for children. "Journaling" Bibles for adults began with wide, lined margins for making notes, but expanded into designed headers and verses, as well as full-page line drawings to color. The inclusion of wide journaling margins *and* designs makes for a large format.

Coloring Bibles are another type of interactive Bible that may appeal to artistically inclined children. However, parents should keep in mind that the main purpose of a Bible is to read it, not decorate it. Getting creative with the design can all too easily distract from the text.

Putting It All Together: Evaluating a Children's Bible

The decision is up to you: You can recycle that children's NIV or KJV that's gone through two kids already, or you can invest in a brand-new one that may be better suited to the individual. We can be grateful for the wide variety of children's Bibles available, but how to choose the best for Shane or Maddie? After considering the usefulness of in-text features and appendices, keep the following questions in mind:

- Are the pages glued or sewn?
- Is the font size appropriate for the child's age?
- Will the Bible be easy to carry? When open, do the pages lie flat?
- If you like the edition but not the cover, are alternate covers available?
- Does the Table of Contents include an alphabetical listing of books as well as canonical listing?
- Are illustrations high-quality and realistic?
- Does the appendix include a dictionary or a concordance?
- Does the appendix include maps? Or (even better) are maps included at appropriate places in the text?

Page through one long book (such as Genesis, Exodus, Isaiah), one short book (Jonah, Micah), one gospel, and one epistle. Do the features seem generally helpful, or repetitive, or bland? Which ones can you imagine your child paying attention to? Which is she more likely to ignore? Taken altogether, would these features encourage understanding, or tend to distract?

Over the years Janie has reviewed dozens of specialty children's Bibles at Redeemed Reader; simply type "Bible reviews" in the search box and start browsing. We encourage you to read reviews, but we also recommend a trip to the local Christian bookstore if you have the option. If it isn't possible to lay your hands on a physical copy of the edition you're looking for, you can still glean information from online booksellers such as Westminster Books.[5] Look at sample pages, font size, number of pages, and cover description. Bibles that are out of print can still be found through used book sellers such as AbeBooks or ThriftBooks.

Youth programs, mission trips, and service projects have little lasting value if children don't learn to study the Bible for themselves. With a little care, though, parents can select an edition of God's Word that will not only be read, but also pondered.

Other Books to Nurture Faith

Once you've chosen a Bible, other resources can help nurture your family's spiritual growth. There are so many good things we want to do! Deuteronomy 6:4–9 teaches us to talk about God all the time: in our homes, in the car, over ice cream, and after movies. Devotionals, hymnals, catechisms, biographies... these are all wonderful tools, depending on the season you are in and what you and your children currently need. The goal is not to use resources because they are recommended by someone you respect, but to shepherd your children's souls wisely, within your human limitations, under the Good Shepherd Himself.

You cannot pour from an empty flask. Our bodies cannot last without breath or water, and neither can our souls. You might try several different approaches to get the Bible in your heart during the day, but consistency may be a struggle. Some days one approach works, some days something else works, and the Lord is faithful through all of it.

---

5. Westminster Bookstore: Children & Youth, https://www.wtsbooks.com/collections/bible-children-youth.

When your children are little, teaching them about God can be woven into every part of your life as a family. Read Bible stories; seek the Lord in prayer; sing a favorite hymn together. Maybe you read just a few verses aloud over breakfast, giving yourself Truth on which to meditate and introducing your children to the language of the pure Word of God. If Jesus satisfied the needs of a multitude by multiplying only a few loaves and fishes, He can nourish your heart with scriptural snacks throughout the day in this season. Listening to Scripture set skillfully to music, such as Fighter Verses or Seeds Kids Worship, can be helpful. If on a particular day you never get to sit down long enough to open your Bible, you might listen to a chapter or more through an app. The children can listen while they play.

Reading or singing a few Bible verses at bedtime is a lovely way to close the day and plant seeds for later family devotions, even if it doesn't happen every night. You might review the same verses you read earlier in the day. Repetition is good. After reading a verse or two, you could read a short Bible story, such as the *Read-Aloud Bible Stories* by Ella Lindvall or one of the Baby Believer board books by Danielle Hitchen. *The Beginner's Gospel Story Bible* by Jared Kennedy is also a good one for young children.

Singing hymns, learning catechism, memorizing the books of the Bible, praying for families in your local church and for missionaries are all important, but it can be hard to fit everything in. Little habits add up. Try a rotating schedule such as "Musical Mondays" and "Theology Thursdays," or just make a loop schedule and do the next thing together. Perhaps you focus on a hymn of the month on a "Musical Monday" and learn a catechism question or read a book like *The Ology* by Marty Machowski on "Theological Thursdays." When you focus on learning a hymn, you might consider reading a brief biography of the author or composer from a book like *Our Hymns, Our Heritage* by David and Barbara Leeman or *Then Sings My Soul* by Robert J. Morgan so the children can appreciate the context out of which these gifts from God were born. See if your church has a prayer calendar for the missionaries your congregation supports and consider praying for one family in your church each day.

As children get older, they can learn to sit for longer readings of Scripture or Bible stories. Enjoying a cup of tea with milk and sugar (or hot chocolate!) is a delicious way to encourage your children to linger while you read aloud. *A Child's Story Bible* by Catherine Vos and *The Biggest Story Bible Storybook* by Kevin DeYoung are some we have enjoyed. Megan's children have grown partial to using proper teacups and saucers or favorite mugs that honor the experience, but you needn't make it this complicated. Betsy's family simply read Scripture and other Christian books over breakfast each morning.

As their attention spans grow, you can begin adding one or two additional readings such as a short biography about a figure from church history, or a children's version of *The Pilgrim's Progress*. *Dangerous Journey* by Oliver Hunkin and *Little Pilgrim's Progress* illustrated by Joe Sutphin are beautiful introductions, worth reading annually, which gradually prepare children for reading an unabridged edition like the ones from Christian Focus.

Classics like *The Valley of Vision* and *My Utmost for His Highest* have nourished the saints for centuries, and there are some excellent contemporary devotionals for families and children. The best ones seek to knit the reader's heart and emotions, which are vital to our makeup as human beings, into the Word of God. Devotionals are introspective by nature, and kids younger than ten aren't always ready for them. Younger children are geared more toward collecting information than pondering it—better for them to focus on what the Bible says as *you* demonstrate (and talk about) how it applies. Of course, we should encourage each other with our thoughts about Scripture, and adults and teens can seek out devotional authors who speak to them. But younger kids might benefit more just from talking over what they read in the Bible with their parents or older Christians.

For books like *The Ology* that have loads of Scripture references sprinkled throughout, you can give your kids a couple of verses to look up. Take a couple of minutes ahead of time to jot the references on little sticky notes, hand them out, and let the kids bookmark the passages in their own Bibles ahead of time so they're ready when you call on them. This helps them participate, and they also become more familiar with the Bible itself!

Some resources, like *The Radical Book for Kids* by Champ Thornton or *Bible Infographics for Kids*, don't fall into a neat box or category. How do we encourage kids to explore these kinds of resources? You can explore one chapter or page spread a week, or you might try reading aloud a portion that sounds especially interesting and then leave the book casually on the coffee table. Since these books are full of all sorts of interesting trivia, you can go with a more subtle approach. At dinner, drop some interesting bit such as: "Did you know that the high priest's breastplate had emeralds, diamonds, and rubies on it?" or "Wow! They also had battle-axes and catapults in the Bible!" (assuming your son has just been showing you his LEGO catapult). Then, model for your kids how to do some research: "Let's find out more about that." The more we turn to certain books (including the Bible itself), the more our children will learn to do the same for their own questions.

Honoring the Church Calendar

Books can be a real asset in appreciating seasons of the year that hold greater significance for Christians. For instance, Advent and Easter offer plenty of special resources, opportunities for changing up devotions and rehearsing the special work of God in redemptive history. Here are some things to look for: Is the text faithful to the biblical account? Does the text accurately represent the emotional weight of the event? Picture books, even for young children, shouldn't retell stories in the Bible in a manner that treats them lightly. Easter picture books often focus on symbols of spring and new life or retell the events of the week leading up to the empty tomb, often from the perspective of a bystander, ignoring the rest of Jesus' ministry and our future hope. This is why Megan wrote *Something Better Coming*, to grapple with both the despair *and* the joy. *Why* did Jesus come to earth? To prove His power over death, save us from our sins, and give us future hope.

Advent is often a busy season. If the thought of adding one more thing discourages and overwhelms you, don't choose a devotional that includes crafts, extra baking, and all the things. Stick with one that is simple and text-based that might encourage a little reflection. If this is a season when your family is looking for extra things to do, find a devotional that is more interactive. Remember to look for something that brings delight to you, the parent, as well as your child.

If you have a regular practice of family devotions, you could swap in an Advent or Easter devotional for a short time. If you don't already have the habit, this is a great time to build one. A Jesse Tree is a fun tradition that lasts through December, leading up to Christmas. Either buy a set of ornaments or make simple ones. Even if you don't make it through all the readings and symbols in a given year, insert a bookmark and pick up where you left off next year (and maybe make a few more ornaments that you intended to finish).

If that's more than you are ready to commit to, pick a devotional that lasts only a couple weeks, enjoy the feeling of accomplishment, and keep going with another one after the holiday. *Promises Made, Promises Kept* by Marty Machowski is a good short devotional for Advent. *Mission Accomplished* by Scott James is only two weeks long, beginning the week before Easter and finishing a week after.

Celebrating Church History

There are plenty of events in the history of the church that are worth celebrating. You may be part of a Christian tradition (such as Anglican or Catholic) that includes many of these along the way as part of the church calendar. If your church does not celebrate church history officially, your family might consider setting aside a month to do so. For instance, Protestants mark October 31 as the anniversary of the day Luther nailed his 95 theses to the door of Wittenberg Castle. Why not use a whole month to appreciate other heroes of the faith?

Select your subject and gather resources in advance. You could focus on one person or enjoy several brief biographical sketches, perhaps by geographical region or period in history. Read a few pages out of *Trial and Triumph* or *Radiant* by Richard M. Hannula, one of Simonetta Carr's picture book biographies, or a few selections of *Church History ABCs* if you have young children. You could also choose to celebrate *The Pilgrim's Progress* by John Bunyan as a theme. This masterpiece was published 159 years after the Reformation began and has been a great encouragement to the church of Christ.

When Life Gets Busy

Having regular family devotions is not the only indication of the spiritual health of your family. Struggling to consistently practice family devotions can be discouraging, because we are often reminded how important it is. Many parents long to know Christ better and to bring their little ones to Jesus for His blessing.

But it is possible to draw near to God with your lips when your hearts are far from Him, and children recognize that. Following a formula or program cannot manufacture hearts that delight in the Lord. Going through the motions of checking boxes brings no lasting fruit.

It is also possible to be biblically faithful without reading through a devotional or even sitting down to read the Bible together every single evening of the week. Maybe your children are too young to sit through a full chapter. Maybe your schedule is inconsistent, and you only have time to pray together before bed most evenings. Thankfully, the Lord has provided a variety of means to show our children that walking with the Good Shepherd brings life and restores our souls, however this looks in your current season.

Consider what spiritual training your children are already getting elsewhere. Some families are blessed with enormous resources outside the home, whether they're in a church with a great Sunday school program, a Christian school, a Bible study or youth group with a focus on discipleship. Where do you need to supplement at home?

If your children are in a public school, or your family is between churches right now, or your church doesn't have an active youth group, you may need to explore other options. Perhaps a faithful brother or sister in your church would be willing to do a Bible or Christian book study with your teen, not only for the benefit of instruction, but also for the older generation to develop a relationship with maturing young people.

If this is a really hard season for preteens or teens, when they think that no one loves them, perhaps you could linger in the Psalms, or share a biography about a Christian who struggled with loneliness and depression. You don't have to do it all yourself. There may be a youth Bible study, and your older children can take responsibility for preparing for the discussion.

God is a God of abundance. Look at all the wealth He has given us! While we are bombarded by our culture on all sides by unbiblical messages, God has provided plenty of resources we can consider. Consider what your children need. Consider what your classroom needs. What would bring delight and discernment? There is no list of "the right books" that will guarantee results, but the Lord will give you wisdom when you ask for it.

BOOKLIST FOR CHAPTER 21

Further Reading

    Children's Bible Guide, Janie Cheaney

For Children/Teens

    Baby Believer books, Danielle Hitchen (Board Book)
    Hymns for Little Ones series, Harvest Kids (BB)
    The Church History ABCs: Augustine and 25 Other Heroes of the Faith, Stephen J. Nichols (Picture Book)
    Emily Lost Someone She Loved, Kathleen Fucci (PB)
    A Light for My Path: An ABC Book Based on Psalm 119, Davis Carman (PB)
    Lily: The Girl Who Could See, Sally Oxley (PB)
    The Promise, Jason Helopoulos (PB)
    Pilipinto: The Jungle Adventures of a Missionary's Daughter, Valerie Elliot Shepard (PB)
    Church History, Simonetta Carr (Middle Grade)
    Exploring the Bible, David Murray (MG)
    God's Timeline, Linda Finlayson (MG)
    The Radical Book for Kids and *The Really Radical Book for Kids*, Champ Thornton (MG)
    Risen Hope: The Church Throughout History series, Luke H. Davis (MG)
    Epic, Tim Challies (Young Adult)

CHAPTER 22

WHO IS MY NEIGHBOR? LOVING AUTHORS

> She learned to trade in kindness and discovered
> the tremendous value in small mercies and selfless giving.
> —Kelly Barnhill, *The Ogress and the Orphans*[1]

When we acknowledge and praise what is good and true and beautiful in a literary work, we are shining a gospel light on both Christian and secular authors. We can rejoice in the common grace present in the work of any author or illustrator. This is a wonderful witness and encouragement to authors, both saved and unsaved.

Often it is easy to relate to the lawyer in Luke 10 who sought to justify himself to Jesus. We want things to be clear. Tell us who our neighbor is, so we can love them. For some, this stems from a deep desire to obey but also from the need to check a box. We need structure. Need someone to tell us how to respond. In our current digital age, it is easy to respond viscerally when we find something that offends our Christian beliefs. But our first response is not always the most loving.

This chapter is not about banning books. As we discuss in chapter 9 on messy books, there is a time and place for discussing problematic books. Instead, let us talk about how we can relate biblically to the authors we read.

For more than a decade Redeemed Reader has had the privilege and

---

1. Kelly Barnhill, *The Ogress and the Orphans* (Algonquin Books, 2022), 16.

blessing of reviewing books by a variety of authors and illustrators. Over the years, we've built connections with many in the publishing world. We've interviewed authors from a variety of backgrounds. During this time, we've watched changes to publishing as Kickstarter campaigns and small presses bring a wider variety of authors to the table.

Our interactions with authors mirror Jesus' interactions with His culture. He sat and fellowshipped with people from all walks of life: disciples and children, tax collectors and prostitutes, zealots and Pharisees.

Concerning Christian Publishers and Authors

As Christian reviewers, we share a common goal and common belief with Christian authors and publishers; we relate on so many things. We agree that children need hopeful, wonderful stories. It is because we agree on all of this, that our team holds Christian authors to a high standard of literary and artistic excellence: They know what is good and beautiful and true. Are their stories mirroring this? Are they reflecting truth and beauty? It is right to hold Christian authors and publishers to a high bar! We find that Christian children's literature can suffer from a lack of literary quality for the sake of a Christian message. Theologian Frederick Buechner's insight into this problem is helpful:

> *If we think the purpose of Jesus' stories is essentially to make a point*
> *as extractable as the moral at the end of a fable, then the inevitable conclusion*
> *is that once you get the point, you can throw the story itself away*
> *like the rind of an orange when you have squeezed out the juice.*
> *Is that true? How about other people's stories? What is the point of*
> *A Midsummer Night's Dream or The Iliad or For Whom the Bell Tolls?*
> *Can we extract the point in each case and frame it on the living room wall*
> *for our perpetual edification?*[2]

---

2. Frederick Buechner, *The Clown in the Belfry: Writings on Faith and Fiction* (HarperSanFrancisco, 1992), 132.

Loving Christian children's literature does not have to entail checking our expectations for quality at the door. It is right to desire illustrations and stories that are beautiful and hopeful and bring delight. Let us encourage and support children's books from Christian publishers that are pressing toward a high standard of excellence.

Rabbit Room press "cultivates and curates stories ... to nourish Christ-centered communities for the life of the world."[3] Meanwhile Bandersnatch Books has "a goal of providing books of substance (that might otherwise be missed) to lovers of all that is good, true, and beautiful."[4] Enclave is a publisher dedicated to getting "Christian speculative fiction into the hands of the fans who love and devour great stories."[5] The Good Book Company, New Growth Press, Eerdmans, Crossway, and Moody Publishers are five examples of well-known Christian publishers dedicated to producing quality children's books. These are only a sampling of the thriving presses, imprints, and publishers that are either explicitly Christian or produced by people of faith.

Let us not settle for poor illustrations and trite stories when it comes to Christian children's literature. Rather, let us strive toward beautiful, quality illustrations illustrating well-written truths. Let us rejoice in well-told stories. When we find something that is good, but not great, we can enjoy it, but let us also keep encouraging excellence in the books we buy and authors we recommend.[6]

Wise, winsome encouragement is needed. We know authors and illustrators have poured much of themselves into their work. With humility and discernment may both Christian readers and Christian makers pursue excellence!

---

3. "Rabbit Room Press," The Rabbit Room Store, https://store.rabbitroom.com/pages/rabbit-room-press?.

4. "Bandersnatch Books," Bandersnatch Books, https://www.bandersnatchbooks.com/about.

5. "About—Enclave Publishing," Enclave Publishing, March 12, 2012, https://www.enclavepublishing.com/about/.

6. While not explicitly Christian, here are two more small presses with goals that will often align with Christian readers: Purple House Press is dedicated to republishing vintage books so families can have wholesome stories. Waxwing Books, founded by Sarah Mackenzie, is committed to producing beautiful books to read aloud.

People of Faith in the World of Books

Moving beyond Christian publishing is a category of people we are so thankful for in children's literature: faith-filled authors who are working in the mainstream publishing industry. These authors, while holding to their faith, are writing stories that reach a broader audience of schools, libraries, and readers. Their faith seems subtle at times, contrasted to the open allegories and Bible-filled books of the Christian publishing industry. However, it still shines brightly. These authors remind us of the faithful centurion in Luke 7.

In his nationally acclaimed young adult literary memoir, *Everything Sad Is Untrue*, Daniel Nayeri writes "Christ has died. Christ has risen. Christ will come again."[7] In his story, Nayeri recounts the conversion of his mother and sister that upended a peaceful childhood and led to arriving in America as a refugee. A Christian himself, Nayeri infuses his stories with Truth. As he says, "I can't tell you all that is Truth. But I can tell you what isn't True: anything that can, or will, pass away."[8]

Mitali Perkins writes beautiful, hope-filled children's fiction and picture books. A pastor's wife, Perkins encourages love of neighbor in her lovely middle grade fiction *Hope in the Valley*. The protagonist's family in the story are not believers, like Mitali's own loving childhood family. However, her main character learns about love and the biblical belief that motivates love of neighbor as she learns more about the history of her town.

Published in the mainstream, N. D. Wilson's Ashtown Burials series reflects Wilson's own philosophy of the world: "I love the world as it is, because I love what it will be."[9] Christian authors writing in mainstream publishing are not always overt. Their books can be messier as they engage with the real world.

---

7. Daniel Nayeri, *Everything Sad Is Untrue : (A True Story)* (Levine Querido, 2020), 196.
8. Daniel Nayeri, "An Interview with Daniel Nayeri," interview by Janie Cheaney, Redeemed Reader, February 11, 2021, https://redeemedreader.com/2021/02/an-interview-with-daniel-nayeri/.
9. N. D. Wilson, *Notes from the Tilt-A-Whirl* (Thomas Nelson, 2013), 17.

Yet, from subtle mentions of Bibles on bedstands, to characters motivated by a deep personal faith launching themselves on quests, these men and women are creating stories with hints of gospel truth, shining a light in our darkened world.

When we read an author we know shares our faith, we delight in the truth of their work. Sometimes we find ourselves reading a book and not knowing the author's faith, but still recognizing some shared beliefs. We love many of Kate DiCamillo's works and resonate with her themes. We've given starred reviews to *The Book of Boy* by Catherine Gilbert Murdock and *The Inquisitor's Tale* by Adam Gidwitz. We do not know about Murdock's faith (Gidwitz is Jewish); still these two titles are good examples of common grace, despite the fact we have not enjoyed all of these authors' books. There are also more liberal writers. Katherine Rundell speaks openly of her faith but is also LGBT-affirming and reflects this is in some of her work.[10] Simply put, the realm of authors writing in the secular world is wide and, as with anything, discernment is needed.

Let us turn to the final category of authors: secular authors who do not share our biblical beliefs. Looking to Jesus, how should we engage with them? This chapter is not about engaging with their content. Rather, it is a reminder that the authors and illustrators behind every book are people.

"And There Was a Samaritan..."

Again and again, whether eating at a table with tax collectors and sinners, or sitting at a well talking to a Samaritan woman, Jesus entered into a person's situation and formed a relationship with them before leading them to Truth. He saw each human as an individual, made in the image of God (Luke 7:36–50).

---

10. "Creative Conversations: Ben Quash with Katherine Rundell," The Visual Commentary on Scripture, https://thevcs.org/creative-conversations-ben-quash-with-katherine-rundell. See also Anna James, "Katherine Rundell | 'I Had a Really Strong Idea of What I Wanted It to Be About, but No Coherent Plot; Plots Are Not My Strong Point,'" The Bookseller, https://www.thebookseller.com/author-interviews/katherine-rundell--i-had-a-really-strong-idea-of-what-i-wanted-it-to-be-about-but-no-coherent-plotplots-are-not-my-strong-point.

In Kelly Barnhill's story *The Ogress and the Orphans*, we delight in the truth she shows, in the gentle acts of kindness and being neighborly. As Janie observes in her review, "the story isn't a political satire or screed. It's about how fear can smother love, but love casts out fear. The emphasis on books and stories as the best way to broaden our minds is by now a well-known theme, somewhat overdone. (The center of the village was the library; there is no church. On the other hand, a long philosophical meditation on Who is my neighbor? will bring the parable of the good Samaritan to mind.)"[11]

When we think of the authors whose worldview we disagree with most, one popular author and his series come to mind. Rick Riordan's Percy Jackson series encouraged a generation of reluctant middle grade readers. However, as Riordan expanded Percy Jackson's world into further series (Heroes of Olympus, Trial of Apollo, Magnus Chase, etc.), he introduced more LGBT themes, a topic Riordan is passionate about in real life. At Redeemed Reader, we still recommend the Percy Jackson series. Were we disappointed by Riordan's venturing into LGBT advocacy? Yes. Yet, the reality is that we still had no issue with Percy Jackson (remember, we found nothing problematic in the original series). In continuing to recognize the good of Percy Jackson (it remains an excellent nudge for reluctant boy readers), we can show Christian forbearance toward Rick Riordan. As a secular author, writing to a secular market, his activist choices are not unusual. As with many authors, we can selectively enjoy a particular book (or in Riordan's case, series) without endorsing, enjoying, or even reading the rest of the author's work.

What if Christians were known for encouraging and praising what was good? Instead of banning, what if we gently shared the truth, explaining how some books and themes do not fit with our worldview?

Forbearance doesn't mean that we will continue to unreservedly recommend Rick Riordan, or other popular authors once we know their views

---

11. Janie Cheaney, "The Ogress and the Orphans by Kelly Barnhill," Redeemed Reader, April 6, 2022, https://redeemedreader.com/2022/04/the-ogress-and-the-orphans-by-kelly-barnhill/.

diverge from a biblical perspective. Rather, we will evaluate their work on a case-by-case basis and continue to praise and encourage specific titles that we find good. This forbearance lets us still encourage books that align with biblical truth at major points and discourages the temptation to "cancel" an author or indulge in frustrated venting when we are disappointed by their choices. Forbearance also allows us to enjoy the excellent work of an author whose private life we disagree with, from classic authors whose lifestyles we would not condone to current authors who have alternate lifestyles.

Scottish theologian John Murray asked, "How is it that men who are not savingly renewed by the Spirit of God nevertheless exhibit so many qualities, gifts and accomplishments that promote the preservation, temporal happiness, cultural progress, social and economic improvement of themselves and of others?"[12] The answer, Murray concluded, was God's common grace. We do well to remember this. We know that stories can reflect truth, even if it is a truth that their creators do not yet know.

Moving Forward in Love and Wisdom

Engaging in a hope-filled biblical manner with authors is a wonderful way to encourage excellence. As we engage with authors, let us be wise as serpents and innocent as doves, shining the gospel light of Truth and Story into children's literature and our engagement with authors and illustrators. May we seek excellence, and praise what is good. May we forbear when faced with disappointing choices, yet continue to read and press on.

For authors holding biblical beliefs, let us be an encouragement and cheerleaders while still holding these authors to a high standard. Let us praise God for illustrators like John Hendrix, who engages the imagination of readers with his Holy Ghost comic panels musing on the Trinity. Let us cheer on authors like Daniel Nayeri, who shares openly how faith changed his life and world

---

12. John Murray, "Common Grace," in *The Collected Works of John Murray, Volume 2: Systematic Theology*, ed. Iain Murray (Banner of Truth Trust, 1977), 93.

in a literary memoir, and let us follow each author we discover, reading and sharing their work.

If an author who has no open profession of faith writes a story that is admirable, let us rejoice and encourage. Let us show publishers and libraries and yes, even authors, that we will read and recommend wonderful books. As we do, may we not forget the truth and pray that the Lord will use our love and encouragement to bring many more sheep safely home.

BOOKLIST FOR CHAPTER 22

Further Reading

Steeped in Stories, Mitali Perkins

For Children/Teens (All authors are professing Christians)

A Little More Beautiful, Sarah Mackenzie (Picture Book)
Zita the Spacegirl, Ben Hatke (Chapter Book graphic novel)
Garvey's Choice, Nikki Grimes (Middle Grade)
Jack Zulu and the Waylander's Key, S. D. Smith (MG)
The Labors of Hercules Beal, Gary D. Schmidt (MG)
May B., Caroline Starr Rose (MG)
The Star That Always Stays, Anna Rose Johnson (MG)
The Wilderking Trilogy, Jonathan Rogers (MG)
Tree Street Kids series, Amanda Cleary Eastep (MG)
Bamboo People, Mitali Perkins (Young Adult)
The Carver and the Queen, Emma Fox (YA)
Embergold, Rachelle Nelson (YA)

CHAPTER 23

FINDING BOOK PEOPLE: LOVING YOUR LIBRARY

> There she worked in a library, dusting books and keeping them from getting mixed up, and helping people find the ones they wanted. Some of the books told her about faraway places. People called her Miss Rumphius now.[1]
>
> —Barbara Cooney, *Miss Rumphius*

Occasionally at Redeemed Reader we receive an email from a reader telling us they have given up on their local library and are now curating their own home library. Some readers tell us they no longer take their children to their local library. This saddens us because we love our libraries.

Lois Lowry, author of *The Giver*, recalls taking two young visitors from France to her local library. They browsed the stacks and chose some books to check out on her card. Afterward, one of the girls asked, "What do you have to pay to belong to the library?" Ms. Lowry was a bit startled by the question: "Why, nothing."[2] Of course it's not technically true since libraries are tax-supported. But still, the public library you see in almost every community in America is one of our nation's better ideas.

---

1. Barbara Cooney, *Miss Rumphius* (Puffin Books, 1985), n.p.
2. Lois Lowry, "An Evening with Lois Lowry," lecture sponsored by the Springfield-Greene County public library at the Springfield Art Museum, Springfield, Missouri, April 2, 2015.

In recent years, some libraries have become flashpoints for controversy. Recently, Betsy's library—as a promotion for a local health group—displayed a table of free condoms directly adjacent to the picture book section. Hayley's library had a display of picture books for Pride Month. Over the years, several of us have had conversations with our local librarians about shelving decisions. But, despite our opposition to some of their choices, we still love our libraries.

As Christians, we know that no library is perfect. We also know that the library's purpose and worldview do not always coincide with our own. Part of our job as parents and educators is to be discerning about what library content our children consume. But we don't believe it is necessary to "cancel" the library over disagreements.

Finding Allies

In Oshkosh, Wisconsin, the library director is a bearded giant of a man, always impeccably dressed. He is also a kind man. He believes in understanding what his staff do, so he fills in around the library. The first time Hayley ever saw him, he was helping a patron at the front desk and chatting with the front desk staff.

One day he paused his rounds at the table where she was working. "What do you do?"

Hayley looked up from sorting through the library archives and smiled, "I'm a Christian book reviewer!"

Looking back, she thinks it was the Holy Spirit prompting her response, recalling, "My job title allows me to share how faith is central in my life."

The library director smiled politely and then asked where Hayley went to church. He asked carefully, treating her as a person of faith but trying not to assume she would go to a church. Hayley noticed the slight awkwardness of the wording and cheerfully told him she went to a small nondenominational church on the north side of town.

After discussing church, the director smiled and said, "You're very welcome here."

Hayley recalls, "While I've never felt unwelcome at the library, I left the conversation encouraged." Sometimes, as Christians, it can feel like we are no longer welcome in some places. Conversations like this remind us that this isn't always the case.

Loving Your Library by Getting Involved

What does it look like to engage with your local library? Depending on your children's age, this could mean bringing your little ones to story time at the library or participating in your library's summer reading program. (Some libraries have both adult and children's summer reading programs!) If your children are older or in school, it might mean volunteering yourself or with your teen children at the library. Volunteering at the local library is a wonderful way to get involved and support your library and build relationships with librarians. Friends of the Library often welcome teen volunteers and as an added perk, volunteering to sort donated books can lead to some wonderful finds for your own collection.

What does it look like to engage with your local library?

Pay attention to the books displayed in your library. You might notice books by authors you love, even Christian authors like Lois Walfrid Johnson or The Prince Warriors series by Priscilla Shirer. This could be a great conversation starter with one of your librarians. As you attend programs and engage with your local librarian, you can have the opportunity to be a Christian witness and share the love of Christ.

Do you have a librarian who appreciates old or classic books? What is your library director like? Getting to know your library is a great way of identifying its needs, being encouraged by what it is doing well, and maybe meeting some allies who love the same kinds of books.

If you'd like to move beyond volunteering to help in the library itself, two more ways to love your library include serving on the Friends of the Library board or your library's Board of Trustees. These roles, often overlooked, provide wonderful opportunities to contribute and speak into your library's decisions.

Loving Your Library by Checking Out Books

Loving your library might simply involve putting good books on hold and checking them out; this helps keep the books you love in circulation. Based on the numbers, your library will see the books you read are still in demand. You can also show support by using the ebook and audiobook checkouts supported by your library system. Libby/Overdrive and Hoopla are wonderful resources for finding a wider variety of books than might be available in your library system. As with checking out physical books, using these digital resources will encourage your library to keep paying for such services.

If all these options still come up short for finding a specific book, consider using your library's interlibrary loan program. Or, ask one of your librarians how to request a book for the library to purchase. Each library has its own procedure. We've noticed books like the Green Ember series by S.D. Smith at our local libraries, and we're pretty certain their availability stemmed from local reader requests. When enough readers ask for a book, there's a good chance your library will purchase it. After all, they want books that will be popular and well-read. Requesting your favorite books also helps authors as you are introducing their work to all the readers in your library system! Depending on your library's policy, you might be able to donate some of your favorite books for circulation, but each library is different, so check before you do.

Remember, librarians can be allies. And by checking out good books, you can encourage your librarian to keep purchasing that type of material so you have more say in the offerings and your children have access to the books you trust.

Loving Your Difficult Library

Maybe this still seems too much. Maybe your hometown library is embroiled in a censorship controversy. Maybe the book displays are over the top. We would encourage you to keep checking out books. This might mean only checking out books you put on hold. It might mean taking a trip to the library without any children in tow. It might mean requesting your library purchase certain books you'd love to see on the shelves.

You might find yourself wanting to do more. Should you take on the system? Should you try challenging some of the problematic books on the teen shelves? At Redeemed Reader, we believe challenging books at your local library can create unhelpful, unhealthy tension. Before an outright challenge, consider discussing shelving choices with library staff. This might prove a much more helpful way of furthering a conversation.

Betsy, noting a problematic book shelved in her library's children's section, had a constructive conversation with her local librarian and learned that the library hadn't prioritized making a nonfiction YA section, leaving the librarian at a loose end. Megan has encouraged her teenage son to have conversations about shelving with their local librarian when he found a book that wasn't appropriate for the area it was shelved in.

Remember, unless we separate ourselves completely from all forms of printed material, the things adults find problematic at the library are also going to be accessible to children at the bookstore, the school libraries (including Christian schools), classrooms, and even in their friends' homes.

At Redeemed Reader, we remember the second part of Jesus' greatest commandment (Matt. 22:39) to love our neighbor (or neighborhood librarian) as ourselves. We believe that loving our libraries is one practical way we, as book lovers, can build up all our neighbors. And we believe you can love your library, too.

Below are some questions to ask yourself as you prepare to more constructively engage with yours.

- What is one thing you appreciate about your local library?
- Do you know any of your local librarians by name? Do they know you?

- What are the volunteer opportunities at your library? Does your library board need members? Can you join the local Friends of the Library? Can you or your older children help sort books for the library book sale? (The early shopping is a great bonus too!)
- What are some favorite books you can check out from the library to encourage circulation?
- What's a new book you're excited to read that you can check out from your library?
- Has Redeemed Reader reviewed a book you can ask your library to order?

BOOKLIST FOR CHAPTER 23

Further Reading

Reading for the Common Good, C. Christopher Smith

For Children/Teens

Miss Rumphius, Barbara Cooney (Picture Book)
The Library, Sarah Stewart, illustrated by David Small (PB)
A Library Book for Bear, Bonny Becker, illustrated by Kady MacDonald Denton (PB)
Library Lion, Michelle Knudsen, illustrated by Kevin Hawkes (PB)
Library's Most Wanted, Carolyn Leiloglou, illustrated by Sarah Pogue (PB)
Love in the Library, Maggie Tokuda-Hall, illustrated by Yas Imamura (PB nonfiction)
The Tiny Hero of Ferny Creek Library, Linda Bailey (Middle Grade)
The Book Scavenger series, Jennifer Chambliss Bertman (MG)
The Legend of the Last Library, Frank L. Cole (MG)
The Lost Library, Rebecca Stead and Wendy Mass (MG)

CHAPTER 24

WHEN THE HEADLINES STRIKE: LOVING YOUR NEIGHBOR AND YOUR WORLD

> There are times when words can't do what you want them to do,
> no matter how much you wish they could.[1]
>
> —Gary Schmidt, *Just Like That*

It's happened again. Something, somewhere is painting the headlines red. A LIVE button blinks urgently. Or maybe the world continues, but your own family or community is rocked with news. No matter if it is big or small, people are talking. Prayers are rising. You know that questions will come. How do you talk about this with your children? What should you read?

We know this because often readers ask us. Surely there is something you can do in response to the latest world event or local tragedy—even if it's just reading a book. We understand the urge to reach for a book. We all know books and stories will not save the world; only the Story of the gospel can save and transform. But in God's grace, whether reading about Afghanistan,

---

1. Gary Schmidt, *Just Like That* (Clarion Books, 2021), 313.

Ukraine, the refugee crisis, or Israel and Palestine, stories can help young readers grow in understanding for their neighbors and the world.

Finding Windows to our World

In chapter 12 we introduced the idea of books being mirrors or windows. Some books, like mirrors, reflect our experiences back at us. These books show us things we know. Other books are like windows. Looking through them, we catch glimpses of unfamiliar landscapes. Such books help us understand different cultures and religions.

What does that look like? Your library is a great place to start. Take the topic you want to learn about, and think about it in these terms. For example, let's look at Israel.[2]

- Geography: Can you find a simple book with photographs about this country? Is this somewhere people travel? A travel guide or book of photography might be a good resource. (Israel is a popular travel destination, so this is easy, with some fascinating books devoted to its biblical archeology that would be of particular interest.)

- Culture: Can you find regional folk tales? Books about a local holiday? How about a cookbook with recipes to try? (Despite a fraught cultural climate, cookbooks are a particularly helpful way of gently learning about some of the culinary differences and similarities between Israeli and Palestinian cuisine.)

- Myths and religion: What is the religion? Can you find a picture book biography about a religious character or religious legend? (While we are familiar with the Old/New Testament era of Israel's history, for example, books about the intervening years, with the birth of Islam and the rise of Zionism will bring readers more understanding of current events.)

---

2. As of the writing of this book, Israel is engaged in the Gaza war.

- History and nature: What historical and natural events have shaped this area? Can you find books about these particular events? (This cradle of the world has been the battleground of many empires: from Babylonian and Persian to Roman to Ottoman to most recently British . . . there is a lot of history to dig into.)

With this framework, use your library's search engine. Enter the name of the country/religion/event you would like to research. Then use your filters to narrow your search results to the juvenile or young adult age group—if you still have a lot of results, select "fiction" or "nonfiction." You might expand to adult nonfiction if you want to find a cookbook or photo book, though remember, these are intended for adult audiences and will need some previewing if you are giving them to young readers. Don't hesitate to put a stack of books on hold. This is a time to take advantage of your library card! Preview the books, and if you discover an author with a connection to the topic that you like, see if they've written anything else that is relevant.

When Russia invaded Ukraine in 2022, we put together booklists at Redeemed Reader that introduced broader regional influences: Slavic folklore, the Soviet Union, Communism, and the Cold War. All the books in these categories helped build a framework for readers wanting to understand both Ukraine and its regional conflict. Following the October 7, 2023, attack on Israel by Hamas, we assembled a booklist featuring both history and Jewish tradition.

When the US withdrew from Afghanistan in 2021, we shared some of our favorite books from that region. As we wrote then:

> For a country many of us can't even point to on a map, Afghanistan has held a consequential place in world history. This mountainous district composed of tribes that barely hold together lies on a crossroad between civilizations and cultures. It's a bridge between east and west as far back as Alexander, who married a tribal princess

from the region. Afghanistan sheltered the terrorists who brought down the World Trade Center and attacked the Pentagon on 9/11, and it was the first rogue government to fall in the backlash.

And now it's fallen again, with consequences yet to be felt by the rest of the world. [3]

Since that post, the world has felt more consequences of Afghanistan's fall. In Hayley's home state of Wisconsin, understanding Afghanistan became more real as refugees arrived in local cities. As a social worker in 2022, books like *In the Land of the Blue Burqas* helped Hayley grasp facets of the Afghan culture she was now working with. No longer was reading about Afghanistan an exercise in geopolitics; it was a way of understanding her neighbors.

Reading to Love Our Neighbor

Who is our neighbor? It's a question we frame in light of Jesus' words:

And one of the scribes came up and heard them disputing with one another, and seeing that he answered them well, asked him, "Which commandment is the most important of all?" Jesus answered, "The most important is, 'Hear, O Israel: The Lord our God, the Lord is one. And you shall love the Lord your God with all your heart and with all your soul and with all your mind and with all your strength.' The second is this: 'You shall love your neighbor as yourself.' There is no other commandment greater than these."
(Mark 12:28–31)

Our neighbor could be someone we've invited to our book club. It could be refugees, recently arrived in our community.

In the parable of the good Samaritan, Jesus defines the term "neighbor"

---

3. Janie Cheaney, "Reading Afghanistan," Redeemed Reader, August 18, 2021, https://redeemedreader.com/2021/08/reading-afghanistan/.

as more than our immediate physical neighbors. Before His ascension, Jesus tells His followers, "You will be my witnesses in Jerusalem and in all Judea and Samaria, and to the end of the earth" (Acts 1:8). We are constantly thankful for that missional reminder.

Following the Great Commission starts at home, understanding our community. Books like Karina Yan Glaser's *A Duet for Home* run through our heads as we visit homeless shelters and read about the local homeless population in the newspaper. A neighbor tells us about her experiences growing up, working the fields with migrant workers. Listening, we are reminded of books from our childhood: Lois Lenski's books and *Blue Willow* by Doris Gates.

During Redeemed Reader's summer reading programs, we have invited families to learn about the history of their city and their church. These programs are ways we can connect with our communities and learn more about our neighbors. For example, every July in Oshkosh, the Experimental Aircraft Association's annual event, AirVenture, turns the local traffic control tower into the busiest in the US for several days. As airplane enthusiasts flood Hayley's hometown, books like *A Higher Call* and *Devotion* by Adam Makos offer a way of connecting with this passion for aviation and understanding its history.

Books also help us connect with our neighbors' experiences. Picture books like *The Rough Patch* or *Emily Lost Someone She Loved* can help us empathize with those who are grieving a loss. Children's literature increasingly covers a variety of topics from *In the Blue*'s gentle picture book introduction to depression, to *My Brother Is Away*, an empathetic picture book about incarceration, and *All the Impossible Things*, a middle grade fantasy that takes on the foster system and trauma.

Whether we are at home or abroad, children's books can spark our

> *Whether we are at home or abroad, children's books can spark our imaginations and help us grow in love for our neighbor and for the world.*

imaginations and help us grow in love for our neighbor and for the world. With nonstop news and social media, we can constantly be on the hunt for books. This may lead to a rising pile of unread books, paired with frustration. Remember, it is okay to return a stack of books, unread. Give grace to yourself and your readers. Stories can't save the world. But, praise God, they can help us fulfill the Greatest Commandment and the Great Commission. As you consider books for your children, here are some questions to help:

- What is your community known for: potatoes, factories, history? Make a list and find books that relate to these topics.

- What do your neighbors care about? What are books that will help your children understand your neighbors?

- What has been on your heart, in your family's prayers, or part of your church's ministry?

BOOKLIST FOR CHAPTER 24

Further Reading

    Operation World, Jason Mandryk

For Children/Teens

    If the World Were 100 People: A Visual Guide to Our Global Village, Jackie McCann (Picture Book)
    Pilgrim Codex, Vivian Mansour (PB)
    All Thirteen, Christina Soontornvat (Middle Grade, nonfiction)
    Chinese Menu, Grace Lin (MG, nonfiction)
    Crossing the Stream, Elizabeth-Irene Baitie (MG)
    A Long Walk to Water, Linda Sue Park (MG)
    Maps, Aleksandra Mizielinska and Daniel Mizielinski (MG, nonfiction)
    When Stars Are Scattered, Omar Mohammed (MG, graphic novel)
    Prisoners of Geography: Our World Explained in 12 Simple Maps, Tim Marshall (illustrated young readers edition; the adult version is also recommended for YA/Adult)
    Window on the World, edited by Molly Wall and Jason Mandryk (MG)
    Emily of Deep Valley, Maud Hart Lovelace (MG/YA, historical fiction)
    What the World Eats, Faith D'Aluisio and Peter Menzel (MG/YA, nonfiction)

CHAPTER 25

PILES AND STACKS: PERSONAL LIBRARY MANAGEMENT

> Over the years, my space on Beatrice's desk has slowly been invaded.
> Stacks of books surround me on every side.
> For some unfathomable reason, the Brindles have collected
> shelves and shelves of them; and still insist on bringing in more.
> It's baffling, I tell you.[1]
>
> —Allie Millington, *Olivetti*

Whether you're curating a home library, a church library, or the New York Public Library, certain principles always apply. Who is the collection for, and what resources will they enjoy using? In our zeal to gather the "right" books, we may forget to love our most immediate neighbors (our families), consider their interests, and make room for books that nourish their imaginations, pique their interest, satisfy their curiosity, and provide just enough silliness and delight to keep them coming back for more.

If your bookshelves are overflowing, and you have been adding more titles to your list while reading this book, and you'd rather not think about where you're going to put those additions to your collection, you may be hoping that this is the chapter that will solve your problems.

The solution may not be what you expect.

---

1. Allie Millington, *Olivetti* (Feiwel and Friends, 2024), 7.

Heart Issues

Betsy and Megan trained as professional librarians. We know the satisfaction of categorizing and organizing and the joy of seeing orderly shelves. But we also struggle with book idolatry, seeking personal fulfillment in really good books and having well-curated home libraries. Are you a kindred spirit?

No matter how many shelves we have, they will always overflow with more books than they can comfortably hold, and rather than honestly assess our hearts and collections, we wonder how to make them all fit. How many of these arguments sound familiar?

- I'm really going to read that someday, honest!
- That book has sentimental value.
- I paid good money for that book, *and* it's signed!
- Do you realize how many good books libraries are discarding?
- This book is out of print now, and it's hard to find.
- I want people to be impressed with the diversity of my reading tastes and know I'm well-read.
- I enjoy loaning books out to people, especially those hard-to-find titles.
- I might need to reference that book again.
- But I have the entire collection of this series!
- Books are my preferred choice for decorating. What else are shelves for?
- Sure, I have eight versions of this story, but each one is uniquely illustrated.
- *This* version is my old copy from high school with all my notes, and *that* version is the updated one that's easier on my old eyes.

Having lots of books doesn't automatically mean you have a great library. Your lifetime accumulation of volumes cannot accurately reflect the current and reasonably anticipated needs, priorities, and passions of your family. If looking at your collection brings a sense of burden rather than delight to you, your spouse, or your children, there is only one way to begin: on your knees.

Have honest dealings with your heart before God. Humbly confess any greed and idolatry, the seeking of security in temporal excess rather than being content and trusting Him to provide your literary bread. Thank Him for providing so many wonderful resources, and for the pleasure of stories and reading. Ask Him to guide you in assessing your collection and to show you what you have been hoarding and don't genuinely need.

Now you are ready to curate.

What Home Librarians Can Learn from Professionals

Even small libraries require several staff members to help library services run smoothly, and none of them are simultaneously managing a family during their working hours. No wonder it's difficult to organize a home library! You're starting the process from scratch, the needs and interests of the children change year by year, and you don't have an unlimited budget for books and additional shelves. (Neither do libraries, actually; that's why it's necessary for libraries to weed their collections periodically.)

A well-managed library takes into account *who* are the primary users of the collection, *what* kind of books would interest and appeal to these users, *where* they ought to be shelved, *when* to add or remove books as the needs of the users change, *which* books are worthy of shelf space, and *who* is responsible for making sure books are returned to the place they belong.

A well-managed library takes into account who . . . what . . . where . . . when . . . which . . . and who.

We book lovers tend to accumulate vast quantities of "someday-I-might,"

"I've-always-wanted-to," and "I-just-found-out-about-this" in addition to the "essential-must-have" books to read. Well-meaning parents spend money on books we think our children ought to read, but sometimes those books honestly aren't all that appealing. Maybe they're old and grungy. Maybe the illustrations are mediocre. Maybe the story is didactic instead of delightful. These are not assets to your collection.

How to C.U.R.A.T.E. a Home or Church Library

When you are ready to bring order out of chaos, one sign that your home library is successful is that the books enjoy heavy use, which may mean they're strewn all over the house. It means that people want to keep favorites on their own shelves, and tidying up probably means that books don't always make it back where you intended them to belong. Be patient through the process, giving thanks that the books are being used. This is reality; embrace it, along with the children for whom and with whom you want to enjoy your books. The goal of a good home library is quality, not quantity.

Before organizing, decide which books are most interesting and important. What will attract readers to the shelves? Give yourself permission to *not* own a book, whether it is currently on your shelf or in your online cart. It is better to develop a high quality, functional, focused collection, rather than have lots of books that are of little use. Spend your organizing time and energy on the best of what you have.

We'll approach the project with the acronym C.U.R.A.T.E.: Clutter/Crowded, Useful, Read, Appeal, Time, Excellent.

While you go through the process of evaluating, organizing, and storing your collection, keep a notepad on hand. Make a list of broad categories (picture books, biographies, etc.) that you notice during the process. Eventually you can decide what arrangement makes the most sense to you and the rest of your family.

Clutter/Crowded

As much as we bibliophiles love books, we must take an honest look at our shelves. The pencils, LEGO, vintage graduation cap, and Christmas snow globe that never got put away from last year don't belong. Set aside torn or dingy books to be repaired or replaced. Extra books lying across the top of other books on a crowded shelf are unattractive.

Useful

Consider publication date. Is the book/series outdated? Just because it's a bargain doesn't mean it's worthy of your limited shelf space. Have you already studied that subject in your homeschool and someone else could use it now? Is your child done with the origami phase? Do you *need* duplicate copies of that title? Pick your favorite. Don't feel obligated to keep everything.

Read

Have you read it? When do you intend to read/reread it? If you have books on your shelf you don't love, whether gifts or book club titles that you won't read again, you're not obligated to keep it.

Appeal

We cringe when moms on social media who, eager to add good books to their library, assume that because something is old, or is a complete set of junior manuals of some kind, it must be worth buying. Do you/your children love the illustrations? Is the book dingy? Dated? Need repair or to be replaced?

Time

Are your children ready for it, or will they ever be? Is the title limited to a particular time of the year (such as Christmas or Easter), and it could be housed in a box or bin until it's needed? At what time of day do you usually use that book? Would it be handier to keep it near where you have devotions or where you usually read aloud?

Excellent

What are your criteria for determining excellence? What are your children's criteria? Please remember to respect their taste, because although it may change and mature, they are persons made in the image of God who might appreciate something that mystifies you.

Invite your children to help you evaluate a stack of books. Try not to be hurt or disappointed if they aren't as enthusiastic about this or that title as you are. Why is that particular book important to your collection? Did a friend tell you how much her children love it? Are you willing to read it aloud? What value does it bring to your shelves?

You may find these questions helpful:

- Why should I keep this? "Because it was free (or $0.25)," is not a sufficient answer. "Because I paid full price for it," is not adequate either. If you don't have space for it and can't honestly justify it in your collection, let it go!

- How often do I use it? Can I borrow it from the library or a friend if I need it in the future?

- Have I read it? Will I really read it again? Remember that your life is a breath.

- Is it attractive? Books ought to be appealing, if at all possible. (There are a few "ugly" exceptions, such as library-sale treasures that are out of print but still have genuine value.)

- Do I have duplicates or comparable items?

- Is it falling apart? If it is really worth keeping, is it worth replacing it or having it repaired or professionally rebound so it's useful? Consider investing in simple maintenance supplies from a library supply company.

- Can you find it in a library or used bookstore if you need it later?

- Are you willing to make space for it? (If not, return to question #1.)

- Is there someone else who can use it?

Allow your spouse and your children to help evaluate whether a book is truly an important asset to the household. If you have doubts about a book, it probably isn't essential, and you can put it aside to decide later whether you have space for it.

If you're struggling, keep asking God to help you be a good steward, to not hold on too tightly to what you don't need. Remember that the Lord is not dependent on our home library collection for His work in our lives.

Ongoing curating will make library management easier. Your literary needs and the reading seasons and interests of your children will change, and we are storing up treasures in heaven, not on bookshelves.

GIVING BOOKS NEW HOMES

Donate to local Christian ministries and schools.

Your local Christian homeless shelter, mentoring ministry, or Christian school may have use for good books you no longer need. Call first and ask if they can use them. Please make sure the books are appealing before you donate them.

Donate to a church library.

Does your church have a library? Ask if you can start one! After you have enjoyed using a devotional or Christian biography, other families may enjoy reading it. Megan's small church doesn't have a full library, but they have designated a bookshelf as a Little Free Library to share resources among the congregation. (See below for further recommendations.)

Give to a Little Free Library in your town.

These are often located in parks or neighborhoods, and you can install one in front of your own house! Look online to find one near you. This is an easy way to offload a few great titles at a time and bless some unknown reader who might happen by.

Are They Worth Selling?

Selling them at a used bookstore is not that lucrative; you'll earn pennies. Unless the books really have value, you're better off donating them. If you have certain titles that are worth your time to try selling online, list them on Ebay or social media sites. Trading a box of books for credit on ThriftBooks or a local consignment place may be a better option. You can improve the appeal of your shelves while giving them space to breathe.

Host a book swap.

Invite friends, serve snacks, and provide a table where you and your friends can glean each other's discards. Be sure to donate the remaining titles at the end. This is especially helpful when you have several families whose kids with a wide range of ages. Do you participate in a book club? Make a regular swap part of the event.

Give them as gifts.

True book lovers may not mind a gently loved book that is still in good condition if they know and love the giver and respect his or her taste in books.

Friends of the Library, thrift stores, and other general donation places.

If your library has a Friends group, their book sales often support summer reading programs that are not possible with regular library funds. Goodwill and other thrift store organizations also take book donations.

CATEGORIZING AND ORGANIZING WHAT YOU KEEP

Choose a broad category to start with. Walk back through your house and pull every item off the shelf that fits that *one* category. Stack them on the floor so you can see how much shelf space you will need. If you come across books with torn pages or dust jacket edges, set them aside.

Next, decide on the best location for each category of books that provides convenient access for its *primary* users. Make sure to leave a margin of space at the end of the bookshelf, both for future collection development and to make shelving as easy as possible. Don't overthink your decisions! You can always move a book if it makes more sense to shelve it elsewhere.

Here are some helpful categories:

- Picture books
- Fiction
- Christian resources (Bible reference, devotionals, Bible story books, hymnals, church history, etc.)
- Nonfiction reference
- Nonfiction
- Poetry
- Folklore and fairy tales
- Hobbies and special interests

You might choose to alphabetize fiction by author's last name because the spines are wide enough to locate a title at a glance. Think thrice before doing the same with picture books, because the responsibility to put them away would likely fall on *you*. Is your goal to find an individual title, or encourage them to be frequently and serendipitously used? Make it convenient for children to put the books away, and allow the occasional minor inconvenience of scanning shelves if you're looking for something.

Betsy has another simple approach. Sort books by reading level category, then group authors together without regard to any alphabetizing whatsoever. Her practical strategy for picture books is to arrange them by size.

Once you have limited your collection to what you really want to keep, it's time to decide how to rotate and manage the collection. Be willing to accept the presence of a few modest stacks as long as the piles are neat and the books are still useful to your family. Did you know that libraries keep statistics on which books are pulled off the shelf and used at the library? Knowing which books engage the interests of your readers in this season provides valuable insight. Then you can put them away.

Protecting Your Collection

Remember the stack of books you set aside because they needed TLC? Tape can be used to carefully repair pages torn from heavy use or accidents. Library supply companies such as Demco sell dust jacket covers, which are worth the investment for reinforcing paper covers over hardbacks. This not only strengthens books purchased secondhand but also protects them from damage when they're set down on a wet or sticky spot. A roll of twelve-inch adjustable book jacket covers will last a long time, and a set of pre-cut sheets sixteen inches high takes care of oversized books. A roll of quality book tape (four-inch width is good) helps paperback spines to endure wear. It's not difficult to tip in loose pages with Elmer's glue (or PVA, if you're ordering supplies anyway) and a paintbrush. Plenty of online videos offer instruction.

Managing the Overflow

Because it is more aesthetically pleasing and easier to manage shelves that have breathing room, and if the books you are sure you want to keep still don't fit your space, consider a few well-curated storage boxes. Labeling and cataloging are entirely optional.

First, buy some banker's boxes. These are inexpensive, more visually appealing than free paper ream boxes, stack neatly without crushing the contents, and the lid is convenient.

If you want to try "circulating" books to keep the shelves fresh and interesting, simply pack away an assortment of books and rotate the contents every so often. This works best for recreational reading choices and seasonal or holiday themed books.

Try putting away a box of miscellaneous fiction, one of nonfiction, and one of picture books for several months and then pull them out, see if any of the titles spark new or renewed interest. This provides an opportunity to rediscover books that they may not have noticed for a while: "I love this book!" "Oh, I don't remember this one." Putting away a random assortment of nonseasonal books changes up the variety of spines you see. If none of the books pique anyone's interest, they might be of interest to only you, and you can apply the C.U.R.A.T.E. model to decide whether or not you should keep them.

Some home librarians may wish to organize and catalog the overflow. If so, you don't have to designate one box per subject. All you need to do is be able to find a specific title if someone is looking for it. First, fill the boxes with whatever books fit in there nicely. Next, choose an app designed for home libraries, designate one box per "shelf," and add books to that "shelf." You can customize each entry as much as you wish. Finally, number the box according to the shelf, and stack it out of the way. If you don't want to use an app, index cards or a spreadsheet also work nicely.

When you take books out of the boxes, consider writing which box it came out of in pencil either on the first inside page of the book or on a small sticky note inside the cover. This makes it easy to return the book to its proper place.

You have the option to move things around, and you can easily update which box a book is stored in. You can record books as you lend them out and note any titles you are missing in a series.

The goal of managing a home library is to bless your family and friends and to encourage them to explore and use it. The purpose is not to have every title you could possibly ever want, nor to have every book always readily available, but simply to be able to find it.

The "All Things in Common" Church Library

When we develop our home library collections, we include books of all kinds, especially titles that are not available in local libraries or ones we plan to use for an extended period. How long do we need to keep them? What if we have enjoyed certain picture books or a particular family devotional, but don't need to hold on to them long-term? Maybe there just isn't room to keep all the abundance on the shelf and your children would like to share chapter books with friends.

Does your church have a library? Is it located somewhere out of the way and full of books for adults? Is there a reason for children to visit, or is it mostly forgotten? Are the books dingy castoffs from families whose children have outgrown them and didn't love them enough to want to keep them?

Nobody wants to borrow those. They're dated, mediocre, and uninviting.

Set a better precedent. Ask if you can C.U.R.A.T.E. the books on the shelves as described above, keeping only the best and most appealing titles. Donate some of the quality devotionals or Christian picture books your family is finished with. If your church doesn't yet have a library, offer to establish a very appealing Little Free Library in the children's Sunday school area.

Appoint a volunteer librarian who will keep it tidy, encourage children and families to borrow books, and invite feedback on what is being read. Ask the church leadership whether there are funds for investing in some new, excellent resources and a cart. A rolling library cart doesn't take up too much space, can be moved around, and could carry a rotating collection of titles so the selection is always fresh. The librarian could curate a wish list of books they would love to have available, including family devotionals, well-written biographies, attractive picture books, and engaging Christian fiction. Most public libraries are not likely to carry such books, but the church family can greatly benefit from sharing what we already have.

The librarian should sort them to make sure that the best, most interesting, and appealing books are available, not bounce-house versions of Noah's ark. Please be sure that whatever is added to the library will attract young readers. Keep the checkout process simple with a notebook in which the children can write the title, their names, and the date. Ask borrowers if they are enjoying the books, or simply keep it casual and allow families to borrow what they like without keeping a record.

If you teach in a Sunday school or Christian school classroom, consider creating a classroom library with engaging, age-appropriate resources that children can borrow to read at home. Keep in mind that some children struggle with reading more than others, so include well-illustrated picture books, chapter books, and audiobooks such as the Christian Heroes Then and Now biographies. The Trailblazer biographies include books about scientists and how their faith worked out in their vocation, which may have special appeal to some children in your class.

Remember to stock informational books like *God's Bible Timeline* or *Bible Infographics* and *The Radical Book for Kids* for those who enjoy nonfiction. If space is limited, try rotating themed "featured titles" each month on a display shelf or table. Or host a book swap a couple times a year to exchange devotionals by Marty Machowski, Starr Meade, Champ Thornton, Scott James, and many other gifted authors.[2]

The early church practiced generosity with the resources God provided them and shared "everything in common" (Acts 4:32). There will be differences in what each family needs and enjoys in various seasons, but what an opportunity to enhance the reading life of the church!

---

2. Please visit the website for our special feature on church nursery libraries: https://redeemedreader.com/2023/02/why-your-church-nursery-needs-a-library/.

BOOKLIST FOR CHAPTER 25

Further Reading

These are great resources for building your libraries. Choose one or two.
Honey for a Child's Heart, 50th anniversary edition, Glady Hunt
The Read-Aloud Handbook, Jim Trelease (6th edition or earlier preferred)
The Read-Aloud Family, Sarah Mackenzie (read-aloud favorites)
Books Children Love, Elizabeth Wilson (primarily nonfiction)
Soul School, Amber O'Neal Johnston (Black children's literature)
The Enchanted Hour, Meghan Cox Gurdon

Children/Teens

See the chapter 6 booklist for Bible story picture books, chapter 21 for other Christian resources, and chapter 23 for children's books about libraries.

THE CHAPTER AFTER THE LAST

> I wonder if we shall ever be put into songs or tales.
> We're in one, of course; but I mean: put into words, you know,
> told by the fireside, or read out of a great big book with
> red and black letters, years and years afterward. And people will say:
> "Let's hear about Frodo and the Ring!" And they'll say:
> "Yes, that's one of my favorite stories."[1]
>
> —J. R. R. Tolkien, *The Two Towers*

> "There are some things you can't share without ending up liking each other,
> and knocking out a twelve-foot mountain troll is one of them."[2]
>
> —J. K. Rowling, *Harry Potter and the Sorcerer's Stone*

Friends, we have come to the end. Can we call you friends? We've covered a lot of ground together. We like to imagine that we're sitting with you on the back porch in our rocking chairs, enjoying cups of tea and talking books. Our heartfelt prayer is that we have helped you learn how to cultivate a child's discernment and imagination through Truth and Story. What do these young souls need from us, the shepherds of their imaginations?

---

1. J. R. R. Tolkien, *The Two Towers: Being the Second Part of the Lord of the Rings* (Houghton Mifflin Co., 1986), 321.
2. J. K. Rowling, *Harry Potter and the Sorcerer's Stone* (Scholastic, 1998), 179.

They need Truth and Story, recognizing that Truth is always measured against God and His Word, not our own understanding. Story is that nearly undefinable quality of artistic excellence, particularly as it hearkens back to *the* Story of Christ rescuing His bride.

Instead of looking to artificial "reading level" metrics as our primary tool for handing books to children, we watch for stories that make us think, invite delight, and expand our understanding. We want to read stories that resonate with our children and teens where they are right now and that foster growth and wisdom.

Sometimes, our children need to journey with Christian as he heads to the Celestial City. Other times, our students need to be prodded to think critically about big contemporary ideas and issues (if you recall, we call those "discussion starters"). We have explored issues like racism, identity, and environmentalism; we hope those discussions offer a model for how you can help your child engage with issues and think critically about what they read.

As we read with our children, we encounter the music of poetry, thoughtful retellings of influential works in literary history, and well-crafted graphic novels. We strive to balance the messy books with the funny (and sometimes find books that are both!). We travel to other worlds in fantastic settings and pore over pictures in illustrated books. No matter the age of our children or students, books can delight and instruct.

As a team, we've already given you many book titles in our themed "micro" lists at the end of each chapter. Those are designed to help you explore the ideas in each chapter further. When you turn the page, you will encounter countless more book titles! Remember, the only required book is the Bible. May you never be too busy to read it. Our booklists are recommendations, not requirements. We hope you find new treasures among them. Others will make you think, and you may choose to pass on some titles or wait a few years before introducing them to your children.[3] We would never ask you to violate

---

3. Each of the titles in the appendix has been reviewed on Redeemed Reader.

your conscience; you know yourself, your children, and your community best. We pray regularly for wisdom and encourage you to do likewise. We do hope this book and our recommended children's and teens' books spur you on to love and good deeds.

All published books are bound by their publication date. Our team was reading new children's books right in the midst of our final edits that we wish we could have included in these lists. And we have reviewed many excellent titles over the past fourteen years at RedeemedReader.com that we did not have room for in this book. We cordially invite you to continue reading with us through our website. We publish reviews regularly, always looking to engage with contemporary culture even as we also try to highlight excellent countercultural resources (particularly biblical ones). Let us know when you find a new literary treasure, whether we introduced it to you, or you want to introduce it to us!

Friends, find a reading community (perhaps in a book club). Consider reading this book with a friend or small group and discussing it. We hope your bookshelves are curated well and that they include old and new books, many genres, and lots of Stories full of Truth. Consider this a waystation as we journey on this earthly pilgrimage, seeking to love the Lord and His people.

Janie, Betsy, Hayley, and Megan

STARRED REVIEWS: THE BEST OF THE BEST

We consider the following lists "library builders" in their respective categories—the best of the best from the thousands of books we have reviewed during our fourteen years as Redeemed Reader. We heartily recommend them to you!

Because we focus on twenty-first-century children's books, you will not notice many "classics" on this list. That is not because we do not recommend the classics; it simply means that we have not reviewed them. Many good resources have already covered older titles extensively. The few older titles in this list are simply the ones we have occasionally reviewed over the years.

Each book listed has been reviewed on www.redeemedreader.com. We recommend checking reviews to determine if a given title is a good fit for your children or students, particularly for books in the older age ranges.

Lists are alphabetical by title within each category. Where books have both authors and illustrators, such as for picture books, we have listed authors first. We update this list annually for our members. You may access the latest edition at redeemedreader.com/truth-and-story/, using the password REDEEMED.

Bible and Devotional Resources (Ages 0-12/General Family)

Picture Books

- *A World of Praise*, Deborah Lock and Helen Cann
- *African Heroes: Discovering Our Christian Heritage*, Jerome Gay, Jr. and John Joven
- *Baby Believer Board Books*, Danielle Hitchen and Jessica Blanchard
- *Bare Tree and Little Wind: A Story for Holy Week*, Mitali Perkins and Khoa Le
- *The Friend Who Forgives*, Dan DeWitt and Catalina Echeverri
- *The Garden, The Curtain, and the Cross*, Carl Laferton and Catalina Echeverri
- *Go and Do Likewise! The Parables and Wisdom of Jesus*, John Hendrix
- *God's Very Good Idea*, Trillia Newbell and Catalina Echeverri
- *He is Risen: Rocks Tell the Story of Easter*, Patti Rokus
- *Jesus Rose for Me*, Jared Kennedy and Trish Mahoney
- *A Light for My Path*, Davis Carman and Alice Ratterree
- *The Lord's Prayer*, illustrated by Tim Ladwig
- *Miracle Man: The Story of Jesus*, John Hendrix
- *Noah's Ark*, Peter Spier
- *Tell God How You Feel: Helping Kids with Hard Emotions*, Christina Fox and Lisa Flanagan
- *The One O'Clock Miracle*, Alison Mitchell and Catalina Echeverri
- *The Prince's Poison Cup*, R. C. Sproul and Justin Gerard
- *The Promise: The Amazing Story of Our Long-Awaited Savior*, Jason Helopoulos and Rommel Ruiz
- *Psalm Twenty-Three*, illustrated by Tim Ladwig
- *Reformation ABCs*, Stephen J. Nichols and Ned Bustard
- *Something Better Coming*, Megan Saben and Ryan Flanders
- *Something Sad Happened*, Darby Strickland and Thaís Mesquita

- *The Story of Us*, Mitali Perkins and Kevin and Kristen Howdeshell
- *Who Are You?*, Christina Fox and Daron Parton
- *Zacchaeus and Jesus*, Dandi Mackall and Lisa Manuzak

Devotionals and Family Resources
(For Teen-Friendly Resources, see the Teen Section)

- The Big Questions series, Chris Morphew
- *The Biggest Story Family Devotional Bible*, Kevin DeYoung and Don Clark
- *Comforting Hearts, Teaching Minds*, Starr Meade
- *Creative God, Colorful Us*, Trillia Newbell and Chase Williamson
- *Easter Stories: Classic Tales for the Holy Season*, compiled by Miriam LeBlanc
- *God's Attributes*, Jill Nelson
- *God's Design*, Sally Michael
- *God's Word*, Sally Michael
- *Heaven and Nature Sing: 25 Advent Reflections to Bring Joy to the World*, Hannah Anderson and Nathan Anderson (Advent)
- *Hosanna, Loud Hosannas*, Barbara and David Leeman
- *Hosanna in Excelsis: Hymns and Devotions for the Christmas Season*, David and Barbara Leeman
- *The Illustrated Westminster Shorter Catechism in Modern English*
- *Little Hearts, Prepare Him Room*, Holly Mackle
- *Mission Accomplished*, Scott James (Easter)
- *The Ology: Ancient Truths, Ever New*, Marty Machowski and Andy McGuire
- *Prepare Him Room*, Marty Machowski (Advent)
- *Promises Made Promises Kept*, Marty Machowski (Advent)
- *The Radical Book for Kids*, Champ Thornton
- *The Sower*, Scott James and Stephen Crotts

- *Training Hearts, Teaching Minds*, Starr Meade
- *Unwrapping the Greatest Gift*, Ann Voskamp (Advent)
- *Unwrapping the Names of Jesus*, Asheritah Ciuciu (Advent)
- *Window on the World*, edited by Molly Wall
- *WonderFull: Ancient Psalms Ever New*, Marty Machowski

Bibles (includes story Bibles)

Note: We have reviewed more than 70 Bibles for children and teens on our website. We encourage you to look for more options! These are a few standouts in the field.

- *Beginner's Gospel Story Bible*, Jared Kennedy and Trish Mahoney
- *The Biggest Story*, Kevin DeYoung and Don Clark (story Bible)
- *The Biggest Story Bible Storybook*, Kevin DeYoung and Don Clark

Church History Resources

- *Brother Andrew: Behind Enemy Lines*, Nancy Drum
- *Church History*, Simonetta Carr
- *Epic*, Tim Challies
- *Evangelical Heroes*, Joel R. Beeke and Douglas Bond
- *The Faithful Spy*, John Hendrix
- *For Christ's Crown*, Richard Hannula
- *Heralds of the Reformation*, Richard M. Hannula
- *Irenaeus*, Simonetta Carr and Matt Abraxas
- *John Newton*, Simonetta Carr and Matt Abraxas
- *Pilipinto: The Jungle Adventures of a Missionary's Daughter*, Valerie Elliot Shepard
- *Radiant: 50 Remarkable Women*, Richard M. Hannula
- *Reformation Heroes*, Diana Kleyn and Joel R. Beeke
- *Risen Hope: The Church Throughout History* series, Luke Davis
- *Wang Mingdao*, Simonetta Carr and Matt Abraxas

PICTURE BOOKS

(All Ages; includes early readers)

Picture Book Poetry

- *And Then It's Spring*, Julie Fogliano and Erin E. Stead
- *Firefly July*, Paul Janeszko and Melissa Sweet
- *Give Thanks to the Lord*, Karma Wilson and Amy June Bates
- *Giving Thanks*, Katherine Paterson and Pamela Dalton
- *I, Too, Am America*, Langston Hughes and Brian Collier
- *Marshmallow Clouds: Two Poets at Play Among Figures of Speech*, Ted Kooser, Connie Wanek, and Richard Jones
- *My Best Friend*, Julie Fogliano and Jillian Tamaki
- *My Daddy Rules the World: Poems about Dads*, Hope Anita Smith
- *The Midnight Ride of Paul Revere*, illustrated by Christopher Bing
- *Sing a Song of Seasons: a Nature Poem for Each Day*, Fiona Waters and Frann Preston-Gannon
- *The Watcher*, Nikki Grimes and Bryan Collier
- *When Daddy Prays*, Nikki Grimes and Tim Ladwig

PICTURE BOOK BIOGRAPHIES

- *A Boy, a Mouse, and a Spider: The Story of E. B. White*, Barbara Herbert and Lauren Castillo
- *Because Barbara: Barbara Cooney Paints Her World*, Sarah Mackenzie and Eileen Ryan Ewen
- *By and By: Charles Albert Tindley*, Carole Boston Weatherford and Bryan Collier
- *Finding Narnia: The Story of C. S. Lewis and His Brother*, Caroline McAllister and Jessica Lanan
- *Gingerbread for Liberty!: How a German Baker Helped Win the American Revolution*, Mara Rockliff and Vincent X. Kirsch
- *Go Forth and Tell: The Life of Augusta Baker, Librarian and Master Storyteller*, Breanna J. McDaniel and April Harrison

- *Granny Smith Was Not an Apple*, Sarah Glenn Fortson and Kris Aro McLeod
- *John Ronald's Dragons: The Story of J. R. R. Tolkien*, Caroline McAllister and Eliza Wheeler
- *Joni Eareckson Tada: The Girl Who Learned to Follow God in a Wheelchair*, Kristyn Getty and Hsulynn Pang
- *Lily: The Girl Who Could See*, Sally Oxley and Tim Ladwig
- *Make Way: The Story of Robert McCloskey, Nancy Schön, and Some Very Famous Ducklings*, Angela Burke Kunkel and Claire Keane
- *The Pilot and the Little Prince: The Life of Antoine de Saint-Exupéry*, Peter Sís
- *The Right Word: Roget and His Thesaurus*, Jen Bryant and Melissa Sweet
- *A River of Words: The Story of William Carlos Williams*, Jen Bryant and Melissa Sweet
- *So Tall Within: Sojourner Truth's Long Walk Toward Freedom*, Gary D. Schmidt and Daniel Minter
- *Sparky & Spike: Charles Schulz and the Wildest, Smartest Dog Ever*, Barbara Lowell and Dan Andreasen
- *Through the Wardrobe: How C. S. Lewis Invented Narnia*, Lina Maslo
- *Whoosh! Lonnie Johnson's Super-Soaking Stream of Invention*, Chris Barton and Don Tate

Nonfiction Picture Books

- *About Mammals*, Carolyn and John Sill
- *The Beetle Book*, Steve Jenkins
- *The Dinosaurs of Waterhouse Hawkins*, Barbara Kerley and Brian Selznick
- *Finding Winnie: The True Story of the World's Most Famous Bear*, Lindsay Mattick and Sophie Blackall
- *Freedom on Congo Square*, Carole Boston Weatherford and R. Gregory Christie
- *God Counts: Numbers in His Word and His World*, Irene Sun

- *Gravity*, Jason Chin
- *Honeybee: The Busy Life of Apis Mellifera*, Candace Fleming and Eric Rohmann
- *If the World Were 100 People: A Visual to Our Global Village*, Jackie McCann and Aaron Cushley
- *If You Plant a Seed*, Kadir Nelson
- *A Leaf Can Be . . .* , Laura Purdie Salas and Violeta Dabija
- Made by God series (I Can Read) (Early Reader nonfiction)
- *The Man with the Violin*, Kathy Stinson and Dušan Petričić
- *Maps*, Aleksandra Mizielinska and Daniel Mizielinski
- *Moon Shot: The Flight of Apollo 11*, Brian Floca
- *National Wildlife Federation World of Birds: A Beginner's Guide*, Kim Kurki
- *Nya's Long Walk*, Linda Sue Park and Brian Pinkney
- *On the Wing*, David Elliot and Becca Stadtlander
- *Saving the Liberty Bell*, Megan McDonald and Masha Gray Carrington
- *Water Can Be . . .* , Laura Purdie Salas and Violeta Dabija
- *Water Is Water*, Miranda Paul and Jason Chin

General Picture Books (Fiction)

- *Adrian Simcox Does NOT Have a Horse*, Marcy Campbell and Corinna Luyken
- *The Amazing Christmas Extravaganza*, David Shannon
- *Bartholomew and the Oobleck*, Dr. Seuss
- *Babble! And How Punctuation Saved It*, Caroline Adderson and Roman Muradov
- *Brother Hugo and the Bear*, Katy Beebe and S. D. Schindler
- *A Chocolate Moose for Dinner*, Fred Gwynne
- *Christmas Is Here*, Lauren Castillo
- The Church Mice series, Graham Oakley

- *DragonQuest*, Allan Baillie
- *Drawn Onward*, Daniel Nayeri and Matt Rockefeller
- *Drawn Together*, Minh Lê and Dan Santat
- *Each Peach Pear Plum*, Allan Ahlberg and Janet Ahlberg
- *The Empty Pot*, Demi
- *Flora and the Penguin*, Molly Idle
- *The Gardener*, Sarah Stewart and David Small
- *The Girl and the Bicycle*, Mark Pett (wordless)
- *The Golden Plate*, Bernadette Watts
- *The Grasshopper and the Ants*, Jerry Pinkney
- *Great Joy*, Kate DiCamillo and Bagram Ibatoulline
- *A House That Once Was*, Julie Fogliano and Lane Smith
- *The Snow Queen*, H. C. Anderson and Bagram Ibatoulline
- *I Worked Hard on That!*, Robyn Wall and A. N. Kang
- *In Plain Sight*, Richard Jackson and Jerry Pinkney
- *It Is Not Time for Sleeping*, Lauren Castillo
- *Jumper: A Day in the Life of a Backyard Jumping Spider*, Jessica Lanan
- *Just Like Millie*, Lauren Castillo
- *Kiyoshi's Walk*, Mark Karlins and Nicole Wong
- *Knight Owl and Early Bird*, Christopher Denise
- *Last Stop on Market Street*, Matt de la Peña and Christian Robinson
- *A Library Book for Bear*, Bonnie Becker and Kady MacDonald Denton
- *The Lion and the Mouse*, Jerry Pinkney
- *Long Ago on a Silent Night*, Julie Berry and Annie Won
- *Mockingbird*, Allan Ahlberg and Paul Howard
- *Moving the Millers' Minnie Moore Mine Mansion: A True Story*, Dave Eggers and Júlia Sardà
- *Mr. Squirrel and the Moon*, Sebastian Meschenmoser
- *My Brother is Away*, Sara Greenwood
- *Nana in the Country*, Lauren Castillo
- *New House New Home*, Megan Saben and Liz and Kate Pope

Starred Reviews: the Best of the Best

- *Noodles on a Bicycle,* Kyo Maclear and Gracey Zhang
- *Press Here,* Herve (Board Book)
- *Rabbit and Robot: The Sleepover,* Cece Bell (Early Reader)
- *Room for Everyone,* Naaz Khan and Mercè López
- *See the Cat: Three Stories About a Dog,* David LaRochelle and Mike Wohnoutka (Early Reader)
- *Sidewalk Flowers,* Jon Arno Lawson (wordless)
- *Simon and the Better Bone,* Corey R. Tabor
- *Sneaky Sheep,* Chris Moore
- *This Is the Feast,* Diane Z. Shore and Megan Lloyd
- *Three Bears in a Boat,* David Soman
- *Tops and Bottoms,* Janet Stevens
- *Unspoken: A Story of the Underground Railroad,* Henry Cole
- *Waiting Is Not Easy!,* Mo Willems (Early Reader)
- *We Are (Not) Friends,* Anna Wang (Early Reader)
- *William's House,* Ginger Howard and Larry Day
- *Yoo-Hoo, Ladybug!,* Mem Fox and Laura Ljungkvist
- *You Are (Not) Small,* Anna Wang (Early Reader)

Chapter Books and Middle Grade (~4th–8th grade; ages 8–12)

Chapter Books

Chapter books bridge the "gap" between straight-up picture books and full-fledged middle grade novels, but the edges can be blurry. Some of these are robust enough for all middle grade readers, and some will appeal to brand-new readers.

- *Anna Hibiscus,* Atinuke
- *Ben Washington Is the Newbie on the Block,* Jasmine Mullen
- *Cody and the Fountain of Happiness,* Tricia Springstubb
- *Lindbergh: Tale of a Flying Mouse,* Torben Kuhlmann

- *A Long Road on a Short Day*, Gary D. Schmidt
- *McBroom's Wonderful One-Acre Farm: Three Tall Tales*, Sid Fleischman
- *Orris and Timble: The Beginning*, Kate DiCamillo
- *Phoebe the Spy*, Judith Griffin
- *Sam the Man and the Chicken Plan*, Frances Dowell
- *Skunk and Badger*, Amy Timberlake and Jon Klassen
- Tales from Deckawoo Drive series, Kate DiCamillo and Chris Van Dusen

Middle Grade Poetry

- *All He Knew*, Helen Frost
- *The Crossover*, Kwame Alexander
- *Edgar Allen Poe's Pie*, J. Patrick Lewis
- *Gone Fishing: A Novel in Verse*, Tamera Will Wissinger
- *I'm Just No Good at Rhyming*, Chris Harris and Lane Smith
- *Twelve Kinds of Ice*, Ellen Brown Obed
- *Voices of Christmas*, Nikki Grimes

Middle Grade Graphic Novels

- *Bolivar*, Sean Rubin
- *Catherine's War*, Julia Billet
- *El Deafo*, Cece Bell
- *Hereville*, Barry Deutsch
- *New Kid*, Jerry Craft
- *New Shoes*, Sara Varon
- *Saving H'Non: Chang and the Elephant*, Trang Nguyễn and Jeet Zdũng
- *Tommysaurus Rex*, Doug TenAppel
- *Treaties, Trenches, Mud, and Blood*, Nathan Hale
- *Watership Down: The Graphic Novel*, Richard Adams and Joe Sutphin

- *When Stars Are Scattered*, Victoria Jamieson & Omar Mohamed
- *Zita the Space Girl*, Ben Hatke

Middle Grade Nonfiction (includes biographies)

- *The Adventurous Life of Miles Standish*, Cheryl Harness
- *All in a Drop: How Antony van Leeuwenhoek Discovered an Invisible World*, Lori Alexander
- *Answering the Cry for Freedom: Stories of African Americans and the American Revolution*, Gretchen Woelfle and R. Gregory Christie
- *Betty Before X*, Ilyasah Shabazz
- *Carry On, Mr. Bowditch*, Jean Lee Latham
- *Crossing on Time*, David Macaulay
- *The Double Dangerous Book for Boys*, Conn, Arthur, and Cameron Iggulden
- *The Genius Under the Table*, Eugene Yelchin
- *The Girl Who Drew Butterflies*, Joyce Sidman
- *Harriet Tubman: Conductor on the Underground Railroad*, Ann Petry
- *Her Own Two Feet*, Meredith Davis
- *Houses With a Story*, Seiji Yoshida
- *How Sweet the Sound*, Carole Boston Weatherford
- *A Long Walk to Water*, Linda Sue Park
- *Look Up: Bird Watching in Your Own Back Yard*, Annette LeBlanc Cate
- *Memories of Survival*, Esther Nisenthal Krinitz
- *The Miracle Seed*, Martin Lemelman
- *Indescribable Atlas Adventures*, Louis Giglio
- *O Captain, My Captain*, Robert Burleigh
- *On the Horizon*, Lois Lowry
- *One Long Line*, Loree Griffin Burns
- *The Promise of Change*, Jo Ann Allen Boyce and Debbie Levy
- *Shakespeare's First Folio: All the Plays, A Children's Edition*, illustrated by Emily Sutton

- *Soldier Bear*, Bibi Dumon Tak
- *Some Writer!*, Melissa Sweet
- *This is Our Constitution*, Khizr Khan
- *Twelve Days in May: Freedom Ride 1961*, Larry Brimner
- *We've Got a Job: The 1963 Birmingham Children's March*, Cynthia Levinson

Middle Grade Fiction – Fantasy and Science Fiction

- *100 Cupboards*, N. D. Wilson
- *Airborn*, Kenneth Oppel
- *The Bootlace Magician*, Cassie Beasley
- *The Book of Boy*, Catherine Murdock
- *Circus Mirandus*, Cassie Beasley
- *Deadweather and Sunrise*, Geoff Rodkey
- *A Dragon Used to Live Here*, Annette LeBlanc
- *Faerie Gold*, Kathryn Lindskoog, ed.
- *Ferris*, Kate DiCamillo
- *The Green Ember*, S. D. Smith
- *Handbook for Dragon Slayers*, Merrie Haskell
- *Inkling*, Kenneth Oppel
- *The Inquisitor's Tale*, Adam Gidwitz
- *Jack Zulu and the Waylander's Key*, J. C. Smith and S. D. Smith
- *Larklight*, Philip Reeve
- *The Light Princess*, George McDonald
- *A Little Taste of Poison*, R. J. Anderson
- *Little Pilgrim's Progress*, Helen Taylor
- *The Miraculous Journey of Edward Tulane*, Kate DiCamillo
- The Mistmantle Chronicles, M. I. McAllister
- *Mr. and Mrs. Bunny: Detectives Extraordinaire!*, Polly Horvath
- *Mrs. Frisby and the Rats of NIMH*, Robert C. O'Brien

- *Nuts to You*, Lynne Rae Perkins
- *Ophelia and the Marvelous Boy*, Karen Foxlee
- *The Ordinary Princess*, M. M. Kaye
- *A Pocket Full of Murder*, R. J. Anderson
- *The Puppets of Spelhorst: A Norendy Tale*, Kate DiCamillo
- *Robin Hood*, David Calcutt
- The *Rwendigo Tales*, J. A. Myhre
- *Secrets at Sea*, Richard Peck
- *The Sign of the Cat*, Lynne Jonell
- *Sweep*, Jonathan Auxier
- *Tales of Wonder* (Vol. 1), Brian Philips, ed.
- *Tuck Everlasting*, Natalie Babbitt
- *When the Sea Turned to Silver*, Grace Lin
- *Where the Mountain Meets the Moon*, Grace Lin
- *The Wild Robot*, Peter Brown
- The *Wilderking Trilogy*, Jonathan Rogers
- The *Wingfeather Saga*, Andrew Peterson

MIDDLE GRADE FICTION – REALISTIC AND HISTORICAL FICTION

- *A Place for Peter*, Elizabeth Yates
- *All-of-a-Kind Family*, Sydney Taylor
- *Almost Paradise*, Corabel Shofner
- *Astrid the Unstoppable*, Maria Parr
- *The Bletchley Riddle*, Ruta Sepetys and Steve Sheinkin
- *The Bridge Home*, Padma Venkatraman
- The *Brixton Brothers Mystery* series, Mac Barnett
- *By the Great Horn Spoon*, Sid Fleischman
- *Bright April*, Marguerite De Angeli
- *Caddie Woodlawn*, Carol Ryrie Brink

- *The Charlatan's Boy*, Jonathan Rogers
- *The Desperate Adventures of Zeno and Alya*, Jane Kelley
- *A Duet for Home*, Karina Yan Glaser
- *The Emperor's Ostrich*, Julie Berry
- *The Father Brown Reader*, Nancy Carpentier Brown
- *Ghost*, Jason Reynolds
- *The Golden Goblet*, Eloise Jarvis McGraw
- *Homer Price* and *The Centerburg Tales*, Robert McCloskey
- *The Hotel Balzaar*, Kate DiCamillo
- *The House of Arden*, E. Nesbit
- Tree Street Kids series, Amanda Cleary Eastep
- *Hope in the Holler*, Lisa Lewis Tyre
- *Hope in the Valley*, Mitali Perkins
- *Insignificant Events in the Life of a Cactus*, Dusti Bowling
- *Into the Jungle*, Katherine Rundell
- *Johnny Tremaine*, Esther Forbes
- *Leaving Lymon*, Lesa Cline-Ransome
- *Linked*, Gordon Korman
- *Little Christmas Carol*, illustrated by Joe Sutphin
- *Lizzie Bright and the Buckminster Boy*, Gary D. Schmidt
- *Magnolia Wu Unfolds It All*, Chanel Miller
- *Mara, Daughter of the Nile*, Eloise Jarvis McGraw
- *Mikis and the Donkey*, Bibi Tak
- *Mishka*, Edward van de Vendel and Anoush Elman
- *The Misadventured Summer of Tumbleweed Thompson*, Glenn McCarty
- *The Most Perfect Thing in the Universe*, Tricia Springstubb
- *North to Freedom*, Anne Holm (republished as *I Am David*)
- *Out of My Mind*, Sharon Draper
- *Pay Attention, Carter Jones*, Gary D. Schmidt
- *The Penderwicks in Spring*, Jeanne Birdsall
- *A Place to Hang the Moon*, Kate Albus

- *The Pushcart War*, Jean Merrill
- *Restart*, Gordon Korman
- *The Season of Styx Malone*, Kekla Magoon
- *The Secret Keepers*, Trenton Lee Stewart
- *The Sky at Our Feet*, Nadia Hashimi
- *Sled Dog School*, Terry Lynn Johnson
- *The Ship of Stolen Words*, Fran Wilde
- *The Simple Art of Flying*, Cory Leonardo
- *Somebody on This Bus Is Going to Be Famous*, J. B. Cheaney
- *Sunny*, Jason Reynolds
- *Super Jake and the King of Chaos*, Naomi Milliner
- *The Swallow's Flight*, Hilary McKay
- *Tangerine*, Edward Bloor
- *Tiger Boy*, Mitali Perkins
- *Time Sight*, Lynne Jonell
- The Vanderbeekers series, Karina Yan Glaser
- *The View from Saturday*, E. L. Konigsberg
- *We Could Be Heroes*, Margaret Finnegan
- *The Wednesday Wars*, Gary D. Schmidt
- *We're Not from Here*, Geoff Rodkey
- *The Westing Game*, Ellen Raskin
- *The Witch of Blackbird Pond*, Elizabeth George Speare
- *The Year Money Grew on Trees*, Aaron Hawkins

Young Adult and Adult

We've broken this list into books recommended for ages 12 and up and a list that should be reserved for those ages 15 and up. Teens over 15 will still enjoy the titles in the 12+ category; the older designation is for books that contain more mature elements. Young adult literature in general contains more "considerations" than middle grade literature. We particularly encourage you to read our reviews for more information on titles with an *.

Young Adult Bible and Devotional Resources

- *10 Questions Every Teen Should Ask (and Answer) About Christianity*, Rebecca McLaughlin
- *Be Thou My Vision: A Liturgy for Daily Worship*, Jonathan Gibson
- *The Dawn of Redeeming Grace: Daily Devotions for Advent*, Sinclair Ferguson
- *Get Your Story Straight*, Kristen Hatton
- HCSB/CSB *Teen Essentials Study Bible*
- *In the Lord I Take Refuge: 150 Daily Devotions Through the Psalms*, Dane Ortlund
- *Is Christmas Unbelievable? Four Questions Everyone Should Ask About the World's Most Famous Story*, Rebecca McLaughlin
- *Journey to Bethlehem: A Treasury of Classic Christmas Devotionals*, Leland Ryken
- *Love Came Down at Christmas*, Sinclair Ferguson
- *New Morning Mercies for Teens: A Daily Gospel Devotional*, Paul David Tripp
- NLT *Jesus-Centered Bible*
- *Proverbs For You*, Kathleen Nielson
- *Surviving Religion 101: Letters to a Christian Student on Keeping the Faith in College*, Michael J. Kruger
- *Transformed by Truth*, Katherine Forster
- *Truths We Confess: A Systematic Exposition of the Westminster Confession of Faith* (Revised Edition), R. C. Sproul
- *Visual Theology*, Tim Challies and Josh Byers
- *Wild Bells: A Literary Advent*, Missy Andrews
- *A Wondrous Mystery: Daily Advent Devotions*, Charles Spurgeon
- *The Young Man's Guide to Awesomeness*, Barrett Johnson

Nonfiction: 12+

- *12 Ways Your Phone Is Changing You*, Tony Reinke

- *Abigail Adams: Witness to a Revolution*, Natalie Bober
- *Carved in Ebony: Lessons from the Black Women Who Shaped Us*, Jasmine Holmes
- *Dorothy and Jack*, Gina Dalfonzo
- *Everything Sad Is Untrue*, Daniel Nayeri
- *The Forgotten Man: A Graphic Novel*, Amity Shales
- *Land of Hope: An Invitation to the Great American Story*, Wilfred McClay
- *Let Justice Roll Down*, John Perkins
- *The Mythmakers*, John Hendrix
- *Nine Days*, Fred Hyatt
- *Pioneer Girl: Annotated Autobiography of Laura Ingalls Wilder*, Pamela Smith Hill
- *Popular: Vintage Wisdom for the Modern Greek*, Maya Van Wagenen
- *Rise*, Trip Lee
- *The Roar on the Other Side: A Guide for Student Poets*, Suzanne Underwood Rhodes
- *Through Gates of Splendor*, Elisabeth Elliot
- *Ugly: A Memoir*, Robert Hoge
- *Unbroken: Young Reader Edition*, Laura Hillenbrand
- *Under Our Skin: Getting Real About Race. Getting Free From the Fears and Frustrations That Divide Us.*, Ben Watson
- *The Year We Were Famous*, Carole Estby Dagg

Young Adult Fiction: Fantasy and Science Fiction (12+)

- *Amber & Clay*, Laura Amy Schlitz
- *Beauty*, Robin McKinley
- Beyonders Trilogy, Brandon Mull
- *The Carver and the Queen*, Emma Fox
- Daughter of Arden Trilogy, Loren Warnemuende
- *Entwined*, Heather Dixon

- The Hungry Cities Quartet, Philip Reeve
- *If We Survive*, Andrew Klavan
- Monster Blood Tattoo Trilogy, D. M. Cornish
- *The Perilous Gard*, Elizabeth Marie Pope
- *Pilgrim's Progress: A Retelling*, Gary D. Schmidt
- *The Sherwood Ring*, Elizabeth Marie Pope
- *Skyward*, Brandon Sanderson
- *Swift*, R. J. Anderson
- *The Thief*, Megan Whelan Turner
- *Watership Down*, Richard Adams

Young Adult Fiction: Realistic and Historical Fiction (12+)

- *Bamboo People*, Mitali Perkins
- *Calvin*, Martine Leavitt
- *Dragonfly Eyes*, Cao Wenxuan
- *Enemies in the Orchard*, Dana VanderLugt
- *Hattie Big Sky*, Kirby Larson
- *Jepp, Who Defied the Stars*, Katherine Marsh
- *Just Like That*, Gary D. Schmidt
- *The Labors of Hercules Beal*, Gary D. Schmidt
- *Marcello in the Real World*, Francis X. Stork
- *Nearer My Freedom: The Interesting Life of Olaudah Equiano by Himself*, Monica Edinger and Lesley Younge
- *One Big Open Sky*, Lesa Cline-Ransome (MG, but recommended for YA readers)
- *Peak*, Roland Smith
- *Red Butterfly*, A. L. Sonnichsen
- Seeds of America Trilogy, Laurie Halse Anderson
- *The Star That Always Stays*, Anna Rose Johnson
- *Two Old Women: An Alaskan Legend of Betrayal, Courage, and Survival*, Velma Wallis

- *What the Night Sings*, Vesper Stamper
- *You Bring the Distant Near*, Mitali Perkins

Young Adult Fiction: Fantasy and Science Fiction (15+)
- *Arthur, the Always King*, Kevin Crossley-Holland*
- *Once a Queen*, Sarah Arthur*
- *The Song That Moves the Sun*, Anna Bright

Young Adult Fiction: Realistic and Historical Fiction (15+)
- *Berliners*, Vesper Stamper*
- *Boxers/Saints*, Gene Luen Yang*
- *Charis in the World of Wonders: A Novel Set in Puritan New England*, Marly Youmans*
- *Cry, the Beloved Country*, Alan Paton*
- *Disappeared*, Frances X. Stork
- *Forward Me Back to You*, Mitali Perkins*
- *Love and Other Great Expectations*, Becky Dean
- *Lovely War*, Julie Berry
- *The Red Palace*, June Hur*

Resources for Adults and Mature Teens (Nonfiction)
- *American History*, Thomas Kidd
- *Broken Pieces and the God Who Mends Them*, Simonetta Carr*
- *Caring for Words in a Culture of Lies, 2nd Edition*, Marilyn McEntyre
- *Confronting Christianity*, Rebecca McLaughlin
- *Echoes of Eden*, Jerram Barrs
- *Finding Truth*, Nancy Pearcy
- *Honey for a Child's Heart*, Gladys Hunt
- *Honey for a Teen's Heart*, Gladys Hunt
- *In the Land of the Blue Burqas*, Kate McCord
- *The Money-Smart Family System*, Steve Economies
- *Ordinary Hazards*, Nikki Grimes*

- *Recovering the Lost Art of Reading: A Quest for the True, the Good, and the Beautiful*, Leland Ryken
- *Same Kind of Different as Me*, Ron Hall and Denver Moore*
- *Seeking Allah, Finding Jesus*, Nabeel Qureshi
- *Steeped in Stories: Timeless Children's Novels to Refresh Our Tired Souls*, Mitali Perkins
- *The Tech-Wise Family*, Andy Crouch
- *Wild Things and Castles in the Sky: A Guide to Choosing the Best Books for Children*, Leslie Bustard, ed.

ACKNOWLEDGMENTS

From the Redeemed Reader team:

When we say we stand on the shoulders of giants, Gladys Hunt is the first name that comes to mind. We are indebted to her work, *Honey for a Child's Heart*. Some of us are products of that book since our parents used it, and some of us have used it with our own children. Thank you to Mark Hunt, who generously provided his late mother's unpublished blog posts to be featured on our website (see "The Hive").

Redeemed Reader would not be where it is today without the initial idea of Emily Whitten; we are so glad she pursued her vision.

We are deeply grateful for the many excellent writers and illustrators who are sharing stories with children today. Mitali Perkins and Karina Yan Glaser, two of our favorite authors, have consistently encouraged us and granted us interviews. We are also indebted to each of our readers who have reached out over the years: expressing appreciation, encouraging us to press on, and extending so much grace when we miss something.

A constant thank you to Herb, our faithful IT guy, who has bailed us out of many a website disaster.

Most authors acknowledge their editors and publishing teams with good reason. This book would not be in your hands today without Catherine Parks, our book's cheerleader from the beginning; Amanda Cleary Eastep, editor extraordinaire; and the entire team at Moody Publishers who shepherded this book through green pastures to the work you hold in your hands. They have been a delight to collaborate with, and we are thankful the Lord opened doors for us with Moody.

Thanks first and last to our heavenly Father. We are each humbly aware of the Lord's great faithfulness and goodness to us, particularly during the book-writing season. We look to Jesus as the author and perfecter of our faith, resting in Him alone for our salvation and thankful that He equips where He calls. May He establish the work of our hands.

Janie:

If I remember correctly, I was the one who suggested to Emily Whitten that we might write some kind of blog together. But she was the one who jumped on it with an enthusiasm that almost overwhelmed me (like, What have I let myself in for?). To her we owe our name, our basic color scheme, our original website design, and our dove logo. Thank you, Emily.

Over the next four or five years I often wondered if I was spending too much time on it: so much reading, so much reviewing, so much thinking about what distinguishes an objectively good book from one I happen to like. Then Hayley joined us as an intern and Betsy and Megan climbed aboard as collaborators, and I began to think this vessel might have a future. Many thanks to you ladies—you each bring something unique and irreplaceable to the enterprise.

Betsy:

To my parents who introduced me to Jesus (and who read so many great books aloud to me). To Mr. Pettit, who introduced me to the scholarly appreciation of children's literature. To Megan, who has been my constant encourager for nearly three decades. To Janie, who has been such a wise mentor in so many ways. To Hayley, for her consistent "Girl Friday" help. To my three amazing children who have grown up alongside Redeemed Reader: You have been my test subjects, and one of my chief delights has been sharing stories with you from the beginning to the present. May you always use Scripture as the benchmark, and may you continue to engage wisely with culture. Last, but certainly not least, to my husband and Renaissance man, Ethan, who has been supporting my love of children's literature since before we were married. Thank you for your many sacrifices that enabled me to actually contribute to a book about children's books! And thank you for the countless discussions we have had analyzing stories in all forms.

Megan:

To my beloved husband, Michael, who listened patiently during a baseball game while I waxed eloquent over children's literature and witnessed my enthusiasm for buying books, then married me anyway. Thank you for many years of delightful conversations about reading and everything else under the sun. To Henry, David, John, Philip, and Edward, who are admirers of Truth and Story. Thank you all for bearing patiently with my passion for writing and then celebrating with chocolate cake. To my three wise and winsome colleagues from whom I have learned so much; I would not have persevered in this dream without you. To Janelle and Amy, with gratitude for your faithful prayers, and to Nellie, my writing cheerleader. Thanks to my parents, who took me to meet real authors and filled one whole wall of my bedroom with bookshelves, and to Mr. Pettit, the librarian whose insight into children's literature became a turning point in my life. Above all, to my Savior, Jesus Christ. May I fill a little space that Your name be glorified.

Hayley:

This book stems from many conversations about what it means to be a Christian and a reader that have shaped me over the years. Thank you first of all to Mom and Dad who shared their love of reading. I was blessed to grow up in a household filled with books and stories. Even more than books, I am thankful for parents who shared their love of the Lord and talked about their faith. I am so thankful for the wonderful women of God at Redeemed Reader as well as Jaclyn, Tamar, and my mother-in-law, Kathy. To all the friends, family, and church members, thank you for your prayers during the book writing process. Finally, I am so thankful for my amazing, book-loving husband, Joel. Thank you for all the discussions and for being a patient soundboard and editor/tech helper extraordinaire as we formatted this behemoth of a manuscript.